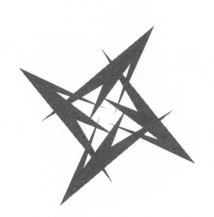

Nanotech Fortunes

Make Yours In the Boom!

Winning Strategies

by

Darrell Brookstein

For every person who wants to make money investing in stocks; for every teacher who changed a kid's life for the better, or made him or her think beyond one's limits; for the teacher within; and for the loves of my life, Helen, Kimbra, and Shannon.

NANOTECH FORTUNES

Make Yours In the Boom!

Winning Strategies

by

Darrell Brookstein

First Edition

PRINTED IN THE UNITED STATES OF AMERICA

ISBN 0-97628-510-X

LCCN 2005925640

10 9 8 7 6 5 4 3 2 1

ACKNOWLEDGMENTS

There are people who helped make this book happen, and there are folks who helped make it better; much, much better than it would have been if left to my own devices. Some did both.

I would like to thank Dr. Erkki Ruoslahti who acted as my nanotechnology mentor, showed tremendous patience, and always supported me in building my company; even lending his good name and scientific prominence to build a nanotech Scientific Advisory Board second to none. Thanks to Dr. Ruoslahti, Steve Perlberg, Michael Tantleff, Richard Goldstein, Chris Radford, Steve Ridgeway, Helen Brookstein, and Allan Silberhartz for giving me the initial encouragement I needed, and so much more. My gratitude to Jay Greenblatt, Thom Yanari, Ed Moran, Eva Ruoslahti, Richard Goldstein, Stuart Pulvirent, Vincent Caprio, Mike Moradi, Erkki Ruoslahti, Nathen Fox, Nathan Tinker, Jeff Phillips, Steve Perlberg, Scott Livingston, Steve Maebius, Dr. Robert Abraham, and Ken Nunes whose writing and editing inputs were invaluable. Many thanks to Stephen Maebius, Ed Moran, Dr. Reza Ghadiri, Dr. Sangeeta Bhatia, and Dr. Evelyn Hu for their support and work on the Corporate Development and Scientific Advisories of The Nanotech Company, LLC. Thanks to Andre Leeder and Dan Maher for wonderful cover and corporate artwork, and to Charlie Niven for organizational and clerical inputs. Thanks to Michael Brooks who was generous with his publishing expertise. Ron Kenner made important contributions in editing, and Laura Shapiro in formatting.

Ph.D. candidates, and nanoscientists, Austin Derfus and Albert Lin made outstanding contributions to this book and the growth of my understanding and awareness of nanotechnology, and I am especially grateful to Austin for his excellent work on our free e-digest of international *small technology* news, *The Best of the NanoWeek,* and to Albert for his help on this book, and in identifying publicly traded nanotech stocks.

Thanks to Mark Cullivan and Jeff Phillips who contributed to the company's development while I was writing. Jeff's super marketing advice is always welcome.

To my wife, Helen, and two wonderful daughters, Kimbra and Shannon, very special thanks for their emotional and clerical support.

Special thanks go to you, the readers, who make my hours at the keyboard worth it if you find value in the hours you spend with my book.

I sincerely hope this helps you make your fortune in nanotech, that you find the lessons applicable across the gamut of investment arenas, and that you enjoy your fortune and your life.

TABLE OF CONTENTS

FOREWORD

TO THE READER:

I t is my distinct pleasure to write these introductory remarks for *Nanotech Fortunes*. I first met Darrell almost five years ago when a colleague of mine, who knew about our mutual interest in nanotechnology, got us together. We hit it off right from the beginning. Darrell had a hunch then that nanotech was going to be the next big business opportunity, and I had decided to move my research in that direction. We starting having brainstorming sessions about the business and science of things nano, usually accompanied with interesting wines each of us had discovered.

Darrell's general business acumen is beyond question, but I have also come to admire his impressive understanding of scientific and technical underpinnings of nanotechnology. He is now, five years after we started thinking about nanotechnology ventures, one of the leading business experts in the field.

Darrell has written this book in an entertaining and provocative style, but, make no mistake, this book was written by a person who has an impressive track record in technology-related business investment and who thoroughly understands (a fact he does not hide in the book) the promise and pitfalls of nanotechnology.

The book critically examines the investment possibilities in the nanotechnology field, and also transmits the current excitement of the field among nanoscientists, entrepreneurs, government funding agencies, and even the general public. And there is much to be excited about: The U.S. government, some of the state governments, and government agencies of many foreign countries are investing vast sums of money in nanotechnology research. My own experience is that it is easier to get funding for nanotechnology projects right now than for any other type of research. This investment in nanotechnology research is increasing the number of scientists in the field and, as a result, new discoveries will be made at an accelerating pace. These discoveries will feed investment and development of new products, and the result will be the growth of nanotechnology into a major economic force. Predictions that this will be the century of nanotechnology and that this technology will completely transform the way we live our everyday lives, and even how long we live our lives, may well turn out to be accurate.

Much of the progress is incremental, anything from surface coatings that better repel moisture or dirt, to better facial creams and ski waxes. Let me take an example from my own field, nanomedicine, that illustrates how this incremental process works and how impressive the results can be. Improving drug delivery is one of the main promises that nanotechnology can bring to medicine in the short term. Taxol and its derivatives are among the most effective anti-cancer drugs currently available. The problem with taxol is that it is too insoluble to be injected as such; it has to be dissolved into an oil and given to the patient slowly over a long period of time. Unfortunately, the oil has its own side effects that compound those of taxol itself. This is where nanotechnology has provided a solution. American Biosciences packaged taxol into tiny nanoparticles made of the most common blood protein, albumin. This product, Abraxane, is easier to administer to a patient than the parent drug, and more effective. Based on these properties, Abraxane was approved by the FDA in 2005.

My prediction is that Abraxane is going to be made obsolete fairly soon by nanoparticles that not only incorporate the advantages of this product but that also actively seek out the tumor. These targeted nanoparticles would be "smart" in that they would concentrate in the tumor and deliver more drug there and less elsewhere. The next stage is to develop a targeted nanoparticle that delivers its drug payload upon command and only at the correct site (the tumor). One can envision a further function that would entail the remnants of the particles returning into the circulation with information on how effective the treatment was. Other nanoparticles might survey the body and give a warning signal if cancer is detected. Similar approaches can be applied to other diseases. All the elements needed for these improvements are already available, but making them work in the challenging environment of the body will require hard work. The payoff may be another revolution in medicine.

Nanotechnology will also bring about revolutionary changes. Most of those, by their very nature, are impossible to predict, but some are widely anticipated. One such quantum leap is the development of a computer in which the equivalent of a transistor is made out of individual atoms. A molecular computer like that could be at least 100,000 times smaller than the current computers. The proof of principle is there, but the speed is not. If such difficulties will be overcome within the next several years, we would be seeing a major deviation from what Moore's law would predict with regard to improvements in computer performance.

The nanotechnology revolution is just beginning, but it will be profound. A lot of money will be made, and lost. All investment booms spawn operators who are riding the wave with little of value to offer. The nanotech boom will be very much science driven, and we will be seeing, and are already seeing a great deal of pseudoscience chasing unsuspecting investors. What I particularly respect in Darrell Brookstein is that his investment philosophy is to be firmly anchored to good science. He has spent the last five years immersed in nanoscience and developing contacts with scientists in this field. Being a scientist, I may be biased, but I think that relying on good science is far likelier to make you money than investing in ephemeral companies supported only by a market fad. Darrell Brookstein's advice in nanotech investing will give you the solid science angle and make you a nanotech investor on the winning side.

—Erkki Ruoslahti, M.D., Ph.D.
Distinguished Professor
The Burnham Institute

PREFACE
FOREWARNED IS
FOREARMED

Nanotechnology has a mortal lock on being tomorrow's gold mine. It will produce trillions of dollars in new wealth over the next century. It's sure to reshape every industry it touches — computing, materials, health care and so on. But which nanofranchises will emerge as comparable to Windows and Pentium? Which CEOs will walk the path of Gates, Grove or Dell? Sorting this out won't be easy. It'll require four talents: deep scientific understanding of nano, the ability to see market forces at work, financial acumen, and an instinct for discerning the Dells from the Waitts."
—**Rich Kaarlgard**, Publisher, *Forbes*

W e know that Michael Dell said he would focus on nanotechnology if he was starting his career again. Jeff Bezos and the Google guys have been investing in nano or have expressed a deep interest in it. Many other well-known high-tech names are quietly building Angel and VC positions in nanotech startups.

What do they know that you do not? This is a book about how, precisely, you can make a boatload of money in nanotech.

And, very importantly, about how to avoid losing money. Let me explain why I am in the unique position to tell you how this can be done.

WHY SHOULD YOU LISTEN TO ME?

I am a grizzled investment and small-cap, boom/bust speculation pro. I am supported by some of leading, world-renowned nanoscientists and nano-oriented financial, investing, and corporate development professionals. My company's Scientific Advisory Board (SAB) includes some of the most prominent names (representing every important discipline) in nanotechnology: chemistry, physics, engineering, biology, medicine, and materials science. Among them are a Feynman Nanotechnology and Japan Prize winner, and National Academy of Sciences, National Institute of Medicine and National Academy of Engineering members. My Corporate Development Advisory Board features two of the most well-regarded nanotech-oriented CPAs and intellectual property (IP) attorneys in the world. The active Senior Directors of my firm are the founder of the premier U.S. nanotech industry association and the former CEO of the nanotech company which won the *First International Nanotechnology Business Plan Contest* in 2003. I am in daily contact with two young nanoscientists, a physicist and a biomedical engineer, both handpicked by my Scientific Advisors to support our mission and help me make this exciting but complex science and technology understandable to non-scientist investors.

Let me give you a little more color on my business and investment background. Since starting as a futures broker in 1973 I have developed proprietary pattern recognition trading systems for everything from silver to cocoa, from T-bonds to index options, and from the Yen to Yahoo. I have owned and operated securities broker/dealers, Registered Investment Advisors, hedge and private equity fund managers, and Commodity Pool Operators. While finishing this book, I am trading a long/short hedge fund in so-called "small technology." *Small Tech* includes nanotech, micro-technology, MEMs and microfluidics, and managing this fund is giving me a great feel for the 140 to 175 international publicly-traded companies currently in this space, the likely winners and the losers, as well as providing a tremendous *listening post* on what is coming.

And, hype aside, let me tell you that nanotechnology is the *gold mine* of the 21st Century.

That has a special ring for me because, for years, in the 1980s and '90s I and my firms were recognized as leading advisors in precious metals mining finance and investing, and in natural resource venture capital.

With 4,000 clients and more than $100 million under management in the 1980s, I provided early financing for some of the biggest stories of the day in international gold mining. In the Carlin Trend in Nevada, the Coeur d'Alene silver district in Idaho, and the Hemlo gold district in Ontario, my name and financing clout were well known. My newsletter, *The Prospector*, my brokerage firm in Washington, D.C., and several of my natural resource investment entities were important drivers through the mining booms and busts from 1980 through the mid-1990s.

By 2000, my offshore private equity natural resource fund had chalked up 80%+ audited returns over three years, and we were early investors and *de facto* directors to private natural gas companies in the incipient Powder River & Green River Basins in Wyoming, and elsewhere, that later grew to nearly $5 billion in market capitalization.

Having read about nanotechnology in 1988, I always thought it was likely to be *the next big thing*; I just had no idea it would take so long. Fortunately, given my long experience in the financial markets, the *stock market timing guru* in me kept me away from nanotech for 13 years until I was introduced to one of the world's leading bionanoscientists, Distinguished Professor Erkki Ruoslahti, M.D. Ph.D., in 2001, and we began a fruitful and collaborative relationship that brings us to the present. He and our carefully chosen diverse scientific advisory board vet the science and technology, while I *cast a cold eye* of business and investment criteria on companies seeking funding and needing our accelerated corporate development services.

By way of ending this introduction, my firm, The Nanotech Company, LLC of San Diego, helps international nanotech companies and nano-focused professional investors make their most important decisions and solve their most difficult dilemmas correctly. We assist them in executive-level hiring, directors, mergers, acquisitions, scientific review and in all the critical success areas of corporate development. Our clients derive measurable benefits from a high level of advice, financial, corporate development, and investment services provided by our outstanding Scientific Advisory and Corporate Development Boards, Senior Directors and executives. We are focused exclusively on the *small technology* space. In addition to our nanotech corporate clients, our professional investment clientele benefit from our being directly in the center of all things *nano*.

Even our website is at the center of it all: www.nanotechnology.com.

Gold mining, natural gas ventures, and nanotech companies have an extraordinary amount in common. In a few pages, we will follow up on this commonality. For now, allow me to leave you with a single key point: With my long experience in natural resource venture capital, I am a proven adept in the boom/bust, speculative investing style that will be the hallmark of nanotech over the next few decades.

A Winning Tip for Making Your Nanotech Fortune

"Do not fight the tape." The IPO market is likely to be weak into 2006 - 2007 timeframe. The tech equity market, in a major downtrend since 2000, seems likely to weaken or be flat at best from the 2004/05 high until an eventual bottom between 2006 and 2008. Finally, that stock market high will likely hold until at least 2006 - 2008. If I am right (and very few people will put such predictions in print), the first MAJOR nanotech equity boom is slated to start between 2006 and 2008. *You cannot push a river.* Trade, play and learn, ASAP; get really serious about positioning in profit-exploding opportunities in nanotech in 2006 - 2008.

Introduction
A Nanotechnology
Boom is Inevitable

Shrink and integrate; shrink and integrate.
—**Andy Kessler**, *Running Money*

(To me) Nanotechnology is like building hospitals on the moon...
—**An unnamed investment banking CEO** in October 2004.

Nanotechnology is a collective term for a set of tools and techniques that permit the atoms and molecules that comprise all matter to be imaged and manipulated. Using these tools and techniques it is possible to exploit the size-dependent properties of materials structured on the sub-100 nanometer scale, which may be assembled and organised to yield nanodevices and nanosystems that possess new or improved properties. These tools and techniques, materials, devices and systems present companies in all sectors of the... economy with opportunities to enhance their competitiveness by developing new and improved products and processes.
—**Irish Council for Science, Technology & Innovation**

So where do we go from here?

Beginning sometime between 2006 and 2008 the U.S. (and other securities markets worldwide) will experience the first of many major nanotech stock booms that will occur periodically for decades – at least until sometime between 2025 and 2050.

Whether you have $5,000 or $5 million to invest, if you are properly positioned you are going to make a killing while having the thrill-ride of a lifetime. To boot, at the same time you will be making the world a better, vastly more fascinating place.

This is not a book about nanotechnology as a science, technology, or school subject. I will spend a few minutes on this in the first chapter and sprinkle such information throughout, but I encourage you to explore the extensive appendix at the back of this book. It's worth the weight of this book in gold, at least, and is chock full of every important source of information you'll ever need to understand what nanoscience and nanotechnology are and are not (unless you are planning an advanced degree in one of the hard sciences).

This book will not try to be a scientific history. You will not find much discussion of the key theories, the disagreements, or the ethical concerns related to nanotechnology (a little, not much).

You certainly will not find this author trying to *out-scientist* the scientists.

You do not need to be a scientist or have received an A in high school physics (or even a B) to obtain value from this book and make your *nanotech fortune*. No equations. No math. No chemistry. No physics. No biology. I "don't know much about biology; but I do know that one and one are two, and I do know"… how you can make a fortune, and, perhaps more importantly, *how to avoid losing one* while investing and speculating in nanotech companies. Remember good old, $P\,V = n\,R\,T$. Hint: It's the ideal gas constant. Remember what "P" stands for? Neither do I.

Internet telephony is having its day. It will be "over" before 2010. Wireless is having its day. This will be over before 2010. RFID, Fuel Cells, the Hydrogen story, satellite radio, electric utility based internet – still another round in biotechnology – they will all have their day in the financial sun. The broadband revolution is ongoing; it is by no means over. However, by 2008 or 2009 most of the battles will have been won or lost and the so-called broadband revolution will be evolving more slowly, with the excitement pretty much over.

But nothing will be like nanotech. Nanotechnology is an enabling and disruptive technology. It is a revolution in the same way the Industrial Revolution was a revolution. Its tentacles will reach into and touch every aspect of our lives, culture and economy. Nanotechnology will be under the surface of nearly every industry, and it will destroy companies and possibly whole industries that fail to focus on it or acquire companies that do.

The internet boom was a small burst compared to what the nanotech boom will look like. Think of it this way. Fire, electricity, and digitization enabled numerous technologies and disrupted (read changed, revolutionized and destroyed) many others. The *Nanotechnology Revolution* will set off a series of rolling booms and busts that will last decades and literally destroy untold businesses – disrupting and leapfrogging technologies that, only a few years earlier, were considered *cutting edge*.

Another thing this book is not: It's not a typical *how to make money investing… book. Those books often tell you such ridiculously obvious things as: save money, buy insurance* before investing in stocks, *diversify*, etc. I am going to assume you are sophisticated enough to know these things, and I will not waste your time on *Investing 101*. That being said, here is my concession to the obvious: Do all the things mentioned in the second sentence of this paragraph – diversify, insure, save – and remember that most non-professional investors should have no more than 5 - 15% of their funds in speculative, volatile, illiquid or small-cap stocks.

Prudence should guide. This is a book about investing in *nanotechnology*. This is not rocket science. It is not brain surgery. It's way beyond that. If you are a *total* investment novice, please, you might want to stop reading now and return the book. While the scientific and technical references will be brief and simple enough for even my non-scientist brain, we are looking at things related to the laws of quantum physics, things as small as a few atoms, the uncertainty principle, carbon nanotubes, fullerenes, quantum dots, *etc*. Even as a novice – hopefully one taking advantage of professional advice – you're more than welcome to peek in to gain some solid familiarity with the topic. Yet all of my tips and expertise will be of little use to you if you are *freaked out* by the science and technology. So please relax. We are not going to go there; too much.

On the other hand, I will not *dumb down* the financial, investing, business, economic and speculative references. I will take it as an article of faith that you are probably a somewhat sophisticated investor and that, while most likely not a scientist, a few scientific terms sprinkled here and there will not send you screaming out of the room.

Do not worry. **This is going to be *a piece of cake.***

On the other hand: Unlike you, typical investors who are not following the guidelines of this book are going to have a tough time getting a handle on how to make a fortune – let alone keep from losing one – in the emerging nanotech industry. One of their problems is that they are not scientists and thus without proper guidance they are going to have their heads handed to them. Even scientists are going to have a hard time with nanotechnology because it is so cutting-edge, so complex, that only some Ph.D.s in physics, chemistry, biology and engineering have the ability to really understand the esoteric concepts related to the infinitesimally tiny, and especially (and much more importantly) the properties and forces that occur or are developed at such an infinitesimally tiny scale: the nano or quantum scale of things.

None of the individual *pieces of the nanotech puzzle* can even be seen with a college chemistry class microscope, much less with a magnifying glass. Remember cells. Remember mitochondria. Remember the *nucleus*. Well, all those things are made up of molecules; many, many molecules. And the molecules are made up of atoms. Well, nanoparticles, like quantum dots or carbon nanotubes are made up of a few dozen, hundred or thousand atoms. Imagine a speck within mitochondria! The important properties or forces that nanoscience and nanotechnology deal with are forces *between* molecules, *between* individual atoms, and even *within* atoms. These forces are very different from the ones we experience in our everyday *macro* lives. Even Einstein called the behavior of matter at the nanoscale *spooky*. Remember, I am not a scientist; so *do not try this at home*, but some of these properties at the tiny scale are spooky because they are contrary to what we would expect. For example if we rub our hands together they get hot. Maybe in some nanoscale application, friction creates *cold*. If I push a ball it goes away from me. At the nanoscale, perhaps the more you push the more what you push sticks to you. If I shine a yellow light on a piece of paper it appears yellow. Maybe at the nanoscale shining a yellow light turns the object shined on blue. By playing with these *spooky* forces, materials, systems and machines can be manufactured that are truly extraordinary; that is what makes nanotech so darn cool.

If you understand that this is the gist of what nanotech is about, you are lightyears ahead of the masses of investors and the public who think that nanotech is about small bloodstream-traveling, cholesterol-gobbling vacuum machines.

While the general lack of real scientific knowledge and understanding presents difficulties for regular investors, brokers and venture capitalists alike, it is not insurmountable. It does not negate the inevitability that many men and women, business people, traders, executives, academics, and professionals will make money – a flat-out, mouth-watering lot of money – over the next ten years!

That is why I wrote this book.

I have made fortunes for myself and others as a financial professional since 1973. My books and newsletters on natural resource stocks gave me a file cabinet of "Thank you" notes from folks who turned a few thousand dollars into tens of thousands of dollars, up to hedge fund managers who, through my expertise, made millions of dollars for themselves and their investors. As an investment banking and venture capital executive of my own firms, I have a history of making outsized profits that spans decades. No one wins every battle, but I have played an instrumental role in obtaining tens of millions of dollars in financing startups and in turning that into billions of dollars in market capitalization for investors.

The gold mine of the 21st century is nanotechnology. That's why I purchased the fundamental domain name (nanotechnology.com) and have been toying with the idea of a nanotech investment business since 1988. It is why I have been furiously studying the space and making instrumental contacts, across the broad spectrum, since 2001.

When I gained my expertise in natural resource venture capital and private equity finance, it was not because I was born into a family of geologists or because my college major was mining engineering. My following came from being a virtual sponge. I absorbed everything I learned in hundreds of meetings and conversations with geologists, engineers, geophysicists, prospectors, promoters of every ilk, brokers, analysts, executives at some of the largest mining firms on earth, and investors.

I was fortunate to learn what works, and what does not. I learned how to communicate complex scientific information in a way that can be related and understood by a stockbroker or analyst, in less than two minutes, so that he or she can convey it to a client in less than thirty seconds.

I watched friends jump into the center of the biotechnology industry and use my model to build successful relationships and strong businesses. I co-invested with them from time to time, and when the internet craze took over I was late to the party (mid-1997) but early to leave (mid-2000) – with several key investments for myself and my clients and with a timely sell signal on the whole stock market on March 21st, 2000.

Today another, far bigger, more far-reaching, considerably more important investing and speculative boom series is about to begin.

I know how the *Nanotech Boom* is likely to play out over the next few decades because I have seen this movie many times before. I am going to share with you everything I've learned over three decades.

Most importantly, I know how to keep you from making the same mistakes I have seen many other very smart folks make while losing fortunes in *Booms and Busts* over the same years.

I am confident that when you finish with me on this ride, you are going to know exactly how you are going to make your fortune in the rolling nanotech booms that are inevitable, and equally confident that you are not going to be among the big losers who are already sowing the seeds of disaster for themselves and their clients.

A Nanotechnology Boom is inevitable. In fact multiple rolling booms and busts, over a period of decades, are inevitable.

How do we know this?

Nanotech has already been developing for a long time. Nanotech is nothing new to the scientific, high-tech, and cutting edge venture capital (VC) communities. It has been under way now for decades, from Richard Feynman's Cal Tech speech in 1959 to pioneering work at IBM and elsewhere from the 1970s onward… to Drexler's science/science fiction musings in the 1980s… atomic force and scanning tunneling microscopes (AFM and STM) that can image individual atoms, specialty chemicals, thin films, and coatings a bit later… to the beginning of venture capital investing in nanotech startups in mid-1990s.

Nanotech has been formally established and confirmed by the brightest scientific minds of our time. By the second half of 2004, we started seeing weekly (if not daily) conferences and seminars for scientists and engineers on nanotech topics at every respected university, national laboratory and high-tech driven corporation. Materials scientists, ceramic scientists, electrical engineers, physicists, chemists, biologists, medical doctors, and many others have committees, magazines, learned journals and interdisciplinary meetings devoted to nanotechnology. While nanotechnology gives its own award, The Feynman Prize, prestigious Nobel Prize candidates and winners, and National Academy of Sciences members such as Richard Smalley, George Whitesides, Alan MacDiarmid, Anthony Leggett and the Chairman of my own firm's Scientific Advisory Board (SAB), Erkki Ruoslahti, have embraced nanotechnology in full.

It is not too farfetched to say that today many if not most Ph.D. candidates in engineering and the "hard sciences" at the top universities consider themselves nanoscientists and nanotechnologists. Simply put, nanotech is a worldwide phenomenon. In December, 2003, President Bush signed a Nanotechnology

Initiative authorizing $3.7 billion for research and for the basic infrastructures for further research. Senators and representatives of both parties are on board for what they say will be a trillion dollar – their (probably ridiculous) number, not mine – industry by 2011.

Furthermore we are not alone. The U.S. has tremendous competition. Japan has authorized more than the U.S.; some $6 billion! Russia, Israel, Switzerland, Korea, China, are players. And every day I am surprised by the nanotech news – you can sign up for a free e-digest of the most important relevant news, *The Best of the Nano Week*, at www.nanotechnology.com emanating from some conference in Finland or Poland; or I get an urgent request for funding for a nanotechnology company from India or New Zealand!

Exactly what is my definition of nanotechnology?

Nanotechnology is any engineered, useful technology that can be manufactured and that derives from nanoscience. Nanoscience is the study of matter and forces at a nanoscale (1-100 nanometers). Nanotech reveals special properties related to quantum physics, not simply the macro-physical properties we see in our everyday world.

If you look at talcum powder, you can easily see how size, by itself, is not the essential, distinguishing characteristic that separates nanotech from mere miniaturization (in a sense, the ongoing quest of all technology). Talc, magnesium silicate hydroxide, is a stone that is the main ingredient in talcum powder. One of its properties is hydrophobicity, a $5 way of saying that it repels water. When crushed into the tiny particles that make up talcum powder, it still repels water. It even repels more water per weight, since the tiny particles have more surface area than a single chunk of talc weighing the same amount.

Imagine the surface area of a spherical chunk of talc weighing one ounce. The total surface area of all the particles in the powder, weighing the same one ounce, is much greater. The property has not changed due to the size of the particles. The hydrophobicity remains the same, yet the surface area increases as particle size decreases. If we were able to engineer nanoparticles of talc only a few molecules in diameter, theoretically the water repelling per weight would be even greater. Interestingly, by some experts' definition, such technology would not be nanotechnology. In nanotechnology, *a property would have to change or a new one would have to arise* as it reached the nano-scale. Not every material, element or compound does this. As far as I know (and the science could advance at any moment), so far, talc does not. **However, a few nanoparticles, like some forms of carbon, cadmium, peptides, titanium, *etc.*, do.**

For a bit more color (and expertise) on the subject, allow me to quote from our SAB chairman, Dr. Erkki Ruoslahti: "Darrell, yours may be too narrow an interpretation. Miniaturization is important, too. New nano-engineered machines are *nano* even if they don't rely on quantum phenomena. In nano-medicine, the challenge is to build nano-devices that work better than Nature's nano-devices (proteins, DNA, etc.). There may not be any new properties from the small size – just clever engineering."

What are some examples of a change in properties at the nanoscale? Some things change color. Some become stronger or harder. Some change magnetically or electrically. Some become more slippery. Some become more reflective. Yet, unlike the talc in the example above, the change is not predicted by everyday non-quantum physics, chemistry or biology, based on size alone. The change in properties occurs because of quantum effects, atomic or subatomic laws and forces.

That is when a nanotechnology effect or property reveals itself.

In my opinion, for there to be a developed nanotechnology the new property must be used in a novel way. A product must actually be engineered; *it must be able to be commercially manufactured in industrial quantities, in a way that allows integration into current systems, for the world as it is,* not as it is imagined to be in the future. **Nanotech investors and nanotech fortune seekers, take note of the above.** Admittedly this is a pretty high hurdle. However, we already have many examples, and the future will bring amazing leapfrogging, disruptive, revolutionary technologies in every field. Today we have sunscreens, ski wax, stain resistant clothing, eyeglass defoggers, micro-displays, scratch-resistant automobile paints, foot warmers, tennis rackets… .

In the very near future (2008 - 2013) we will see our lives affected in very dramatic ways by nanotechnologies that are now in late stages in the lab. Look for nanotech-driven filtration, decontamination, and purity detection solutions aimed at the massive worldwide "pure water" problem. Early detection of a variety of diseases from arteriosclerosis to Alzheimer to cancer by nano-detectors, *lab-on-a-chip*, and bio-tagging will catapult beyond current techniques and will no doubt save lives. Nanotech applied to imaging within the human body, mirror-like TV displays, and computer monitors have the capability to leapfrog a generation of so-called *high definition*. New packaging will increase shelf-life of an amazing variety of foods we now deem highly perishable. Nanocatalysts will also provide new, unimagined efficiencies across a broad swath of the energy industry. *Time release* will take on new meaning as *intelligent* nano-coatings might allow the elderly to take a pill once a week instead of three times per day. We will see the earliest beginnings of highly customized (nearly down to the DNA level) health care.

On a lighter note, we will likely see a wrinkle cream that actually works.

In the more distant future, say 2014 - 2024, you may be amazed at what is *not* science fiction and by what is likely. Personal mobile computers and micro-displays could be built into clothing. You might have practically all of the knowledge there is at your finger-tips, along with the ability to communicate, at any time, with whomever you want. Actually the preceding could happen in the timeframe above without dependence on nanotechnology, but look for *small tech* to accelerate development dramatically and lower energy consumption and costs.

Non-nanotechnologies are fully capable of developing incredible futuristic products on their own, but it is safe to assume that nanotech inputs will enhance, leapfrog, speed up or make processes more efficient. *Intelligent* paint on your wall may well change color or display a veritable museum of art at your wirelessly communicated whim. Cancer, if not cured, will more often be detected in advance, removed early, or, in many cases, irradiated non-invasively. Individualized medicine will become more common.

The trend toward tailor-made pharmaceuticals based on the genome will continue.

Investors should keep their heads. Unscrupulous and unknowledgeable (we will cover these characters, and how to actually MAKE money from their shenanigans, in another chapter) promoters, brokers, executives, and, even, scientists are already painting a near-term future for technologies that are either decades away, at best, or *on the never, never plan*, at worst. **Learning to separate science from science fiction is an important lesson** that, once learned, will keep you with the winners. I will show you how you can begin to do this for yourself, shortly.

That is my "What is Nanotechnology?" speech. I have included voluminous resources for further edification in the appendix. Within the confines of the covers of the book you now hold in your hands, you have all you need to be well on your way to making a *Nanotech Fortune*.

Getting back for a moment to the inevitability of the *Booms*, we know they are coming because serious governments have JUST BEGUN (2002 - 2005, for gosh sakes) to invest billions of dollars, as well as the best of their brains in *small technology* (usually referring to nanotech, microtechnology, micro-fluidics, and MEMS – microelectronic mechanical systems). New, exciting, explosive pure science is **only just starting** to manifest itself. While truly *disruptive technologies* are extremely rare and often emerge unintentionally, the disruptive technologies that nanotech will probably create (those that leapfrog and **destroy** existing multi-billion dollar, incumbent industries) are now appearing on the horizon. Similarly, biotechnology started in earnest in the 1970s, became public in the 1980s, came into its own profits in the 1990s, has come through multiyear *booms and busts*, and will still be shining strong in 2015; nanotechnology circa 2005 (which is even BIGGER, and will touch far more of our lives in many more ways) remained roughly at the stage of the biotech field in 1980 (maybe 1984).

Remember, nothing goes straight up. Sharing an awareness of this is how I and this book can help you win big. I can show you advanced techniques that account for those weeks, months, or years, when nanotech stocks and fortunes are not going straight up, and how to use them for your advantage. Using the **Winning Strategies** I reveal here, and avoiding the proven *losing strategies*, you will overcome the fact that you are not a Nobel Prize winner, and, amazingly, you will even beat Nobel Prize winners (who may have not read this book) to your **Nanotech Fortunes** objective.

A WINNING TIP FOR MAKING YOUR NANOTECH FORTUNE

Winners will know how to play the boom/bust game and will not get wedded to a starry-eyed, rose-colored-glasses picture of investing in a "hot, new" technology. We may take profits when stocks are overhyped. **Sell whenever people you least expect (cabbies, housepainters, gardeners, schoolteachers, *et al.*) start talking about nanotech stocks.**

NZZ, Switzerland's most prestigious financial newspaper, interviewed me in mid-2004 on the state of nanotechnology investment in the U.S. I understand the taped interview also ran on German financial news radio. The short interview is helpful in setting the stage.

Tobias: *How can a retail investor invest in nanotechnology in the U.S.? How many mutual funds are out there? What can we say about investors' demand for nanotechnology in general?*

Darrell: In the U.S. the retail investor can only invest in individual publicly traded shares, of which there are about 10 - 30, pure play companies at this time depending on your definition of nanotechnology and your definition of "pure play." I have heard of one closed-end, unmanaged fund which some promoter brought out just to earn the fees, and there is Harris & Harris, a publicly-traded venture capital fund focused on nanotech, but it is currently trading at an unreasonable valuation of more than 5X NAV. My firm may be starting a U.S.-oriented nanotech venture fund, and at our website we will be in contact with those who indicate interest (*www.nanotechnology.com*). I have a VERY different view of investors' demand in the U.S. for nanotechnology shares and for private equity placements than do my fellow experts. I believe it is almost NIL right now. I see no current interest whatsoever. The vast majority of even university educated investors, aged 35 - 70 cannot even give a vaguely correct definition of the term; most have never indicated even a passing interest to a stockbroker in this field. I know, because I actively canvass brokers and individual investors and speculators on this subject.

The Nanosys and Nano-Tex IPOs, and the movie, *Prey,* may put nanotechnology "front and center" in the popular press in the U.S. and begin to trigger active investment over the next 18 months. So these are really VERY early days.

Tobias: How are Nano-companies financed in the US? VC (venture capital), public subsidies? How many are already listed on Nasdaq?

Darrell: Government grants combined with Angel and then VC funding are typical. Entrepreneurs, financiers, and promoters team with scientists at the university or national laboratory level and try to bootstrap to an IPO (Initial Public Offering – extremely rare as yet) or an M & A (Mergers & Acquisitions) resolution, sometimes involving only the IP (intellectual property). Some government agencies, such as the CIA (Central Intelligence Agency), have "investment" arms that can make limited direct investments in shares, but this is very rare in the U.S. where 99%+ is private. (That being said, government grants for research do play a large role in the development and viability of early stage nanotech companies) See my reference above on the number of companies. I am not including IBM, Hewlett-Packard, Texas Instruments, DuPont, BASF, *et al.,* who are all relatively HUGE into nanotechnology even though they currently receive only a tiny fraction of their revenues from nano-related sources. There are no nanotech companies developing in people's garages.

Tobias: Which companies are interesting from a financial perspective? How many have a solid business model? Which criteria do you

*apply for an investment decision? Is a portfolio of patents sufficient?
Or application platform? Or final products?*

Darrell: Of course there is a somewhat different criterion for public vs. private companies. I look closest at four things, in this order:
management, science, market, and valuation. If I'm not impressed
by management I go no further, since, with poor management,
everything that can go wrong will go wrong, while great management can "cure" just about ANY ill. If the science is not sound, if
it is science fiction or if the scientists are not top-notch (and you
require world class experts as we do with our Scientific Advisory
Board to recognize as much), there's no reason to press on.

Good managers can be fooled or mislead and yet cannot be
expected to succeed unless they themselves are top scientists; and
the chances of a truly top scientist being a truly top manager are
slim, indeed. The market for the product must be large, profitable,
and ready. *For a market that does not exist, great products are going
nowhere.* For a company seeking financing, this insight is sometimes very difficult to grasp. The science must turn into a technology through engineering. Then the technology has to turn into a
product. Then the product must be economically manufactured,
and in mass production quantities. And then it must be integrated
into already existing or easy to modify processes. Typically, it must
also offer dramatic benefits at small additional cost. AND especially it has to meet real, ALREADY EXISTING market needs.

Of course a company could meet each of the criteria above
and still not be a good investment, due to valuation. Here we
work with an IP valuation expert and the other financial and valuation pros on our advisory board to actually put a price per share,
or total market capitalization number, on the corporation. We
apply many of the same standards already used in the high-tech
and biotech industries, such as discounted future cash flow models, to help us arrive at a range based on something other than the
entrepreneur's asking price. Clearly, unless the cost to us is significantly less than the arrived at "value" or unless we can see an eventual surge in revenue growth (or a natural corporate buyer with
different criteria than ours to provide a profitable exit), we pass.

Tobias: After an expected Nanosys IPO in 2004 or 2005, will we experience a flood of IPOs? Which companies are likely to go public in the near future?

Darrell: I don't think we'll see a flood of IPOs. Nano-Tex within 18 months seems likely; I would bet on NanoFilm in 12 - 24 months. In addition, there will be an assortment of low-quality promotions, reverse mergers and the like. I would look for a relatively serious IPO period starting in 2006 - 2008. Because of the huge barriers to entry, you will not see anything like the Internet IPO boom occurring in Nano. As in the example of Biotech, I believe many of the companies my firm will be investing in over the next 2 - 3 years will be bought out by major companies or their IP will be licensed before and instead of an IPO exit strategy. Investors will be well-rewarded.

UNLIKE Biotech (maybe because we have already seen that "movie") investors will demand a short timeframe to profitability, multiple competing technologies will find it much more difficult to find funding, and pure science will NOT get funded by private investors at all. It will stay the purview of universities and national labs where it belongs.

Tobias: Besides the Merrill Lynch Nano-tracker: Are there any other indices that track the U.S.-nanotechnology industry?

Darrell: The brokerage firm Punk Ziegel has an index, and my firm may have one before the end of 2005. I'm just concerned about clear definitions and properly weighting the index we're developing so as to give investors something meaningful and useful.

Tobias: Are there any caveats that investors should be aware of?

Darrell: Absolutely: 1) Don't chase the hype unless you are a seasoned speculator. And have an equal willingness and enthusiasm for going *short* as well as *long*. 2) Involve yourself with a financial or money management team that understands the science, because this is really beyond *rocket science*. 3) Do not put more than 5 -

15% of your investible funds in *small tech*. This is a highly speculative area. 4) The "industry" will follow a repeating Boom/Bust
scenario for 2 - 3 decades. Unless you are literally putting away
money for 15 years or more, don't even think about a *buy and hold
strategy*. While the downdrafts will be severe, firms such as ours
should be able to maneuver profitably in this treacherous terrain.

1 Science Fiction vs. Science Fact

Probably like you I do not feel incredibly confident when analyzing machines that one cannot even see with a high school microscope. Also, I do not possess an easygoing understanding of the variables that quantum mechanics imposes on infinitesimally small forces. As seen in the *Heisenberg Principle*, particles and forces may change simply when viewed with light, the particles of which are larger than the particles they are viewing. These are not facile concepts for my non-scientific mind that has lost most memory of even high school chemistry.

If someone told you in 2005 that a gold deposit had just been discovered in Nevada, that it has 300 million ounces of easily recoverable gold, at the surface, in the middle of the Carlin Trend, you might have no reason to disbelieve them. However, there would be hundreds of analysts and brokers in the U.S. who could tell you that was fantasy. (The Carlin is one of the most picked-over geological trends in North America. "Everything" at surface is well known and understood.) If you heard that an OLED display will never make it in the marketplace because it uses too much energy, you might just accept it. Yet thousands of folks throughout this great land, and tens of thousands around the world, know that one of OLED displays' advantages is its low use of energy.

What if someone claims a discovery that cobalt nanoparticle encrusted quantum dots have been found effective in treating feline nanovirus? Who are you going to call? You cannot call *Ghostbusters*. Where are the hundreds, the thousands who even know that the sentence does not even make sense, much less that the science is mumbo-jumbo-science-fiction? They are in universities and laboratories. Currently, these individuals are not working on Wall Street in any significant numbers.

If a mine is "a hole in the ground with a liar on top," nanotech will be a natural gusher for science fiction passing as science. Furthermore, do not imagine that the lines of demarcation are clear and absolute. Quite the contrary; two high school chemistry students can agree on what is an acid and what is a base, yet a professor of biology might be fooled or fail to grasp a nanotech phenomenon for lack of the physics training of a Feynman Prize winner or Nobel candidate. It gets better (or worse). Recently a bio-nanoscientist noted that an award-winning internationally renown chemist and nanoscientist was about to make a major basic blunder in the bio-mechanism that controlled how healing occurs in some injuries. Because his background was in chemistry, he was blind to the fact that his medical "advance" could never really work. Meanwhile, a biologist would have been aware of decades old research that would have kept him from the folly of his approach.

This is not a *nanotech only* phenomenon.

Economics-trained mining engineers are forever killing the dreams of geologists and geophysicists. A trained geologist with a review of properly conducted sampling and drilling can tell you that a $150 million worth of gold lies 600 feet under the ground. The "economic" mining engineer can tell you it will cost $400 million to get it out and into gold bars!

After I had been a stockbroker for about six years (and had been through several strong bull and bear moves) I thought anyone who used a broker with less experience than that was taking their financial life in their hands. Physicians have had years of schooling and on-the-job training before they are called "Doctor," but would you have a new surgeon perform your heart surgery?

If one thinks of nanotechnology as an extremely cutting-edge science that only the most skilled, knowledgeable practitioners are proficient and conversant in, it is easier to understand how a Ph.D. in biology, chemistry or physics (much less a Master's) may completely miss the fine points. As my case above proves, even an eminent *nanoscientist* with background in an inappropriate discipline may miss something (everything?) that is important.

My belief is that very few of any profession's "professionals" are truly gifted. Stock brokers, engineers, CPAs, lawyers, hairdressers, chefs, cab drivers, salesman, actors – for any profession you could name, many of the so-called professionals manifest weak areas. The gifted few are really special (and are probably reading here, now, no doubt!).

Separating science from science fiction involves deep understanding of the scientific method *as well as* a deep understanding of the facts of the relevant field of science.

The vast majority of us (not 72% of us; 99%) are capable of making foolish mistakes in nanotechnology. Make sure you get the highest level of expert advice, or put your trust in a firm that uses a strong SAB who is current on science and preferably possesses broad diversification across the disciplines of nanotechnology: physics, materials science, biology, medicine, engineering, and chemistry.

It is difficult enough to win the battle for a fortune on the fields of the business model, management, product, and financial inputs. Do not make it even more difficult for yourself by inadvertently embracing science fiction.

A Winning Tip for Making Your Nanotech Fortune

You receive an unsolicited piece of junk-mail touting a nanotech company stock. The author is a newsletter writer and self-proclaimed stock market expert. *Throw it away immediately.* **Sharp traders will find a way to short the stock** (usually the only way to benefit from these solicitations). The newsletter writer has a zero chance of being able to separate science fiction from science fact and you are likely being sold worthless paper from folks who know its worth and want to shove it onto you. Read the *fine print* in the disclosure at the bottom of the page of these promotions. Invariably the recommendations are *for pay* in stock or cash, or both, and are nothing more than advertisements. Assume there is even more incentive, under the table or offshore. **The stocks are almost always Canadian and/or Bulletin Board deals because they can more easily tread in the greyest of securities law areas**. In this *pump and dump* game the newsletter writer really does not care if you subscribe to his or her letter; the profit is already made.

SMALL IS NOT NECESSARILY BETTER (OR EVEN NANOTECH)

One place an investor can start to become nano-savvy is by recognizing, as noted, that nanotech does not refer to size alone. If the features of a thing or force can fit in a cube 100 nm X 100 nm (think 1/1,000 the width of a human hair by 1/1,000 the width of a human hair) that is a good start, but then the "properties" question comes into play. To my way of thinking, *true nanotechnology* involves matter that exhibits unique properties due to its size. Quantum effects and properties are exhibited. So if a material is a catalyst, there's a very good chance it will be a better catalyst when processed to the nanoscale ? for no other reason than that there will be much more surface area with which to react. "Nanotechnology" of that ilk will be much more common than what I like to call "true" nanotechnology. The nanotech that impresses me the most happens when a material that is not a catalyst for a chemical process in the macro might become one at the nanoscale.

Variations at the nanoscale itself are very interesting. For example, quantum dots, all of them extremely tiny by any standard, emit very different colors of light depending on their size. Sometimes size does not matter at all. There could be no actual quality change for the purpose needed; perhaps no property changes at all once a critical size is achieved.

How is this knowledge going to help you make money, and avoid losing it?

You will not be fooled by either of what are likely to be the two most over-used and simplistic claims by the *hypesters* of nanotech: 1) it is nanotech because it is at a nanoscale (not everything at the nanoscale is nanotechnology; after all, a molecule of water is at the nanoscale; most small molecule drug development and a lot of material science like polymer plastics take place on the nanoscale) and 2) we made it smaller, so it is better nanotechnology (a property may or may not change when an already tiny nanoparticle is made smaller, but, clearly, smaller size alone is not necessarily an "improvement."

A Winning Tip for Making Your Nanotech Fortune

Fade (sell short) good news. When everyone already invested in a stock expects good news, and the expected good news is announced, there is a natural sigh of relief and shrug of the shoulders as if to say, "What else is new?" Assuming that no new, better news is expected in the near term, this is a perfect time to sell and take profits. It might be hard to do the opposite of what everyone else is doing but it is usually right. Small and micro-cap nanotech companies will not typically have a run of very important news over a period of more than a couple of months at a time. Especially use good news to "blow out" of stocks you do not want to own long-term.

THE ILLUSIVE KILLER APPLICATION

To my way or thinking, e-mail was a *killer application*. So was word processing. So was gene splicing, as was recombinant DNA, the steam locomotive, internet, and the invention of commodities futures markets. Something discovered is applied or engineered into a product or platform that changes the world, becomes a standard, and makes multiple whole industries exist and grow that did not exist before.

How this will occur in nanotechnology was unknown in 2005.

Transistors were invented years before transistor-driven calculators and radios. Integrated circuits existed long before there were personal computers. From Ben Franklin to Thomas Edison to cathode tubes and television, it's a strange road for electricity and lighting to have traveled. But it happened. Who could have predicted it? Look at the industries, much less the companies, that have risen and fallen during the course of that investment history.

The applications of nanotechnology will come fast and furious, and worldwide, billions of dollars will be made and lost, even over the relatively short timeframe of 1997 - 2012. Every VC and investment professional will think he or she is investing in a technology that could possibly serve as the base for a *killer app*, but they will be universally disappointed. Serendipity combined with economic demand will produce now unseen *killer apps*. There is a high likelihood the sought-after application will derive from something invented at a large corporation, or by a lone scientist, or by an entrepreneur toiling in anonymity. Along the way, the best we can realistically hope for is to invest in excellent companies that create valuable products and improvements for their customers and society. There's nothing wrong with that.

A WINNING TIP FOR MAKING YOUR NANOTECH FORTUNE

The *XYZ cures cancer/XYZ causes cancer* conundrum. Early in my career, I had an extremely high opinion of my long cocoa position and had made my biggest single speculation to that point. An acquaintance asked why, since I was so sure, did I not "back up the truck," and literally mortgage my home and "bet the ranch" (hmmm, are there any more clichés I can employ?)? I replied then (and have repeated it often since), "Hey, I don't know that tomorrow morning they're not going to announce that chocolate causes cancer." This is short-hand for being aware that **outlier events do occur**. Heaven help you if you are caught short when they announce that cocoa cures cancer. These events happen all the time. In late 2004 the *big pharma* powerhouse Merck announced that its #2 drug, Vioxx, for arthritis, increased risk for heart attack and stroke. The stock lost $26 billion of its market cap in the next day of trading. At the end of 2002, nanotech giant GE made an announcement that sent its stock shooting from around $23 to $29 in a few, quick days, tacking on billions and killing short-sellers. For better or worse, it can happen to you. No matter your level of confidence, be prepared – maintain a responsible risk profile.

FAIRY DUST

Tinkerbelle threw "Fairy Dust" on people and things which had amazing, magical properties to change the way things were. It could make seeing men blind and put children to sleep. It could make you super light – light enough to fly. It came out of a fairy's pouch: it was invisible. It was cool stuff.

No one had a clue how it worked. It is the same today with many of the materials sciences' nano- "additives" that I like to call *Fairy Dust*. The science behind the activity of action of some nanoparticles such as those added to make bowling balls harder, Mercedes paint jobs more scratch resistant, or Dockers pants unstainable is well-founded and understood. However, more and more we read about particles that somehow, seemingly serendipitously, affect materials and actions in unexpected yet helpful ways.

For example, when silicon computer chips are passed through a fog of extremely small particles of a certain compound during a key point in the manufacturing process, the processor speed is found to increase substantially. The science behind this result is poorly or not at all understood (by physicists, chemists and Ph.D.s in electrical engineering, much less you or me!) It could be found that a super nano-catalyst dramatically increases the efficiency of gasoline combustion. Now, imagine that the "catalyst" does not work for any possible or understood chemical reason. Maybe the reason it "works" is based on the physics related to the electrical charge of the particle. Maybe it works because of an as yet unidentified or poorly understood tiny, biological event.

Maybe it works because we clap our hands.

The point is, more than they'd like to admit, scientists are hard put to explain how or why many of nanotechnology's most promising outcomes work. That does not make these outcomes any less useful or interesting, and we can be certain that scientific explanations will eventually be found for all of these phenomena. No doubt, the correct scientific explanations will come sooner rather than later.

Do not take this as encouragement to invest in *snake oil*. Solid science should always be the necessary basis for investing. I am simply making the point that occasionally science works *backwards* from "the observed," rather than from the hypothesized.

Additionally, sometimes our technology is ahead of our knowledge. A good friend of mine had twins, and a sonogram during his wife's pregnancy showed that each one had slightly enlarged kidneys. After birth, x-rays showed the same condition. Now the kids are ten and in perfect health, each with a slightly enlarged kidney. New technology can show us things we never saw before, that have little or no impact on our lives or that are just not well understood.

For investors, this is all very interesting but does it help us make money? I think the key is to remember that story of 3M and "post It" notes. True or not, the story is that in trying to discover an innovative, strong glue some goofy engineer at old Minnesota M & M slopped together a pathetic glop that not only was not very strong, it was downright lousy. It was terrible glue. So terrible that it of course turned out to be fantastic as *weak glue.*

As long as the Luddites, Lilliputians and other anti-knowledge gang members are kept at bay by bold, honest men and women, the serendipity that marches science forward will keep driving nanotechnology to greater heights. The result will be technologies that enrich the world and the shareholders of the companies that create and develop them.

A Winning Tip for Making Your Nanotech Fortune

Be aware of *Fortune 500* competition. Some small companies are naïve enough to insist that they are working on something so unique, so cutting-edge that no large company is competing with them. **Get worried**. Assuming they are correct means they are likely targeting a tiny market or that large companies have already written off the science. These are big red flags. Assuming they are incorrect (more likely), you have to assume they are remiss in doing their homework, are trying to pull something over on you, or do not understand what competing technologies exist or what near-term, potential technologies science might produce. The correct answer is a complete list of all of the important large and small company (as well as lab and university-based) competing technologies; an intelligent discussion of the pros and cons of each, how the company's technology is positioned to win, and exactly what *unfair advantage* it provides. Of course, all of this should be seen in the context of an exceptional business model and a customer service orientation. Depending on the stage of a company's development, it is always fun to ask how they will provide follow-up services to the customer and who will be doing it and how these people will be trained. Expect that with a few rare, extremely important exceptions, *Fortune 500* companies will dominate the commercialization of nanotechnology. Early stage companies will be merged, acquired, or joint ventured with these mammoths. Small and micro-caps that ignore this reality will be trampled out of existence in a few years.

BETTER MOUSETRAPS ARE A DIME A DOZEN

The world is littered with better mousetraps, better technologies, better restaurants, and better music. **The world does not reward better.** *It rewards those who provide what people want.*

Since college days, I have loved the quote on Yeat's tombstone. "Cast a cold eye on life, on death. Horseman, pass by." We cannot change the world; we must see it as it is in the cold light of day. The Big Mac is not the world's best hamburger. Windows is not the world's best operating system. (Hamburgers, I know. As for the operating system, I'll take the word of my friends who are computer mavens.

A nanotech company is more than its IP, science, technology, and even its products. Marketing must come together with PR, and a high-demand market must greet a motivated, motivating, exceptional CEO. Creativity and mundane planning and operations must meld with a total commitment to serving the customer. The company and its products must add value, and drive out or trump competition.

This is a pretty complex mix that requires thoughtful reflection to succeed in achievement. The bottom line is that better (even best) is usually not good enough.

Meanwhile, there actually is a better mousetrap for sale at your local hardware store. I tried it. It works amazingly well. I am told that it does not sell nearly as many units as the traditional model.

A Winning Tip for Making Your Nanotech Fortune

Look for *film and camera* and *razor and razorblade* companies. Old-fashioned as it sounds in this age of digital cameras, everyone understands intuitively that if you have to keep purchasing film, razorblades, reagents, catalysts, quantum dots, disposable diagnostic kits, whatever, from a specific company for its star product to work, you have a great start at an excellent, sustainable business model. In fact, often the "razorblade" becomes the profit center while the so-called name product becomes a commodity. Just prior to the digital camera age you could probably buy a decent Kodak camera for $19, the film for which cost about $4 per roll, the Kodak developing of which cost about $6 per roll. It appears that profits rose along the chain. Look for models like this. Making a widget for $1,000 and selling it for $2,500 is good work if you can get it, but nothing beats a product that keeps generating sales, revenues and profits by its mere use. The cost of those little ink cartridges that go in my super-cheap Lexmark All-In-One printer, scanner, copier, fax gizmo drives me crazy. In *small tech* there will be special reagents that make certain lab-on-a-chip features work and there will be other consumables in diagnostic tests of all sorts.

One Good Scientist Can Ruin the Soup

Beware the good scientist; especially if he or she is articulate and persuasive. This is not a criticism of scientists in general. Obviously the good ones – better yet, the great ones – are the keys to developing the science behind nanotechnology, the industry, and to creating all the tools and products that compose the nanotech revolution. Yet without benefit of commercial direction and financial controls, a single good scientist can keep a company hard at work on his or her *science project* instead of growing a viable business.

Geologists like to "turn the drill bit to the left"; investment bankers like to do deals; scientists like to do science. This is not hard to understand. Where it becomes a problem is when corporate focus is lost to scientific research. This is especially prevalent when a scientist leads a corporation, and this is more common in a cutting-edge field like nanotechnology, where the scientist may be both a founder as well as the only person in the company who truly understands the science and technology.

It is no exaggeration to say that there have been ongoing science projects disguised as public companies trading on the NYSE, ASE and NASDAQ for decades. At some point in a company's development between its third and tenth years (and usually well before its fifth), this problem becomes clear to all but the most gullible investors. After that, each investor must decide for himself or herself whether to trade the ups and downs, the lab successes and failures, or find "entertainment" and profit in greener pastures where a sustainable, growing, scalable business is the goal.

A WINNING TIP FOR MAKING YOUR NANOTECH FORTUNE

Spotting major trends early and leveraging off them is a great way to build and invest in scalable businesses. You do not have to be first. You do not even have to be very early; just be reasonably early. The Starbucks example is a good one. We all saw Starbucks growing. We saw the trend of Americans drinking better and more expensive coffee. It did not take a genius to see this. Whether you became convinced this was a trend, not merely a fad, in 1992 or 1998, really did not matter. You could find scalable enterprises in the space in which to invest. Espresso machine makers, coffee roaster manufacturers, and coffee-growing acreage in quality areas in Indonesia all had or are having bull markets, I am sure. Examine the unintended consequences, and unanticipated results of this one trend. We have high-end coffee bars in grocery stores. There are exotic, previously unheard-of coffees costing $45 to $100/lb. You can take a course on becoming a barista. Coffee ice creams and candy seem much more popular than when I was a kid. High end tea bars are popping up. Nanotech companies that sell more and more of whatever they are selling as a true, scalable trend grows are the ones to buy. If you cannot identify the trend that the company is leveraging off do not buy the stock. If the scientist, entrepreneur, broker, or executive pitching the deal cannot clearly identify and articulate it, run.

Nanoscience and nanotechnology will grow for years in the areas of health care and medicine.

In 2005 the co-founder of The Nanotech Company, LLC, our SAB Chairman, Erkki Ruoslahti, M.D., Ph.D. was awarded the prestigious Japan Prize. The Japan Prize is awarded for original and outstanding achievements in science and technology that are recognized as having advanced the frontiers of knowledge and served the cause of peace and prosperity for mankind. Dr Ruoslahti is a member of the National Academy of Sciences, American Academy of Arts & Sciences and the National Institute of Medicine. Here's what this noted bionanoscientist, had to say about the future of medicine.

The Future of Medicine

"Will biotechnology and medicine go nano? Will we see microscopic machines coursing through the body, monitoring vital activities and correcting problems? Very likely, and here is why: nanodevices can potentially do more than current drugs and diagnostic tests.

Applications in the management of cancer exemplify the potential of nanotechnology. The National Cancer Institute and NASA have a cancer nanotechnology program with the goal of producing devices. First generation nanoparticles are already in development. Magnetic particles for in vivo diagnostics are in use in the clinic, and various lipid-based nanoparticles capable of delivering drugs or genes are in advanced preclinical testing.

However, for the full potential of nanotechnology in medicine to be realized, nanomachines have to get 'smarter'. They have to home in on the appropriate target, respond to its recognition by sending a signal, and effect a treatment. Finally, the device should be capable of recognizing changes caused by the treatment and report back on the results. These tasks require built-in sensors for target recognition and molecular switches to convert the sensor signal to a response.

The sensor aspect has essentially been solved. Peptides, proteins, antibodies, and nucleic acid molecules with recognition properties suitable for sensor functions are available. We work on guidance molecules that could serve as sensors to direct a nanodevice to the appropriate target in the body through the bloodstream. We use bacteriophage, a virus that infects common bacteria, as a tool in probing the vasculature for specific changes. The phage can be engineered to display a vast collection of peptides on its surface. By injecting these into the bloodstream of a live mouse, one can select peptides that make the phage home to a given target.

It turns out that essentially every tissue puts a specific signature on its vasculature and that pathological lesions, such as cancer, impose their own changes on the vasculature. Tumors make blood vessels grow as a way of securing a blood supply for themselves, and growing tumor blood vessels are different from normal ones. The tumor environment also causes other changes in the vessels, changes that can be specific to a degree that even allows one to distinguish the vasculature of a pre-cancerous lesion from normal vasculature, and from the vasculature of a full-blown tumor in the same tissue. This specialization is not limited to blood vessels; tumor lymphatics also differ from normal lymphatics.

The phage that helps elucidate much of the vascular address system is a natural nanomachine. It functions much like a nanoscale syringe, binding to the prospective bacterial host and injecting the phage's nucleic acid into it, so that the host supports its multiplication. Following this model, researchers have designed targeted viruses and synthetic nanoparticles that can home in on tumor vessels and deliver a gene or drug that destroys the vessels and the tumor. The specificity of these devices relies on the targeting (and possibly a specific action of the drug or gene); the delivery part is passive.

One can envision that more complex nanodevices capable of being altered by an encounter with a target could survey the vasculature and come back through the circulation to report on the findings. Other nanodevices could similarly survey the gut or bladder for precancerous and cancerous changes. An encounter with the target could induce release of the device's payload for treatment purposes. Alternatively, an external signal – such as the magnetic field of a diagnostic magnetic resonance imaging instrument – could trigger the treatment step. A two-way interaction with an imaging instrument would be particularly desirable because it would link diagnosis to a treatment.

Finally, another set of sensors operating in the same way as the homing signals but designed to detect apoptosis, cellular distress, or cell proliferation, could monitor the treatment's success. The goals outlined above are within reach, but achieving them will require collaboration among a diverse group of scientists. The sensor technology, which has already been designed by bioengineers, will have to be combined with work by chemists who can convert the sensor signals to specific action and by materials scientists who can provide the framework for functional nanodevices. Forging such collaborations is likely to usher in a new era in medicine."

—Erkki Ruoslahti, M.D., Ph.D.,
Distinguished Professor
The Burnham Institute
La Jolla, California

—*MATERIALS TODAY, Vol 6, No 12, Supplement 1 (Nanotoday), 2003, pp 13, E Ruoslahti, "The Future of Medicine?"* with permission from Elsevier.

3 THE NANOTECH ROADMAP 2005 - 2030

IF YOU COULD PICK ONE AREA OF NANOTECH IP TO INVEST IN FOR 2006 -2011, WHAT WOULD IT BE AND WHY?

I have great expectations for investments in nanoparticle advanced materials, especially products developed for coatings and lubricants. I also think think film and high resolution display technology excellent investments.
—**Roger Attick**, President, CeMines

Tools! They're the picks and shovels of the Nanotech gold rush.
—**Tim Stultz**, President, Imago Instruments

Nanoparticle catalysts. They will be used in everything from energy systems to improved chemical processes, and they offer phenomenal increases in efficiency.
—**Bryan W. Bockhop** of the law firm *Arnall, Golden, Gregory.*

HOW DO YOU SEE THE COMMERCIALIZATION OF NANOTECHNOLOGY SEQUENCING?

VC Steve Jurvetson sees it this way:

Early Revenue:
- Tools and bulk materials (powders, composites).
- 1 D (One Dimensional) Sensors, larger MEMS scale devices

Medium Term:
- 2D Nanoelectronics: memory, displays, solar cells
- Hierarchically structured nanomaterials
- Hybrid Bio-nano, energy, drug delivery & diagnostics

Long Term:
- 3D Nanoelectronics
- Nanomedicine
- Machine-phase manufacturing
- The safest long-term prediction is that the most important nanotech developments will be the unforeseen opportunities, something that we could not predict today.

Investors (as opposed to speculators whom we will cover later) will want to participate in the areas of nanotech that are likely to prove profitable first. In the alternative, if you choose to invest in a long-term payoff proposition you will at least want to be clear about what you are getting yourself into.

I am always amazed by investors who will write $5,000 to $5,000,000 checks for a high-tech medical device or biotech company's shares for which the commercial payoff is a dozen years away. These folks get carried away by some molecule that killed cancer cells in a test-tube or helped mice live 5% longer, yet overlook that chlorine bleach kills cancer cells in a test-tube, or that Phase 1, 2, and 3 human studies in the FDA approval process can be 12 - 16 years from mice studies to pills for humans. This is not to say one should never invest for the very long term; ignorance of the critical timeframes and processes will not help you develop a winning investment strategy.

This is how I see significant nanotech profits developing over the next few decades (remember, some of the first areas are already producing profits for companies). The timeframes set forth below are not meant to be limiting. The ranges are the years in which I expect these areas to develop explosive profitability. I have included the tools of nanotech itself in this list; though they are constantly being developed and improved and are a major "sector" in the pantheon of nanotech industry and profitability. Devices and instruments for weighing, designing, manipulating, measuring, and viewing nanoscale particles, forces and engineered matter is a growth industry. Nanotech companies need these tools for everything they need to do. You cannot weigh a quantum dot with a bathroom scale. In addition, some companies are creating platforms for creating tools and for creating nanotechnologies; these are amazing products, the best of which are and will be in high demand. It is useful here to remember that companies such as Intel, IBM, Amgen, GE, and DuPont are among the strongest customers for these types of tools; it's not just nanotech micro-caps.

THERE ARE TWO TIMEFRAMES BELOW THAT I EXPECT WILL BE QUITE CONTROVERSIAL:

1. **2007 - 2013: Materials.** Nanotech will be used to improve everyday materials, making them stronger, harder, softer, more durable, etc. We have already seen prosaic products such as anti-stain fabric that feels like the untreated fabric, car paints that retain their color better and are almost scratch-proof, tennis balls that hold their air several times longer than regular ones, and thin films that coat glasses, rendering them fog-resistant. Down the road, we should see *smart* packaging materials that can change temperature or permeability, wirelessly controlled paint that changes color on command; metals that mimic plastics, inks that penetrate seemingly impenetrable materials, and disease-resistant seed coatings among thousands of even more useful and interesting products.

2. **2008 - 2015: Instruments.** Among many other nano-enhanced products, tools for doing nanotechnology will enjoy increasing worldwide demand – from microscopes, special software, scales and accelerators to everyday instru-

ment improvements that result from nanotech such as more sensitive automobile crash sensors, diagnostic thermometers, low-cost, high school atomic force microscopes; supersensitive, gas and explosive *sniffing*, anti-terror devices; and blood testing equipment that makes 2005 technology look primitive.

3. **2009 - 2016: Nanoparticle Manufacture/Packaging.** This is one of my controversial earlier-stage choices. Most financial folks' current thinking is that nanoparticle manufacture will be a commodity business, at best, with steadily declining margins. I think *know-how* and trade secrets will catapult some eventual manufacturing leaders into a highly profitable business supplying custom-designed and very rare nanoparticles to the nanotech industry and labs. In addition, expect to see novel packaging of nanoparticles that will create a value-added proposition for manufacturers. For example, different nanoparticles, properly encapsulated, manufactured and packaged could be water filters, fuel propellants, or agricultural nutrition pellets. If well-patented with defensible claims, what looked like a mere "commodity" product (manufactured nano-nickel, for example) can evolve into a real high-profit item (such as an efficient, low-cost replacement for catalytic converters).

4. **2010-2018: Medical Diagnostics and Devices.** Given the lower FDA approval threshold of non-invasive healthcare-related products, combined with the aging *baby boom* population, I expect the market for diagnostic tests, lab-on-a chip, and myriad nano-driven medical devices and instruments to explode. We should see significant products begin coming to market as early as 2008-2010, but sales and profitability will really take off and accelerate in the timeframe referenced.

5. **2011-2020: Environmental Solutions.** The international fresh water problem, with issues of filtration and purification, air pollution, groundwater problems, new mining, petroleum

product extraction technologies, and more, will keep the pressure on in this important area. As the populations of China, India and (in later decades) even Africa really begin to aspire to the middle class, there's no turning back on the growth of pollution, and the acceleration of the problem. Nanotechnology should be in the forefront of the solution, and companies and investors that focus here could be huge winners by that decade.

6. **2012-2022: Nanoelectronics and Computing.** This is my other controversial pick, with regard to timeframe. A ton of money is being focused in this area from 2003 to 2005 (see Zettacore, NVE, Nantero, Nanosys, and others), but I believe that display and chip technology are not going to be leapfrogged by nanotech anytime soon. Other investors clearly think otherwise; they envision returns much earlier than I. When I hear Intel's leading scientists and technologists saying that current technology will advance Moore's Law through 2013 - 2016, at least, I take them at their word. Don't forget that the imbedded investment in *fabs* (chip manufacturing plants) keeps growing, representing hundreds of billions of dollars. It will not be tossed aside lightly.

7. **2013 - 2024: Energy.** This is almost too big. Old tech-nology, and non-renewable resources, "new" technology and renewable resources, fuel cells, some aspects of a potential hydrogen economy, not to mention the possibility of some new kinds of energy, should be enabled and made more efficient by nanotechnologies. The large companies (oil, utilities, *et al.*) that embrace nanotechnology will bury those that do not. Again, expect nanotech to impact the energy industry well before 2010, but huge profits are unlikely to comfortably manifest until a bit later.

8. **2014 - 2026: Optical.** The use of nanotechnology to manipulate light of various wavelengths for use in switches, as well as new, yet unforeseen opportunities in telecommunications,

computers, microscopy, and wireless could be an exceedingly important profit area. Imagine products based on nanoscale reflecting "mirrors" used to direct and manipulate streams of photons, potentially individual photons, for myriad uses in electronics, display technology, photography, artificial sight for the blind, etc.

9. **2015 - 2028: Health and Nanomedicine.** This is the grand-daddy of them all. Since the quest for healthy, long life is never ending, more money will be made in bio-nano than any other area. Individualized pharmaceuticals, nearly Star Trek-like medical devices, self-targeting, wirelessly communicating, cancer-killing nanoparticles will become realities. As we discover in greater detail how the body and mind work, we should see incredibly effective psychotropic drugs and, based on the brain-medicine interface, whole new platforms for eradicating or ameliorating disease. Look for nanotech-enhanced medical devices and artificial organs and limbs that really improve the quality of life of the ill. Do not underestimate the contributions in dentistry, nutrition, veterinary medicine, crop engineering, and beauty products. While the health and medical areas will be fraught with the danger of hype and will attract the most "also-rans" and shady characters along the way, relying on a team of experts can keep one from wandering into science and medical fiction.

THREE WORDS: DEPARTMENT OF DEFENSE

One cannot underestimate the importance of the Department of Defense (DOD) in the development of nanotechnology. Call me a cynic, (I prefer "realist"), but, clearly with a debt to history, I believe the war on terror, the Institute for Soldier Nanotechnology, and the need for better, stronger, faster weapons and tools of war were the most effective drivers to the formulation and eventual passing of the National Nanotech Initiative by Congress in 2003. Its $4.6 billion investment in national nanotech education and infrastructure, envisioned under

Clinton and birthed under Bush, was the beginning. But, as much or more than NIH (National Institutes of Health) or any other motivator, the Department of Defense will continue to drive the development of the nanotechnology industry far into the future.

Without doubt, companies and products targeting the defense of the country, building weapons, and preparing for new, higher-tech, soldier-focused wars will be a major area for nanotech fortunes. Imagine a hand held device that can read a single molecule of anthrax in a room. Imagine an armor vest that mimics the extreme forgiving hardness of the shell of an abalone. These are being developed now. "Smart Dust" may allow pictures and data to be wirelessly sent across the world from seeming dust particles floating through the air of a room.

NASA (National Aeronautics and Space Administration) and NOAA (National Oceanic and Atmospheric Administration) are other major US supporters of nanotech development in universities, labs and private companies. Their grants and contracts, along with DOD, DARPA (Defense Advanced Research Projects Agency), NIH and the National Cancer Research Institute constitute the hugest capital investment in the future of nanotechnology.

A WINNING TIP FOR MAKING YOUR NANOTECH FORTUNE

The road to corporate profits is not the same as the road to investor profits. In drug development, mining, biotech and oil exploration, corporate profits do not arrive until a pill, ingot, or barrel is actually sold. It is counterintuitive, but once these landmarks are achieved, investor profits usually come <u>more slowly</u>. The highest rates of investor returns typically occur between the time prior to FDA approval (or an initial mine feasibility study) and the day a factory or mine is financed. For nano-investors, this means keying in on the time between the days a profit-producing product *seems likely* and the day financing for manufacture becomes available. **Besides Angel or VC investing, winners will focus on investing during the most important investor profit-potential timeframes.**

Rocks & Bots: The Unusual Linkage between Nanotech, Biotech and Mining

In your pursuit of nanotech profits and the boom/bust cycles you must navigate, it will serve you well to consider the examples offered by the biotech and mining industries. The long histories of boom and bust cycles in mining, and the shorter history in biotech (since 1982) are roadmaps to investing in nanotech for different reasons.

In mining, geologists, geophysicists, and mining engineers, along with assay labs, induced polarization technicians, and others, test a theory that a deposit exists, and can be mined with a positive economic result. Land claims are established or joint ventures are made to ensure the rights of ownership to the hoped-for rewards. The companies involved do several tests and take surface samples before making a determination to drill underground. Then they do test drilling, and, if confirming results are found, they commit to drill much more extensively. Once a deposit is confirmed, it becomes *ore* only after certain commercial tests are applied. Every step requires a new, huge capital commitment, while the results are never known in advance because "no one can see underground." After all this, a decision is finally made about whether to build a mine – another immense capital cost.

So, along the way, for a gold mining situation, gold may be in the ground somewhere but it may not be a *deposit*. A deposit may exist but it may not meet the economic standard to be called "ore" (actually, it very rarely is). Ore may exist but a decision still might not be made to mine it. A mine could be built but – depending on the price of gold and how well the engineers and contractors met the *feasibility study* targets – it might not prove profitable.

Furthermore, in all of the above, we have not even begun to discuss environmental regulations, labor expenses, political risks, or competition from other mines, all of which may have drastic consequences for a new mining operation.

Nanotech has strong corollaries to mining. Physicists, chemists, electrical engineers, biologists, lab technicians and others test a theory that something they cannot see exists, has economic value, and that they can profitably extract that value. Each step along the way is fraught with tremendous economic risk, and significant capital requirements. Clean rooms and AFM microscopes, alone, cost a fortune. Even leasing them, like leasing mining drill rigs and hiring planes and pilots to shoot seismic pictures on geological settings, is an expensive proposition.

After a particular *intellectual property* is developed and *staked (patented)* by the nanoscientists, they still have to worry that their idea will be copied (usually with some minor change) or made obsolete. After significant investment of time and money, a nanotechnology must prove itself through much testing, establishing that what it does is significantly better (and often, significantly cheaper) than existing technologies, and that there is a ready market for it.

Last but not least, after these hurdles are overcome, a product must be produced in significant quantities, subject to stringent manufacturing tolerances for errors, breakage, etc. So-called simple things like how you count or keep track of these infinitesimal things become highly problematic. Furthermore, there are atomic and subatomic forces at work that can play havoc with elements that seem so straightforward in the macro world.

So a nanotech theory can make scientific sense, yet not *prove out*. A proven theory can still result in <u>no</u> developed, significant, marketable technology. A cool technology can result in no product. A product can meet a non-existent, weak demand or immature market. A product may meet a market that is too small to justify the expense of manufacture, or the difficulty of the manufacturing process itself may stop the development in its tracks.

Yet there's more. Environmental regulations, labor expenses, political risks, competition from other nanotechnologies, or even traditional technologies, can have drastic consequences for a new nanotech company.

I do not think it necessary to go through the same exposition with the biotech corollary. Suffice it to say, taking a crafted molecule from discovery or invention to a drug you can pick up at your pharmacist is at least as daunting as (and quite comparable to) the mining and nanotech processes. The FDA, EPA, codes, regulations, agency oversight, laws, bureaucrats, Luddites, competitors, *etc., et al.*, for better, or for worse, can stop a new mine, drug, or nanotechnology at any stage in its development. And when one is talking about a goal of profitability and a winning strategy for investing, each stage of development is critical.

Dr. Evelyn Hu, a member of my firm's Scientific Advisory Board, is working on an incredible new science and technology, well on the Road Map, that is stirring passions in the technology and financial worlds. Scientists on the frontiers of the *small technology* revolution are doing things unimaginable only a few years ago.

Attempting to employ genetically engineered viruses to create – via the power of biological self-assembly – tiny, sophisticated electronic components for the semiconductor industry, Hu and brilliant protégé, Angela Belcher's company, Cambrios, is doing fascinating, somewhat surprising work. In a manner roughly related to the way an abalone shell grows, viruses – with an affinity for gallium arsenide, indium phosphide, or some other electronically important material – are used to infect a bacteria (yes, it sounds crazy), which then act as a kind of manufacturing plant for producing much more of the focal material. What's really exciting is that the self-assembling nature of the viruses lines up the quantum dots or other nanoparticles sought into a useful, evenly-spaced array. Getting other things to stick or connect is also possible, so "building" can be envisioned.

Is this the next step in how Intel (or Cambrios) will one day build the nanoscale circuits and components they are using more and more and will eventually rely upon? Will this prove to be a much less capital-intensive, disruptive technology, away from the current trend toward multi-billion dollar fabrication plants? Time will tell, but aren't the concepts amazing?

When I asked Evelyn about how scientists themselves viewed nanotechnology in late 2004, she said it was more "like a state of mind; a way of thinking about things" and that "the edges between and around nano, MEMs, microfluidics and microtechnology were blurry." As a non-scientist, I found this marvelously freeing.

A Winning Tip for Making Your Nanotech Fortune

Bull markets really do crawl up a *wall of worry*. This is one market chestnut that has *the extra-added benefit of being true*. If investors are very bullish, if you are at a conference and everyone around you is smiling, if confidence reigns supreme, and folks you do not even know give you *high fives* on a recent profit (especially in a company you do not even understand), "be afraid; be very afraid." On the other hand, if you are long (own the stock), and feel mild discomfort with your position, and folks are shaking their heads, and wondering out loud if nanotech could just be a fad, or that government, ecologists, regulators, the public, bad science (take your pick) are going to be the ruination of the growth in nanotechnology, dig your heels in and strongly *consider increasing your positions.*

It is 2011 – Are You Too Late?

If you are reading these words in 2011 you are clearly late to the party. However, are you too late? Have all the profits been reaped from nanotechnology? Was the most recent boom the last boom? Short answer. Short chapter.

"There is no way that you are too late."

Nanotechnology will dominate every field of hard science and drive technology in every industry for at least 20 to 30 more years, possibly 70. This is only the beginning.

Remember the story about *post-It notes?*

Here is another story that should convince you that a killer application or just a plain old fantastic product can serendipitously occur anywhere, anytime, 2011, 2017 or 2027.

Few people know it, but the invention of the microwave oven can be traced back to an inquisitive engineer's sweet tooth. It happened one day in 1946, the story goes, when Percy Spencer noticed that a candy bar had melted in his pocket while he was testing a new magnetron vacuum tube for Raytheon, as part of its radar research that began during World War II. Intrigued, he placed some popcorn kernels near the tube, and an egg, the next morning – and discovered that the intense heat had similar effects. "Scientists familiar with magnetrons knew the tubes generated heat at the same time they radiated the microwave energy that made radar possible," reads the official history of the company, which was founded more than 80 years ago here near Harvard University, the Massachusetts Institute of Technology and other crucibles of advanced research.

Spencer was the first, however, to discover that one could cook food using microwave radio signals. History is full of accidental inventions like this, especially in the United States: Teflon, Coca-Cola and nylon all emerged as serendipitous offshoots of unrelated research.
—**Mike Ricciuti**, **Ed Frauenheim** and **Mike Yamamoto**
From an article in MIT's Magazine of Innovation

A WINNING TIP FOR MAKING YOUR NANOTECH FORTUNE

Bear markets slide down a slope of hope. Everyone knows, or at least has heard about the proverbial "wall of worry." However, far fewer know about, and fewer still understand, that *hope*, in and of itself, is the prevailing emotion that marks *bear* markets and downward moves of intermediate and long-term duration. (*Fear* dominates in short term crashes.) Watch and read interviews with nanotech pundits and analysts, and listen to your own self-talk and the comments of fellow nano-investors. As inevitable declines occur, *caution* and *fear* sometimes get replaced with a hopefulness that stock prices or company prospects will improve or return to previous levels. You do not have to be an expert in human analysis or even sensitive. The actual words *hope, hopeful, hopefulness, and hoping* will keep popping up. That is your cue to sell. The start of the hopefulness is the beginning of a full-scale bear market; the longer the hopefulness goes on, the longer the bear market.

How to Analyze Nanotech Companies Like a Pro

What questions should Nanotech investors be asking that they are NOT asking?

How will your technology be manufactured with scalable processes and tools?
—**Maximillian M. Schroeck, Ph.D.,**
Managing Director, Agilent Ventures
Director of Strategy, Agilent Technologies

Is this a truly 'enabling' device, material, or tool, with scientific merit or just sexy fodder for the press? Is there even a commercial market that justifies its development?
—**Tim Stultz**, President, Imago Instruments

Here is the step-by-step procedure that my firm, The Nanotech Company, LLC, uses to analyze a public or private nanotech company.

First: We analyze Executive Summary, Business Plan, Annual Report and most recent SEC filings – We review and make a basic assessment of the company based on these documents. This is an art honed by reviewing hundreds of early-stage business plans at every stage of development, and usually weeds out 75 to 95% of all businesses at the venture capital level. For a more seasoned public company, this analysis brings us to a basic understanding of the science, technology and business of the company, an overview of basic investment criteria, and a basis for knowing who the company's customers and competitors are or are likely to be. We proceed, assuming a project has passed this cursory review by one of our researchers and is found strongly interesting on some level.

Second: Science – The Nanotech Company, LLC draws on seven internal scientists (including National Academy of Sciences members and a Feynman Nanotechnology winner, as well as a Japan Prize winner) and additional consulting scientists to first determine whether a company has sound science that poses opportunity for relatively near-term commercial exploitation. If a company is unable to pass this common sense test on both counts, science and commercialization potential, there may be no reason to proceed further. Without the filter of highly qualified scientists, you are at a disadvantage to the pros, **but you can still compete adequately simply by reading and researching commentary and input by legitimate scientific sources, such as leading university and learned journals, and getting confirmation through respected high tech securities analysts in the field**. Goldman Sachs, Lehman, Bear Stearns, Alex Brown or Merrill Lynch (and the like) analysts are not perfect, but wandering into science fiction or missing the commercialization date of a technology by half a decade or more is not likely to be one of their mistakes. (In the science big picture these analysts' reports can be most helpful to confirm other research you have done.) On private equity deals or investing in venture capital startups, I strongly encourage you to become your own expert as an Angel (more on this in another chapter), or align yourself with a VC firm with proven nanotech expertise.

Third: The Management and Scientific Team – Once a business/investment review, and the science, the technology, and the nearness of commercialization have been positively assessed, my corporate development team and I analyze the capability and integrity of the management team. While third in our review order, management and scientific team assessment is the single most important consideration. While professional money management clients typically have their own significant expertise in this area, the cutting-edge nature of nanotech itself requires an additional level of screening. Our association with a leading nanotech human capital firm, as well as our scientists' ability to accurately assess a company's scientific and engineering teams' capability to actually advance, what may be good science, is critical to investing success. **Any lapse in integrity, sign of not putting the investors' interests first, or weakness in the board of directors or scientific team must be addressed.** What can be done if a science is good, but taking it to next stage or commercialization requires a higher level of knowledge and expertise than the target company's team possesses? How do you remedy a weak link, such as a VP of marketing who shows too much interest in when he can sell his shares to the public? *You require some hiring and firing prior to your investment.*

Fourth: Business Model – Assuming one has gotten this far, the business model itself must be meticulously scrutinized, because "the best laid schemes o' mice an' men gang aft agley." A company could have a *better mousetrap*. They could have it priced right to build, and priced right to sell in the marketplace. That is not enough. A complete plan recognizes that competition does not stand still. It assumes the worst case for itself and the best case for the competitors, and still *comes up roses*. At this point, winning investors in nanotech will look closely at the ability to seamlessly integrate the key product or nanotechnology into existing manufacturing processes, and see eventual profitability based not on wishful thinking but on a well designed plan. (Practically, at this point, we should have already convinced ourselves that we have the right team to execute the plan.)

Fifth: Deal Structure and Capitalization – After decades of analyzing good business plans (and seeing many more horrible ones), I have seen bad structure kill more than a few potentially sound businesses. This often refers to the *insider's* inability to see the value of capital, or to the VCs and investment banks taking too much of the equity. Both kill deals. There is a *happy medium*, and a fair structure that builds incentives for all parties, and leaves room for additional increases in shareholder value for years after the IPO. This is not brain surgery (or nanotechnology), but it is an art form of sorts and requires experience and practice to create and enhance the right winning, success formula. Too much capital, too soon has hurt many of the early nanotech deals from 1997 - 2005. Simply, if a company needs $1.5 million to answer the next questions about its technology, you do not give them $800,000 or $4 million. You give them $1.5 to $1.9 million. If a scientist spent three years of his or her life and $4 million in grant money developing a platform science that now forms the technological basis for a nanotech startup, no matter how bright and intelligent he or she is, the company cannot get $30 million from investors and keep 65% of the company.

Sixth: Financial Public Relations Plan – Many of my financial professional colleagues miss the importance of this one key area for a new, small or even larger nanotech company. When a company comes before us to be analyzed for its investment potential, I want to also see a **marketing plan for its stock**. I want to see the company's commitment in time and funding stated, and I want it to be significant. *Ivory Tower* types need not apply. Every investor has dozens (in coming years, perhaps hundreds) of private and publicly traded nanotech companies to choose from, and literally thousands of high-tech companies and others compete for every investing dollar, pound, franc, euro or yen.

To think that *if you build it, they will come*, is just wishful thinking. Financial PR (**not** paying brokers under the table to hype your stock – that happens – or bribing newsletter writers with cheap options to promote your story – that happens, too) is important to support and grow shareholder value, and to *create a strong currency* out of the company stock itself. **Remember, a growing company cannot spend cash to acquire a company, important IP, or key employee. If not using its fully valued stock, it is are hurting existing shareholders' value.** Keeping legitimate investment analysts, financial writers, brokers, institutional investors and the public well-informed by putting your company and its story in the best possible, honest light is the **duty** of any management team. I would recommend you not invest a penny in a nanotech company whose leaders do not understand this simple reality or who are unable, for any reason, to make a good go of it.

Seventh: Technical Analysis – Clearly, privately held or venture deals do not *trade* in the usual sense of the word. However, once public, stocks trade and their charts offer significant information to those who use technical analysis. So, for publicly traded shares we analyze those charts using proprietary, pattern recognition tools that I developed between 1973 and 1991. In other chapters, I will spend some time on technical analysis tools you can employ; for now, keep in mind that even a *great company*, that meets all of the criteria of the six analyses above, can still be a *lousy investment*. Consider 1995 – 2005. Consider, Yahoo, eBay, Qualcomm, Intel, Microsoft, Wal-Mart, and dozens of other great companies. Review the charts. Would you rather have bought them at 3-year highs or at 3-year lows?

Eighth: Exit Strategy – No nanotech company wants to discuss an investor's exit strategy (although they smile and pretend to like it), but it is an important part of a serious, winning investor's strategy, and it is an important final step in analyzing whether to make a capital placement or encourage clients to do so. Furthermore, the exit strategy can refer to the company's exit strategy as well. *For example, not all private companies will "exit" in an IPO.* Many (if not most) in nanotech will be absorbed into larger, well-established companies through M & A (mergers and acquisitions), or their IP will be licensed in exchange for royalty payments, or sold. An early-stage investor may be looking for an IPO, a sale of some sort to an existing company, an upgrade in valuation due to some event or significant, repeatable, growth in revenues and earnings. No matter what our exit strategy, **before an investment is made** and no matter how much we like the company's other positive features, the winning strategy takes into consideration timing, process, type of sale, amount of profit expected, and all possible risks. Do not be remiss in assessing management's *exit* *strategy*. I like to see a minimum of a 4-year commitment by key executives and scientists. Clearly, locked-up stock serves investors better than "strong assurances and solemn commitments." Obviously, do not deal with those you do not trust and don't like; but, in the words of one spiritual master, "Have faith in God, but tie up your camel."

For our nanotech company clients, we use the same eight-step advisory discipline noted above. Private companies seeking investment, and the highest level of expertise in preparation for investors, as well as public companies seeking to enhance shareholder value, find the road to their goals made explicit by utilizing a proven discipline as presented above. There are no secrets, no shortcuts; above, I have presented the same investment analysis parameters, criteria and priorities that we use for ourselves and our clients.

It is worth reiterating a point made in strategy eight, above. You should not be disabused or put down out-of-hand a management team or investment group's plan to sell out BEFORE a product is manufactured or even before a technology is fully developed. The most intelligent and profitable investment plan may include an early exit strategy along the way to becoming an ongoing company. In fact, I am always on the alert and sensitive to entrepreneurs, executives, or scientists who verbalize the desire to "build the next Genentech" or "build a huge, sustainable business." These sentiments seem noble at first, but professional investors want to make the most profitable investments and, at most, very few expect or plan to be around for more than three to ten years. Yes, one hears of early investors in Microsoft, Wal-Mart or eBay who still own shares more than a decade later, but they are the exception, not the rule. (Besides, they can still make that claim even if they only have 1% of their initial position left).

For every Sand Hill VC that was an Apple shareholder in 1980 and still is, there are 20 who "lost" their shares before 1985!

Note to Nano-Execs: Do not expect your VC to be your CEO or have the same commitment as your CEO. If he or she did, believe me, they would be your CEO. Passion, proven ability and dedication to achieve a worthwhile goal are extremely important virtues that a management team must possess and demonstrate. Every investor wants to be part of a team with a vision to change the world for the better. Every investor wants to be part of a team with a clear plan and ability to build a huge, profitable company. However, throughout history, very few CEOs, much less whole teams, have been able to pull this off successfully.

It is not a flaw to understand and limit one's goals and aspirations.

I wouldn't mind seeing and being part of making a $10 million dollar investment in a company with a clear, intelligent vision to merge itself with a major company and a high probability of success in doing so in three years at a $70 million valuation. That would get my vote before making a similar investment in a small company with big dreams yet only a small chance of a $1 billion dollar valuation in six years by virtue of an IPO in a hoped-for bull market.

Allow me to tell a couple of short, pertinent stories that illustrate different points about what we have just covered.

THE BOBBY D STORY

By 1984, I had invested significant natural resource venture capital, particularly in precious metals mining, and was gaining national recognition in my field. I had moved my family to Santa Barbara (why not?), and a local high-tech investment maven, eight years my senior, with 20 times my money, named Bobby D for our purposes, called me to ask my opinion on a multimillion dollar investment he was planning in a gold mining stock. We had a few lunches and I discouraged him from that investment. Later, I was able to help him make and, more importantly, save millions, in mining shares and private placements.

Bob's area of expertise was high-tech investing, and after studying investment analysis under a beloved professor in the UC System, he focused on that area. His claim to fame was that he was the recognized "axe" in one particular mid-cap, high-tech company. This was unusual because the "axe" or leading, market-moving analyst in any public company is almost always a large securities firm employee, and he was not. Any important institutional trader or money manager with any interest in this stock, long or short, would contact him for his input before making a move in that company.

The key to his analysis was his ability to assess the leadership ability of any high-tech CEO. He told me the leader of "his" company, despite it being a relatively small one, was one of the five or six leading high-tech CEOs in the world. Gates of Microsoft, Welsh of GE, a couple others and this guy! Then he said something which struck me as ridiculous at the time but which has rung truer and truer over the years, "Darrell, how many da Vincis or Beethovens do you think there are in the world? There are only five or six truly gifted high-tech CEOs. That's it! The rest are pretenders or really not in the same class at all. **To truly understand the technology, to be a gifted leader and manager, to have foresight, to be a tough negotiator and competitor, and then to drive leading, high-profit products into the marketplace to be able to do all these things and, then, to get up day after day, year after year and do it all over again… that is really, really rare."**

THE RESPECTED GEOPHYSICIST COMES UNGLUED

A Canadian engineer and a respected geophysicist with a Ph.D. set out to build three mines over a 3-year period in a renowned gold district of California, and I was enlisted to help them raise some of the early capital. While the mines were not long-lived and eventually ran into problems due to lower gold prices, my investors and I did quite well because the stocks shot up dramatically over several consecutive years.

The engineer and geophysicist each made more than $100 million.

Fourteen years later, I was running a private equity hedge fund, and heard the geophysicist (whom I had known fairly well, but lost contact with) was promoting a new project in South America that he claimed to be *the largest discovery in history*. My partners and I watched the stock quadruple in price, before we sent our consulting geologist down to check out the situation on the ground. While we were all skeptical of the numbers, I said to anyone who would listen, "Look, I knew this guy well a little over a decade ago; he's a brilliant geophysicist, respected by his peers, and RICH. He either has really got something down there or he has completely lost his mind and thinks he will be able to pull off the scam of the century without being sent to jail. The second of those alternatives is so unlikely as to be ridiculous."

Two days after our geologist left the U.S. we gathered around the speakerphone for his call. "The host rock is completely dead," he stated flatly, declaring, in geologist terms, the very worst news possible: the rocks were just rocks, with absolutely no evidence of gold mineralization, much less potential ore. We (especially I) were dumbfounded. The only saving grace for my ill-advised comments was that, luckily, we had not invested until our *due diligence* process was complete, with input from an unbiased scientist and expert (a good lesson or reminder for us all). The other lesson is that despite the importance of the key employee and the fact that every successful company must be driven forward by a single individual, you cannot depend on a single human being to save a company from failure.

Soon after the call, we started blowing the whistle. With the exception of Bre-X (on which we were also early to blow the whistle), I believe this was the biggest mining scam of the last 20 - 40 years; somehow, a drastically different man than I had known suffered dire consequences and lost the reputation of a lifetime.

A WINNING TIP FOR MAKING YOUR NANOTECH FORTUNE

While I believe that 70% of the time the emotions dominating a market are spent in either *worry or hope*, 20% of the time *fear or greed* rules supreme. After investors have been hopeful for a while as a market, a stock or group of stocks declines and then eventually there is a feeling of *resignation*, as if to say, "This is really bad, and it's really going to stay bad for a long time. I give up." Markets spend about 5% of the time in this mode, and this is the start of the bottoming phase and pattern. After a period of time, in the presence or absence of more bad news, the decline begins anew from this bottom-ing area; *fear* sets in. This strong emotion hits holders in the pit of their stomachs, and, with the desire to stop the pain pounding in their brains, and the strange, sudden confidence that their long position is idiotic, they capitulate and sell; maybe even reversing their position and going short. During this period, bear markets end and the bull markets begin. Rising out of this tremendous fear, the stock or market starts rising to ever increasing *worries* that the decline is going to begin again in earnest and that even lower lows will be made, yet it never happens. Market participants and onlookers keep reminding the players of all the problems and obstacles to success, but the market rises. *The more the worry increases, the higher the bull climbs the wall.* After some time, *complacency* arrives and the market spends 5% of its time in that mode until everyone looks back on the previous huge up-move, decides it is likely to be "endless," at which time *greed* takes over. No one wants to be left behind. In a paroxysm of futile buying, the fools rush in, only to be slaughtered by the wait-ing bear. Like the tale of Sisyphus, the emotions and markets replay again and again.

SHOW ME THE MONEY!

Sometimes the smartest of the *smart money* make mistakes.

In March of 2004 articles began appearing that pointed out the weaknesses of companies without near-term earnings or even revenues, like Nanosys, while extolling some nanotech companies that were already selling and making profits in the marketplace, like Nanofilm and Nano-Tex.

Much was made of the glamour image projected by the fine Nanosys team headed by a super-successful biotech serial entrepre-neur and eminent Harvard and UC Berkeley scientists, with mar-quee joint ventures with and investments from nanotech giants such as IBM, DuPont and GE. Contrasted with that was the *down-home, seat of the pants* image presented by low-tech and tex-tile industry giant-invested Nano-Tex, and the rough and tumble, long hard slog, single-minded entrepreneurial attraction of chemist Dr. Scott Rickert's story at Nanofilm.

Nanosys talk/hype reached a peak of promotion about that time with the VCs and investment banks involved, using the good offices of one of the premier PR firms in high-tech, bombarding the mass print media, particularly, with stories extolling the wonders of the company and its unusual business model. At the time, Nanosys boasted a large, broad, diversified and, many would say, quite significant portfolio of IP and no revenues to speak of. The plan or model as I understood it was to leverage this IP into licensing agreements and joint ventures with major companies (Intel, BASF, Texas Instruments, *et al.*) to develop and commercialize products which, as yet, did not exist. Despite the blue-chip credentials of the team and the financiers (the top nano VCs, as well as two or three *first tier* investment banks), this *blind pool* approach is often *a dog that doesn't hunt* even in some shadier realms of the investment landscape.

Be that as it may, most of the nanotech world was convinced beyond a shadow of a doubt that the company would make its IPO debut between April and July of 2004.

In May of 2004, as a member of the IPO Panel (also featuring our Corporate Development Advisory Board Chairman, Ed Moran, Head of the Delloitte & Touche Nanotechnology Practice), I warned that an attempted IPO of Nanosys prior to September 10th, 2004, or prior to a successful Google launch could be a disaster.

While coming from solid experience, the insight didn't require genius. From June 10 to September 10 EVERY year, about 10% of professional investors are vacationing at any point in time, and retail clients and brokers do very little. Why have a sale when more than 10% of your customers were sure to be absent? For the company raising funds, summer IPOs almost never make sense.

As for the Google connection, I just assumed that they would both be lumped together in the public's mind – improperly, of course – in the same *high-tech* basket, and that Google was the clear leader between the two in terms of capitalization and fame. Thus I presumed that a weak tech and IPO market (which were current in the summer 2004 market) would not help anyone; especially anyone like Nanosys which possessed an essentially public "IP Portfolio" *pro forma* business model.

I saw no good reason (for potential, new public investors) to try for the earlier IPO than Google or September 10th, and, as it turned out, I was right. The Nanosys IPO was pulled completely from the calendar by Merrill Lynch, Lehman, *et al.* at the last minute, after a lowering of the initially announced terms, with not a little embarrassment.

No knock to Nanosys, which has many fine features, but companies that can actually "Show me (and you) the Money!" probably have a better chance to trigger a more generous release of nanotech IPOs.

A Winning Tip for Making Your Nanotech Fortune

In the fine details, early-stage IP valuation is for professionals. The traditional tools of investment analysis are tough enough without trying to apply a discounted cash flow model to the potential royalty flow from a patent that may or may not be defendable and that takes a Ph.D. in physics to understand. Do not attempt to go there. You are much better off focusing on target companies with products or services where costs, competitors, and prices are known and at least better understood. Treat an investment in a technology or group of patents as a *call option*, rather than as straight equity, and speculate only 5 - 15% of the money you would normally invest in a single stock.

How Knowing Too Much Can Kill You

It was a bone-chilling autumn day in 1983. I was tromping around silver mining property in the Coeur d'Alene district of northern Idaho with a grizzled "seat of the pants" geologist who was president of the tiny public company that owned it. As we brushed aside some overgrowth in an area he had not previously hiked, we exposed a huge surface vein, 12 - 30 feet wide, that we measured for more than 200 feet before weather, darkness, and tiredness returned us home. Later, chip samples we took graded 9 to 22 ounces of silver per ton, and my friend found yet another 200 feet of "strike." In a part of the world where silver mines run extremely deep (a mile or more!), it was clear this could be major news for the small company, assuming drilling and economic confirmation by geologists and mining engineers of what we had found.

Even so, had anyone bought shares that day it would have been a very long time before the "advance" knowledge paid off. The old man got sick. His daughter took over the company. She was not persuaded to exploit the new discovery, as she preferred to exploit the "easy pickings" of *tailings* (silver-containing leftovers from previous mining and processing endeavors) and rich ore piled right next to the small $350,000 mill and concentrator that they had just built with great difficulty.

I finally saw a press release about "my" discovery about four years later. By then everyone was bored with the company's stock; it hardly registered a blip.

Every investor has heard the phrase, "Timing is everything." When it comes to market success, truer words were never spoken. It will be a major truism in the rolling booms and busts of the Nanotech industry. A key to making long-term money in stocks is to buy quiet (little news good or bad), sideways-moving stocks just when they start to show signs of strength. This can indicate accumulation by "smart" buyers who are anticipating important, good corporate or scientific developments.

If you believe you know something the rest of the market does not; **tread very carefully**. Most often it will be better to wait for confirmation by other investors and you will not suffer by delaying. Your *go signal* will be rising prices on higher volumes, coming out of a long, quiet trading range.

A WINNING TIP FOR MAKING YOUR NANOTECH FORTUNE

Cynical stock market professionals use *hot tips to short* shares! The feeling (proper, I think) is "why would I be getting this

great news, for free, from an acquaintance or unsolicited letter, unless the true feeder of the news stood to gain, probably
by <u>selling me</u> his or her shares?" Of course, I am not referring
to the professional of integrity, who recommends stocks to his
or her clients, customers, or subscribers. I am also not
impugning your real friends who are undoubtedly unintentionally helping the promoter spread his or her story.
However, one should use care when considering potential conflicts of interest. While rare, the opposite of bullish *pumping*
and *puffery* does occur: someone who wants to buy a stock
intentionally *bad-mouths* the shares. Contemplate this certainty a moment: No one who wants to buy shares at a low price
(with the obvious fiduciary/client exception above) intentionally tells others about it, thus driving the acquisition price up
for themselves and their clients. On the other side of the coin,
you can take a lesson from the pros and get comfortable *shorting* hyped, promoted and *tipped* nanotech stocks. There is
nothing illegal or immoral with assisting *The Market* to value
shares appropriately through *going short*. Of course, this brings
up another issue; professional *shorters* who actively, negatively,
promote shares of stocks when they are short. They are a rare
breed; but rest assured, they are out there.

How You Can Survive Micro-Cap Hell

As more nanotech companies go public, I expect the vast
majority will have sub-$1 billion market caps for years to come. In
fact, many will have market capitalizations well under $300 mil-
lion, placing them, depending on your definition, squarely in the
mini- and micro-cap arena. These are difficult stocks to trade and
invest in for many reasons related to their size. (I am going to resist
any reference to *nano-cap* stocks; although it now appears I was
unable to avoid such a reference.)

Micros are generally not *followed* by analysts. They lack *sponsorship* among investment banks. Unless they trade high dollar volumes (difficult when a company has a total 30 million shares outstanding, trading at $3/share – it may be expected to trade 100,000

shares per day), they are not favored by *market-makers*. It remains for these types of stocks to be *sold* to investors, usually by individual retail brokers, or value- or growth-oriented financial newsletter writers. Company PR and IR (Investor Relations) can only go so far, and the SEC, NASD and state securities regulators have rules and penalties that strictly limit what a company may do in this regard.

The result is that micro-cap shares tend to be illiquid, and to have very high costs of trading. This is a recipe from hell for trading or investing in nanotech shares. Luckily, there is a **winning strategy** for surviving and even profiting from those same elements that make micro-cap investing such a loser for the average investor.

Knowledge is everything. A micro-cap nanotech stock may appear on your screen or in the paper at $6.33 X $6.56. This is the *inside market*. If a reference to *size* exists at all it must be tempered by two facts: **large traders and sophisticated speculators disguise their trading, and lower bids and higher offers are on-view to many participants**. Get a Level II quote machine or a friend or broker who has one, and inquire about where the volume bids and offers lie. Remembering the caveat about "disguise," you might be able to see a preponderance of bids around 6.04 to 6.16 and a preponderance of offers between 6.61 and 6.70 for example. In such case, you may safely assume the truer market is roughly 6.10 X 6.65. This is incredibly important whether you are a buyer or a seller, and should be an eye-opener with regard to the true liquidity and size of the market. Case in point: if you own 10,000 shares and there are only 3,900 bid for between 6.04 and 6.33, you have a real problem. Barring certainty that a crash is imminent (in which case sell as fast as you can), do not sell at the market, do not sell at the bid, and do not sell at a limit below the best bid. Assuming you have low commission rates of under 2 cents/share, *work out* the shares, 300 to 800 at a time, over a reasonable period of time between $6.30 and $6.60. Because this range is below the area of volume selling overhang, you have a good chance for success, and you do not give up your option to sell lower.

Reverse this concept for buying in volume.

Eventually the downtick rule for short-selling will be eliminated because it makes no logical sense, but, until then, you can only *sell short* on an up tick or flat tick preceded by an up tick. Again, do not show your hand all at once, and try to play in the area between the best offer and the high volume offer area.

FOUR HIGHLY IMPORTANT ADDITIONAL POINTS:

1. Do not short micro-cap stocks that do not show a significant high volume offering band above your selling point on the Level II.

2. Do not buy stocks that do not show a significant high volume bid area below your buying point. The reasons become self-evident should your timing and position be wrong and you need to cover or sell at a loss. When things go wrong, you do not want to say "Sell!" and hear your broker ask, "To whom?"

3. A bought $6 stock can only, theoretically, drop to zero, but,

4. A shorted $6 stock can, theoretically, rise to infinity – well, let us say $1,000, anyway.

Clearly, all else being equal, if you are able to buy a stock with no significant overhang or sell one short that has no solid bid, you are going to have a better opportunity for profit. As a further caveat, I would caution retail investors to own no more than 10% of a typical day's volume in a stock, and caution professional investors to own no more than one or two days' worth of trading unless they are very long-term investors (2 - 3 years or more) or are willing to shoulder the higher risks involved.

Winners will use illiquidity, volatility, and lack of information to their advantage; *losing investors will be misused by the same.*

I've managed a hedge fund for institutional and accredited investors in a "long/short" strategy in international "small technology" stocks. Should we manage an "index" fund in these stocks as well, I will try to apply the same rules of trading in these micro-technology, MEMs, nanotech and microfluidics stocks for the professionally managed funds as well.

For your information, a "long/short strategy" is "market neutral" in that you maintain the same dollar amount short in the account as you have long in your nanotech or "small tech" shares. You are not making a directional bet on the trend of the nanotech shares. If you buy $25,000 worth of shares and "simultaneously" short $25,000 worth of other shares, your bet is simply that the long shares outperform the shorts.

You may want to try your hand at a long/short strategy on your own. If the market for these shares generally moves up, you are betting that your longs will go up more than your short shares. If the market for them generally declines, you are betting that your longs will go down less than your shorts. When the market is roughly flat, you are betting that the spread between the longs and shorts will widen. This is a low-risk approach to speculative markets like these volatile micro-cap stocks tend to be.

A Winning Tip for Making Your Nanotech Fortune

Bad news comes like roaches. When a nanotech company misses a deadline, reports a bad quarter, loses a grant, fails to meet *guidance*, is left behind by a joint venture partner, has SEC problems, loses an intellectual property mediation or litigation, or a contract, or announces any one of myriad other pieces of bad news, do not assume that you've heard the end of it. No matter the company's assurances, assume more bad news is coming. Have you ever seen a single roach, and not seen others later? If you do not want to risk being out of the stock, stay in, but have no illusions about the potential for further declines. If you have no stomach for that, use the inevitable *dead cat bounce* to exit. A *dead cat bounce* refers to the morbid observation that even a dead or dying stock – like a dead cat – will bounce a little if dropped from a high enough height.

The strength of the IP protection for nanotech relates to the business models that can be safely pursued. For example, if the composition of matter patents afford the nanotech startup the same degree of protec-

tion as a biotech startup, then a "biotech licensing model" may be possible in nanotech. For example, a molecular electronics company could partner with a large semiconductor company for manufacturing, sales and marketing, just as a biotech company partners with a big pharma partner for clinical trials, marketing, sales, and distribution. In both cases, the cost to the big partner is $100 - 300 million, and the startup earns a royalty on future product sales.
—Steve Jurvetson

Part of analyzing a nanotech company is valuing the company's IP. Intellectual property includes patents, trademarks, licenses, patents pending, know-how, and trade secrets. This area of evaluation is especially important when looking at early stage, developing companies in all the "small technologies."

McDonald's did not patent the hamburger, yet many of its manufacturing processes and machines are patented. In fact, even in a business as prosaic as making burgers, shakes and fries, IP has played a significant role in McDonald's history.

Ray Kroc was selling a patented five-spindled milk shake maker called the Multimixer when he found the McDonald brothers' hamburger stand in San Bernardino, CA in 1954. Everyone who had the need to sell multiple shakes of different flavors in a short period of time needed Ray's machine, but they were running an unheard of eight at a time. This left the astounded Kroc entranced, counting customers from his car, and imagining how many Multimixers he could sell if only every hamburger stand were a "McDonald's." The brothers' model was certainly built on many aspects of know-how, but by the time Kroc was running the show everything from cleaning schedules to a factory line burger manufacturing process to the invention of special "french fry" cutting and frying machines, and many other things, were part and parcel of the operation. Much of it was trade secret or patented.

For all this, far beyond McDonald's, in any high-tech business the importance of IP is so much more.

It is fair to say that in nanotechnology, the importance of IP is above that of high-tech businesses in general.

The battlefield of the nanotechnology IP litigation wars has not even been outlined yet. But rest assured this space will be bloody in the 2008 to 2015 timeframe. As money is made and arguments ensue, it is a certainty that patents will be infringed and disputes will feature prominently in the nanotech landscape.

Further muddying the water is that the U.S. Patent Office and other equivalent agencies around the world have not been the best at early stage (1995 - 2005) assessment of patentable claims. My Corporate Development Advisory member, *nanotech IP attorney extraordinaire* Steve Maebius, tells me that overlapping claims, intentional and unintentional, are rife. There are few disputes now because revenues and profits are not great yet, but wait a few years. Seemingly simple, straightforward claims, such as who invented the carbon nanotube or buckeyball, may be legal minefields.

I hate to say it, but in some cases, whole corporate and business futures may depend more on whoever has the better lawyers and the better documentation than on who has the best management and business model.

Nanotech IP Valuation: An Established Process for a New Age

As investors look to evaluate investments in nanotech companies, they open the door to yet another challenging science: the valuation of emerging companies and technologies.

DO I NEED TO UNDERSTAND THE SCIENCE?

In order to determine the value of a nanotech company or investment, it is helpful to understand the science behind the technology. But as we will see, understanding the science is probably less critical to a valuation than understanding the markets and economics of the company's industry.

We saw evidence of the relative importance of technology vs. industry economics during the dot.com boom when e-companies gathered market values far in excess of the market value of their brick-and-mortar counterparts. An easy example is Webvan. Webvan was a high-profile dot.com business that offered consumers the opportunity to order groceries online and have them delivered to their door. (A brief favorite of my wife.) At the time it went public, Webvan's $8.5 billion market capitalization put it on par with Safeway, Albertson's and Kroger's even though it had a fraction of the customers the three stalwarts had.

The failure of the markets to value Webvan properly was not the result of a failure to understand the technology of ordering groceries over the Internet; it was a failure to understand the economics of the grocery industry. More specifically, the price sensitivity of customers, the desire for customers to see the products they are buying, the size of the margin advantage (or lack thereof) of storing inventory in a warehouse and delivering it. These are all basic business issues requiring market research and intelligent cost modeling. Investors failed to do their homework and their investment in Webvan failed, not because they did not understand the technology but because they did not understand the industry and the customer.

FINDING THE RIGHT VALUATION FRAMEWORK

Before we set about measuring the value of a company, we must first answer some basic questions:

- What are the target markets of the product or service?
- Does the product or service compete against other existing products or services?
- What is the competitive environment in the industry? For example, are there large oligopolies that control distribution or customers?
- Will the company attempt to manufacture and/or distribute the product?
- How significant are marketing and customer acquisition costs compared to the cost of the product or service?
- What is the rate of technological innovation and what are the barriers to entry in new technologies?

Answering the first question is easy when the technology improves on an existing, conventional technology. It is more challenging when it breaks new ground. When a technology opens new markets, it is easier for investors to make valuation mistakes and lose (or make) a lot of money.

In many cases, nanotechnologies will compete against conventional technologies. Though groundbreaking in many ways, most nanotechnology – whether a drug, semiconductor or specialty material – seeks to improve the performance of existing technology. That means that the technology will compete against conventional technologies where the economics of costs and benefits have been established by the marketplace.

For example, recent innovations have led to a handful of nanotechnologies that promise to provide cooling technologies based upon more efficient, non-refrigeration technologies. (By refrigeration technologies, we mean those based upon the ideal gas law.) Because these companies would operate in the market for cooling technologies, we already have data about the numbers and types of customers. Some of these customers have consumer needs: air conditioning in automobiles and homes and refrigeration; some have industrial needs: cooling PCs or temperature-sensitive machinery or electronics. But in each of these cases we already know something about the number of customers, the technology constraints in their applications (amount of cooling available, power and product size constraints), and pricing: how much each segment will pay for cooling.

So, in the first steps in valuing our company we need to ask:

- How many customers are in the current market?
- How much do they pay for conventional technology?
- What is their apparent price elasticity as it relates to product performance (will they pay twice as much for a product that cools twice as fast)?
- What portion of the current market can the new technology capture? (The answer to this question requires us to answer more questions about the competitive environment as discussed below).

- What profit margin is realistic once the company captures its market share?

Answering these questions will allow us to gather fundamental information about the value prospects of the company. This information is fundamental because, when properly applied, it will prevent over-valuation of the type so common during the dot.com boom and will help illuminate the diamonds-in-the-rough.

In the dot.com boom, many companies were overvalued because investors failed to pay adequate attention to these highly pertinent questions. They often anticipated markets far beyond the conventional markets, expected customers to pay far more than they would for traditional products and services, assumed impractical gains in market share by new technologies, and had unrealistic expectations about profit margins. This last point is probably the most critical.

EXPECTED PROFIT MARGINS

New technologies often hold the promise of doing something twice as well at half the cost. Many investors wrongly conclude that a company based upon this technology would have substantially higher profit margins than what large competitors achieve using conventional technology.

But technological efficiencies do not establish profit margins; markets do. Margins tend to revert to the mean and that mean is often modest. Even though a company might suggest that a new technology should have better margins than the norm, there are other aspects of the new company that will push margins back down:

- High customer acquisition costs,
- Entry of other new technologies,
- Competitive pricing strategies from existing companies using conventional technology, etc.

More often than not, sustainable high profit margins are observed when a company is the leader in the market and switching costs are high, or alternative technologies are blocked from the marketplace. For example, from 1999 through 2004, Cisco Systems acquired 60 companies – most of them very small companies that had yet to bring their technologies to market. Cisco's strategy was to acquire these companies so that the technologies didn't go to market and compete with Cisco or, if they did go to market, they went with a Cisco label. It was a low-risk strategy for Cisco to pay what seemed to be a high price for these companies to keep competition at bay and protect its customers and margins. Without its market power and the power to use its stock to acquire emerging competitors, could Cisco maintain its margins? What aspect of the emerging nanotechnology company will allow it to maintain high margins?

STRATEGIC VALUE OF TECHNOLOGIES AND EFFECTS ON MARKET SHARE AND PROFIT MARGINS

What happens when the technology opens new markets? In the example of cooling technologies, undoubtedly these technologies will replace some conventional cooling systems; but their unique abilities may also establish new markets where cooling technologies are not currently utilized, such as using novel cooling devices in cars or aircraft. For example, some nanocooling technologies will allow car companies to provide drink chillers in their cars, opening a new market for refrigeration.

Here, estimating the market and profit potential for a new market like this is more difficult; yet we can still rely upon some traditional analysis. How much more effective will the new technology make the products and services of the target customer? If the technology allows car companies to have cooling cup holders in their cars, how much more attractive will the technology make those cars?

The reality is, not a great deal more; cup coolers are not among the top 10 reasons consumers by cars. And we would not expect extreme profit margins in this particular segment. Moreover, car manufacturers are notoriously price sensitive and difficult to negotiate with. Here is an example of how the economic power of the end customer may trump the advantage of a new technology. The customer does not "need" the product and has a substantial amount of negotiating power, so it would be wise to presume only conventional margins in this particular new marketplace.

SUMMARY

In our analysis, we rely upon existing economics and demographics when we examine a situation where the product will compete in an existing market against conventional technology.

When the product opens a new market, we have to draw more inferences about what to expect in terms of the size of the market, pricing and profitability. When dealing with forecasts for new markets, as with existing markets, it is important to remember the factors influencing customer and competitor behavior: the power of suppliers and customers, the rate of technological innovation, barriers to entry, and so on: the classic analytical factors in a competitive strategy framework.

MARKETING AND CUSTOMER ACQUISITION

One of the mighty failures during the dot.com era was the mistaken impression that customers would come from the Internet for "free." In other words, the cost of acquiring a new customer would be low to non-existent. This mistaken assumption led to a deluge of business plans with "hockey stick" revenue and profit projections based upon the cost of fulfillment (product design, manufacturing and delivery costs), without consideration of the cost of customer acquisition (sales and marketing).

Since many *dot.coms* sold information, their business model was like that of a software company: high design costs, low manufacturing and delivery costs. The real key to these companies was (and is) the cost of acquiring the next customer.

As we see more and more new business models emerge from the nanotech world, we should strive to keep the lesson of customer acquisition costs in perspective. Any business plan or investment offering has missed the mark if it spends 95% of its message on the market and the technology. **How much will it cost to get the next customer?**

Even the cure for cancer will have customer acquisition costs.

In pharma, there are multiple "customers": physicians, insurance companies, patients, etc. They all have to be convinced of a new product's value. The first customers won't believe in the product. Performance will have to be demonstrated over time prior to technological acceptance. Time and performance mean customer acquisition costs: the time salespeople have to spend (while they collect a paycheck) attempting to convince the next customer.

A good business plan will show the results of a thoughtful analysis of customer acquisition costs. In some situations, one should expect to have no significant traction with customers for 12 to 18 months after product launch, sometimes longer. Does the company have the capital resources to survive this long? How will these costs affect margins in the short term and long term?

For some emerging companies going public, this situation will present a good "short" opportunity: the market may be thrilled with the innovative aspect of the technology yet completely underestimate the cost to "convince" the market and build a customer base.

BUILD VS. BUY

Another fundamental customer issue is: Does it make sense to build marketing and distribution functions to acquire customers? The answer for many new technology companies is no, simply because the distribution channels for their products are already established and owned. Drug development and medical device companies make classic examples. Why would they attempt to build a distribution network when a larger company with a pre-existing network distributing to their target market can buy their technology and distribute it without incremental marketing costs? The answer is that they simply won't (or shouldn't).

TECHNOLOGY

Finally, we arrive at the issue of assessing the technology. Above, we saw how determining the value of a company starts with basic concepts about business economics: How large is the market? How price sensitive are the customers? How much will it cost to attract customers to a new company and/or new technology? By the time we develop comfortable answers to these questions, we have general ideas about the size of the market and the expected margins.

RATES OF INNOVATION

At this point, our analysis is still based upon a static world of technology. But what happens if we let the technology variable free up? What happens if another company comes along with another nanotechnology that competes with our target company? What happens if the pace of scientific achievement accelerates to where nanotech innovations become likely every 18 months?

Here the analysis gets much more difficult. If the underlying technology is subject to frequent innovation, we can't feel too comfortable with the static analysis described above. The reality is that we will have to soften our market share expectations and our profit margin expectations. We might have to share the nanotech portion of the market with three or four other players.

In these situations, access to capital and management credibility and depth will have significant effects on value. The first to market (with the right mix of capital, management and technology) stands to win while the rest stand to lose. If the technology is good but friable, company management and backing ought to be top-shelf; otherwise the investment won't be compelling.

SWITCHING COSTS CAN BE MORE IMPORTANT THAN INNOVATION RATES

But short-lived technology does not necessarily translate to a short company life span. Sometimes the critical asset is the customer, not the technology. In many technology-based marketplaces, the technology is so sophisticated and not well integrated into industry-standard manufacturing processes that migrating to the new technology is too costly. Switching to a new vendor with new operating systems is very costly to Microsoft customers. But companies such as Microsoft can offer something less than cutting-edge technology and still dominate the marketplace.

A short technology life is not a death knell. Oftentimes the nature of the technology makes the customer want to (or have to) return to the company. Even though technological innovation may occur every 18 months, product-line lives (which are different from technology life) may last 4 years and customer relationships may last 8 years.

These last two items are often the primary intangible assets of the firm.

If the technology requires the customer to adopt a technology platform upon which future innovations will be built (a foundational architecture), then the rate of innovation is a secondary issue. The cost of switching to another technology platform becomes the critical valuation issue.

When considering the effects of technology innovation rates, customer and product lives often are the critical factors in risk adjusting the static valuation framework.

WHEN INNOVATION IS SLOW AND COSTLY

At the late stage of a technology (for example, semiconductors), many of the tools and processes become well known. Even the most sophisticated techniques are taught in schools and openly shared. Innovations come quickly and frequently.

But for many nanotechnologies, processes are still closely guarded in research facilities and have not reached mainstream as of 2005. Furthermore, the cost of research tools and equipment puts research and development out of reach for many companies that could market nanotechnology.

In 2005, an engineer with a top-end Dell PC could design semiconductors, send the design over the internet to Taiwan and ship product back to the customer, all from his or her garage. In 1965 this would have been impossible. But should we expect the same parameters of innovation rate changes in nanotechnology? How would these conditions affect valuation and investment?

It would seem that in the earliest days, operations that can most afford the tools of nanotechnology (the most heavily financed) should be the most likely to succeed. But if that was true, we would all be running IBM operating systems on Xerox PCs. Much has been written about the failure of these companies to realize the value of the computing technologies they had developed. And we know that having deep pockets alone is not always a critical success factor.

More important is the entrepreneurial environment and marketing savvy. This was plain to see in the computer and information revolutions. The greatest successes did not come from the best technologies; they came from the companies with the most driven, marketing-savvy leaders. Though the Microsofts and Intels had strong CTOs, ultimately their greatest successes were in marketing and positioning.

It is Important To Not Simply Invest in the Resumes of the Researchers

How long will it take for a marketing-savvy manager — someone from a company that has developed unique technologies — to spin-off and take those solutions to market in half the time? Yes, the tools are expensive; but if the technology is proven and a motivated leader is behind them, a VC won't hesitate to bring the capital necessary to catapult a spin-off.

Thus the high cost of R&D in nanotechnology will create a few early investors: large pharmaceutical, petroleum and chemical

companies, for example. But the best investment opportunities are likely to come from those leaving the large, stifled environments so as to nimbly take the technologies to market.
—**Ken Nunes**
Managing Director, Caliber Advisors, Inc.

A WINNING TIP FOR MAKING YOUR NANOTECH FORTUNE

Beware of hyped IP valuations, and be on the lookout for the rare "too modest valuation." Strict, tough-minded venture capitalists say an idea is worth what has been spent developing it, or how much would be spent defending it; no more. I would give a bonus for well-spent funds that produced an ever closer and accelerating track to commercialization, and I would deduct for wasted money or efforts that advanced science but failed to move toward commercial applications with a ready market.

How do you know what a company has spent developing its IP? You read their SEC filings and ask. The answer, while couched with caveats, should be fairly direct: "Six of us spent 2 years and $2.5 million of Angel funding to build this prototype, and we have a patent pending; we worked on our own dime, so you can add another $1.5 to $2 million." A "too modest valuation" is harder to spot. Usually, it involves a *re-casting* of purpose, or discovering a new, often completely different market. For example: A nanoparticle designed as a lubricating factor for the aerospace industry is discovered to have immediate application in keeping internal organs from binding after injury or surgery. Great investors, VCs and investment bankers might see these types of relationships even before the scientists and executives at the company. I like to ask executives and entrepreneurs how much they would spend defending a patent if they were sued for infringement, or how much they would spend suing others for the same. It is not a hard, fast rule, but if the answer is not in the millions, I must assume their protection is weak, or worse, that the "winner" has little to gain by way of position in a large, profitable, growing market. You should be especially on-guard if either alternative is the case.

5 BOOMS & BUSTS
GETTING IN ON THE GROUND FLOOR

WHAT ARE THE THREE BIGGEST, UNCORRECTED NANOTECH MISTAKES THAT BIG COMPANIES, START-UPS, SCIENTISTS, EXECUTIVES, VCs, ANGELS, INVESTMENT BANKS, ATTORNEYS, ACCOUNTANTS, ANALYSTS, TECHNOLOGISTS, UNIVERSITIES, AGENCIES, AND NANO-INITIATIVES ARE MAKING IN 2005?

Too much talk about science. Too much thinking about markets that don't exist.
—**Robert Nolan**, NanoMarkets

The idea that "build it and they will come" still dominates. Truly disruptive technologies and paradigm shifts take longer, require more money, and suffer more casualties before achieving commercial success than most estimate.
—**Tim Stultz**, Imago Scientific Instruments

Over the years, many of my friends have asked me how they can get in on the ground floor of some investment or trend. The usual easy answers about getting IPO shares or being in the right place at the right time are not helpful to most people. Peter Lynch's story about his investment in Supercuts, is more on the mark. He liked his haircut, and he liked the price. He thought other people would, too, so it was easy for him to envision growth and profits.

I have a close friend who went to a Sizzler steakhouse in the late 1970s. He loved the gigantic, all-you-can-eat, salad bar, and that the steak, while it would not be confused with Smith & Wollensky's, was an excellent bargain. It was an easy choice for him to buy and accumulate the stock, doing so before the price explosion in the 1980s. He loved and used the product and could visualize others discovering and loving it too.

Another friend is a pharmacist. He has been accumulating Pfizer and Altria (old Phillip Morris) for decades, because every day he sees what sells well in his drugstore.

When other financial professionals criticized me for liking the stock of Starbucks in the early 1990s when the market capitalization of the company represented millions of dollars per store, I told them it still had room to grow. I was not speculating. It is somewhat difficult to remember how bad coffee was, universally, in the U.S. prior to 1985 and, especially, prior to 1975. In Italy in 1973, I remember thinking that what they were drinking (ambrosia?) was so much better than what I was drinking in The States that it should not even be called by the same name. Furthermore, while there were two Starbucks in the relatively small town of Santa Barbara, there was, then (1993), not a single one in Baltimore County when I visited relatives there!

Room to grow? Easy to see? Definitely.

When it came to stocks in my then particular field of expertise, it was even easier. To other financial pros, natural resources were fraught with speculation, danger and, since no one can see underground, fear. To someone who had studied the mining cycle, to someone who had the counsel of expert geologists and engineers, to someone who visited mines and drill sites regularly, it was not something to be feared at all.

It was a smorgasbord of opportunity, and the problem companies stuck out like proverbial sore thumbs.

It will be difficult for anyone (including scientists and high-tech venture capitalists) to buy cheap shares of the nanotech version of Starbucks or Pfizer. Of all the companies that went public over the last few decades, what a tiny percentage it is that have become household names. That being said, nanotech growth companies and products could be just as easy to spot as the examples in the paragraphs above.

Even though the science is nearly impenetrable, once the companies gain some traction the winning products will emerge; *those investors who take professional counsel and are observant of fairly simple guides will be deemed exceptionally astute and will dominate the investment landscape while earning tremendous fortunes.*

You can be one of them.

You did not need to buy Wal-Mart, Microsoft, Amgen or eBay on their IPOs to make a fortune. You will not need to buy any particular nanotech IPO. Sometimes the early cavalry troops end up with arrows in their backs.

Just ask the venture capitalists who poured millions into nanotechnology between 1997 and 2002.

Look for **hot markets.** Wherever unrelieved demand exists, wherever there is real demand for the solution to a problem that is easily recognized, wherever a market exists that does not have to be created or have participants "educated," that's the prime spot to be. Look for companies that solve a recognized problem. Solutions looking for problems are a dime a dozen. Stay away from any company with a product that does something cool, but does not solve a problem that begs to be solved.

Hot Markets are typified by products that save money, build profits, or make one stronger, better looking, healthier, happier, and/or richer. Can a nanotech company or product do these types of things? It had better, or there will not be growing demand and the market dynamics necessary for building a sustainable business.

What might a poor product, poor company, *non-solution* look like?

A nanotech company has a nano-lubricant that decreases friction in jet bearings by 40%. It costs 10% more than the industry standard lubricant, and can be shown to save 3 times that amount because it is longer lasting. This sounds good on the surface. However, with very little digging you discover that the industry does not care about this savings at the current time and that the nanotech company expects to have to *educate* (read "strong-arm") the buyer about his or her "need" for the lubricant. Picture someone's 14-year-old putting their extended thumb and forefinger to their forehead: "LOSER!" This is the opposite of a *Hot Market*. Red lights should be flashing, and you should be *passing*.

Unless you want to finance science projects, your portfolio should not include business models and products that do not solve real problems for real companies or real people; products for which there is no blunt, simplistic, growing market. Beware of the paradox here. If one had not bought Amgen until there was a product, let alone hot demand for its specific products, one would have missed years of tremendous profits and several booms and busts. Furthermore, one could cogently argue that Amgen was indeed a science project for a decade or two. The difference is that Amgen was able to communicate that it would, and, in fact, was creating products for which there was and is huge demand. Yes, it was a speculation. Yes, they could have failed. However, the vision was clear, the "dream" was explicit, and people and companies wanted to be part of it.

Lubricant that solves a "problem" the customer does not believe it has? – Loser. Lifesaving technology that everyone wants? – Winner. It's paradoxical, but, hopefully clearer now.

A Winning Tip for Making Your Nanotech Fortune

Waiting for the right moment to buy is a strong winning strategy. Often, when the going gets rough for investors, "the baby gets thrown out with the bathwater." Every one to three years, expect a major disillusionment with all things *nano*. **After a long period of decline in nanotech stocks, watch for a capitulation of major proportions as the stocks move to even substantially lower levels. Wait until they begin to rise out of this funk (usually three to seven months later), then "back up the truck," and accumulate as they emerge above their low level trading ranges.**

Rambus, Nvidia, and JDS Uniphase, Oh My!

Not that long ago the three names above, among many others, soared to unimaginable heights during the crazy days of the tech boom in the late 1990s. We nanotech investors can learn much from the performance of these stocks, but I want you to note two specific points. At their heights in 2000 - 2001, these three stocks traded at insane multiples of earnings and had market capitalizations of many billions of dollars. And, oddly, even in 2005, even after HUGE declines, they are still trading at insane multiples and multibillion dollar market caps. *A billion dollars can be added to a small cap stock in one day*. It does not happen every day, but, as in the case of AtheroGenics in late 2004, rightly or wrongly, the perfect announcement at the perfect time, even without the suitable scientific confirmation, can explode a stock in a single hour.

The enduring lesson is that exciting technology can be valued by the market in the most extreme ways. Nanotechnology is THE most "extreme" technology, so expect to see extremely insane valuations from time to time in nanotech stocks. To reiterate, we <u>expect</u> to see some insane valuations, we believe they are likely. If they are likely, that is surely the way to bet. All things being equal, one should HOLD OUT FOR INSANE VALUATIONS. That does not mean to hold out forever, but it does mean to be a "pig."

No doubt you've heard the market gem, "bulls make money, bears make money, but pigs get killed." For long-term investors this makes some sense. From the point of view of a speculator, I think this pearl could have only been voiced by a loser. Look, you cannot make a lot of money unless you are a "pig." It is a somewhat disgusting picture, but put porcine images aside for a moment. What I mean is that you must hold on to winning, high-momentum stocks for all they are worth, and then some. *If you sell at "fair value," you will lose in the long run*. To repeat, the certainty of "losing some of them" is such an inherent part of any speculative endeavor that the math alone of selling all your winners as soon as they simply do well, instead of "insanely well," will kill you.

Many nanotech companies are likely to go through the same progression as the high-tech stocks mentioned above. We will see many companies without any revenues, much less earnings, trading as if they are the next Amgen or Genentech. (In fact, back in 2004, some VCs and investment banking-types began calling one private nanotech company, the "Amgen of Nanotech.") Remember, neither Amgen nor Genentech had significant revenues for much more than a decade after going public. Their first <u>earnings</u> were in 1998 - 2000! So it's not unusual for great companies, especially those in the forefront of science, to fail to demonstrate growth company statistics for a decade or more. (They were always excellent companies; they just didn't make any money!)

But when we review the stock price action for Amgen, Genentech, Nvidia, Rambus or JDS, we are struck with the immense volatility and with the importance of timing in purchases and sales. I could have used any of 50 other well-recognized names to make these points, but these examples work well.

You could have bought Genentech in 1999 for $36, and been doing pretty darn well with it at $120. But wait. Could you have held it with equanimity as it declined from $122 to $26? Could you have held it all? More to the point, should you have? Amgen was at the equivalent of $0.42 in 1986. About five years later it had soared over twenty times in value to more than $9 per share; if you sold then and never returned, you missed the move from $9 to $76 over the next nine years! But you would not have suffered two intervening 40%+ declines to get there! Think it was easy to buy Nvidia at $4.25 in 1999 and hold on for $70 in 2001? Think again. Nvdia had *two* declines of more than 60% in that very short timeframe.

Take off the rose-colored glasses and look at it another way. You could have bought JDS Uniphase in 1998 for $4. It spent most of 2000 between $85 and $130! "Good work, if you can get it," I like to say. However, how would you have felt if you bought it for $0.26 in 1993 and had the opportunity to sell 14 times higher at $3.75 just three years later in 1996? Is there a chance you would have been tempted to sell? Be honest, own up to it; of course you would have. Rambus began its life as a public company in 1997 at about $6 per share. On its way to $127 only three years later in 2000, it declined by 50% or more FIVE SEPARATE TIMES.

We could review any boom/bust industry besides high-tech or biotech and see the same patterns repeated again and again. Tremendous volatility typifies certain major inflection points, while dramatic trending markets, both up and down, mark 2- to 6-year timeframes.

It will not be different for the nanotechnology industry and nanotech equities.

As of 2005 the Nanotech Boom has really not even begun, and we have already seen two major bull moves (July 1999 to March 2000 and October 2002 to April 2004) **and two major bear markets** (March 2000 to October 2002 and April 2004 to August 2004), in what could pass for a "small-tech" index (micro, MEMs, and nano). Most of these companies are absolute startups. Some of them are genomics companies or instrument companies (or worse) tarred with the mark of nanotech because they have "nano" in their name! Through the years, we have seen this game played over and over again. How many "dot-coms" that were only vaguely internet-based sprouted in the late 1990s? How many "golds," "energys," "tronics," "biotechs," etc., in years past owed their name changes to pure *marketing*.

This is not new. More than a century ago, when railroads were *hot*, companies routinely added "railroad" to their name. Some 90 years ago, when the U.S. had hundreds of *automobile* companies, do you suppose they all produced and sold cars?

Get ready for "nano" everything. To mangle Dylan, you are really going to "need a weatherman to tell which way the wind blows."

Let us examine the best strategies for making and saving money, and keeping our heads, while all around us are losing theirs.

A WINNING TIP FOR MAKING YOUR NANOTECH FORTUNE

Shrewd boom/bust investors know *another train is always coming*. When I gave my "book" of investors to a now well-known resources broker, I told him that I was certain that "gold and mining stocks had put in a major top that would last for four to six years, and there would be nothing but crying, for now." Of course, I had given them all my best advice, which at that time was to book the huge profits they had made over the previous eight years, and leave what had become almost a religion. That was 1988, and I was dead right. Except… my friend *knew another train is always coming*. After years of tedious handholding and promises, seven years later, that broker was worth $150 million, having continuously invested in private placements in the speculative mining securities. Others have dozens of similar biotech stories. There is no reason to hold on through the inevitable declines, but *never* is a long time. Stay in touch with the market; another nanotech boom is around the corner.

WHEN THE GUN GOES OFF, ALL THE TURKEYS WILL FLY

I published and edited a book in 1982 called *Small Fortunes in Penny Gold Stocks*. The author's premise was that it was useless to analyze micro-cap mining shares; the only thing that mattered, he argued, was their leverage to the price of metals. So, he said to buy a random portfolio of 20 - 30 stocks and to hold on, because "when the gun goes off (the price of the metals soars), all the turkeys (the micro-cap mining stocks) will fly."

Strangely, his hypothesis was correct, and the results have been borne out in every major precious metals boom from the late 1960s silver boom to the gold move from 2001 to 2005. In the second half of the early 1980s boom, a portfolio I chose at random went up more than 200% in seven months; one I chose through research and analysis rallied 312% in the same timeframe. The turkeys flew, but thoughtful, expert analysis flew higher by a large margin.

Some investors believe *the turkeys* (any stock with "nano" in its name) will fly in the nanotech booms. Don't bet the ranch on that.

A WINNING TIP FOR MAKING YOUR NANOTECH FORTUNE

Periodically good, bad and indifferent nanotech stocks will all rally for periods of two to eight months at a time. Use this time to weed the stock of weak companies out of your portfolio. These bouts of unreasonable enthusiasm are used by smart investors to get rid of the "dogs" before the inevitable declines that follow. If you buy a stock just because it has "nano" in its name or is touted by a promoter, come clean to yourself with the game you are playing. Take profits early (leave something on the table for the next guy or gal), and do not be tempted to imagine yourself anything but lucky.

WHY THE NANOTECH BOOMS WILL LOOK NOTHING LIKE THE INTERNET

With the National Nanotech Initiative signed in December, 2003, I look for federal funding to continue to push nanotech research through 2010. Now nanotech, the space race, and cancer research will vie for the historical lead in government funding of science. And the U.S. is not alone in funding nanotechnology. Furthermore, unlike previous technological areas, we are not in the lead. As mentioned before, Japan outspends the U.S. each year on nanotech research, and I am sure that already others do, too, on a *per capita* basis.

Where in the world was the federal internet funding? Well, one could easily argue that it did actually start as a federally financed DARPA project, decades ago. While the internet is a passive platform for moving information, while a highway, copper wires, or railroad tracks are passive platforms for transporting other things, nanotechnology is an all-encompassing set of tools and theories for improving everything we use.

The internet is one developmental outgrowth of many technologies; nanotechnology itself will create many developments; some, by themselves, are likely to be significant as or more so than the internet.

In mid-1998, with the internet in full bloom, I told my private equity fund partners that we needed to get on board. We would have to change horses in midstream since our mandate was for a natural resource venture capital fund. Nothing could be further away than the high-flying world of technology into which we were to land. Our fund made great profits for the next two years in that space. We even started an internet deal in-house and, in a matter of months, took it public on the American Stock Exchange.

Our fund had a prearranged close date of August 2000, so we had the good fortune to cherry-pick probably the best two years of the boom and then get out before the eventual declines. Many others were not so fortunate.

The bars to entry in the internet were practically nil. Literally three folks in a garage with a talented programmer or two and $60,000 could start something (dogfood.com?), and create a huge, yet ephemeral, valuation within 12 - 18 months. That is extremely unlikely in nanotechnology. A few AFM microscopes, clean rooms, other lab equipment, Ph.D. salaries and patent filings, and pretty soon you are talking about tens of millions of dollars. Do not look for *garage* startups in nanotech.

All of the capital that went into the internet created only a few viable businesses. Yahoo, eBay, Google, and Amazon are clear winners, but in the end the billions (in the internet and in laying undersea fiber optic cable alone) that were lost by investors overall, redounded to the benefit of consumers and businesses everywhere in astounding gains in productivity and efficiency. That is less likely to occur in nanotech. Of course, some investors will get burned. Flameouts will occur. There will be over-investment. However, the public will gain untold benefits from the font of nanotechnology. Furthermore, it is more likely that the benefits will be created with just reward for investors, because (despite the simplistic "history repeats itself") they will be more careful this time around, and the dollar amounts needed to gain any traction are just so much greater.

Furthermore, although there will be tremendous competition in nano it will not be the sort of "they have dogfood.com, so we can do doggyeats.com" type of pseudo-competition you saw in the internet days. One may get away with that for $60,000; it's a lot harder to do when $20 million is at stake.

Importantly, competing nanotechnologies (for instance, how to target tiny cancer tumors in the human body, or how to make a better computer display) have the potential to contend like multiple statin drugs do in the pharmaceutical industry today, with huge markets, and the ability to traverse to other uses.

A WINNING TIP FOR MAKING YOUR NANOTECH FORTUNE

When my private equity firm created an internet deal in-house, made one of our partners (who could not program a single line of code) the chairman, took it public, and got it listed on the American Stock Exchange in 1999, you could buy early private shares or IPO shares in ANY internet company and make substantial profits. Many stock players see the same potential in nanotech. Do not be among them. They are just plain wrong. If the nano-equivalent of dogfood.com does happen (count on it), only rip-off artists and rubes will play.

6 THE MOST LUCRATIVE NANOTECH INVESTMENTS

THE ULTIMATE NANO-COMPANY

Laugh not, because here is what the ultimate nanotech company product looks like. The closer a company gets to this "ideal," the more powerful their investment story will be.

The ultimate nano-product is a bionanoparticle-infused, nano-engineered, nutraceutical (a food, usually a drink or bar with nearly drug-like properties) that is delicious, non-fattening, makes you thin, feel and look great, keeps you young and healthy. The ethics of using drugs to enhance life rather than simply treat disease are going under debate similar to that, decades ago, related to using surgery to enhance one's looks. No matter who wins the ethical debate, my guess is that people will use whatever they think is valuable for themselves, and the winner of the fundamental commercial, real, debate will be a foregone conclusion.

This type of nutraceutical is not far-fetched. Encapsulated, time-released, nanoparticles (perhaps vitamins and minerals) could be mixed into a delicious, low-calorie bar. By 2022 it is easy to imagine safe, effective, mild, consciousness-raising, concentration and memory-restoring drugs might exist that could be nano-encapsulated and join the recipe, along with new, powerful, but safe, strength and youth-building "nano-steroids". In late 2004, *The Wall Street Journal* reported on the "recreational" use of Ritalin by white collar types for everything from increased multi-tasking ability to improved golf scores.

With the nanoproduct, a bar a day would strengthen bone, muscle, organs, make your teeth stronger, eyes clearer, hair and skin more lustrous, keep you stronger and happier, sexier, and more relaxed all day.

I have no doubt such a bar will be available by 2022 (in fact, I expect we will see a "preliminary" NANO/Protein Bar on the market by 2010), I'm just not sure it will be legal.

While we are on this subject, winning investments in nan-otech, those that focus on the consumer market (largely ignored by the nano-cabal of scientists, "cutting edge" financiers and pro-moters until 2004, when it became clear what early financial suc-cesses Nano-Tex and NanoFilm were becoming) ? will follow Peter Lynch's guidelines *in spades*. He would invest in The Bombay Company or Pier 1 because his wife liked to shop there. The story goes that he immediately bought shares in Supercuts for Magellan Fund when he had an inexpensive haircut that he deemed as pro-fessional and a good deal less of a hassle than the high-priced salon he had been frequenting.

Pay attention to what friends and relatives say. Better, try to imagine, in advance, what they are likely to say. When Nano-Toothpaste is available, with nanoparticles that make your teeth stronger and whiter, will people say "I want my Nano-Toothpaste," or "I can't use that old brand anymore, I have to have that nano-brand, because it's so much better"? You bet they will.

A WINNING TIP FOR MAKING YOUR NANOTECH FORTUNE

One of the most important things about the markets that you can take from this book and apply tomorrow to making your investing more profitable is that *"technicals precede funda-mentals."* This seemingly odd phrase simply means that the well-regarded technical analysis indicators predict or foreshadow fundamental news either bullish or bearish. This is totally at odds with those who believe that technical analysis looks backward, but that does not make them any less wrong.

Occasionally (only occasionally) fundamental news trumps technical analysis. (The president of a company is suddenly arrested. A scientist makes an amazing lab discovery.) But, more often than not, the stock has already made a new low when the president's arrest is announced, or it is already in a strong uptrend prior to the new findings. Technical analysis looks at supply and demand for the shares of the company rather than at supply and demand for the company's products. The simplest, correct challenge in technical analysis and its solution is this: Define a bull market (one in which you want to be long). Define a bear market (one in which you want to be *gone* or short); bulls have a bar chart pattern of higher lows and higher highs; bears have a bar chart pattern of lower lows and lower highs. I am fond of saying "fundamental news is just an excuse to justify the stock move." There is a kick to being a little controversial, but in "the moving paper fantasy" that is the stock market, I believe this tip is true. Use it to enter or exit trades or to ameliorate surprise in your investing.

NANOTECH MAKES THE THINGS YOU USE BETTER (CREDIT TO BASF)

At the nanoscale, the bulk approximations of Newtonian physics are revealed for their inaccuracy, and give way to quantum physics. Nanotechnology is more than a linear improvement with scale; everything changes. Quantum entanglement, tunneling, ballistic transport, frictionless rotation of superfluids, and several other phenomena have been regarded as "spooky" by many of the smartest scientists, even Einstein, upon first exposure... ."
—**VC Steve Jurvetson**, Draper Fisher Jurvetson

As previously discussed, in nanotechnology a new, different, or unusual property is exhibited by the material. It is largely these interesting properties that are the agents of change and improvement in the new products that nanotech is bringing. Stain-resistant fabric, anti-scratch paint and fog-defying glass are only the beginning.

Investors can win by focusing on consumer product improvements in areas where they, themselves, clearly understand the benefit being touted, and more than welcome, actually demand, the improvement. With *technology*, corporate and investment winners all understand that bland improvements in products or services, even if accompanied by cost or efficiency savings, are rarely sufficient to take significant market share from the incumbent product.

There is sound logic for this. Individual consumers know better than anyone what is important to them.

When I was developing and back-testing securities and futures trading systems in the 1970s and '80s, I started with computer punch cards (physical holes – without infamous *chads*), moved to an Apple IIe, and thought I had found nirvana when I got my super 486 in 1991. I was running calculations that took seventeen (17 - yikes!) hours on my previous computer. When I got my result, I usually wanted to tweak one variable, and run the back-test again. It would take me a month or more to get a model I liked. Suddenly, with the 17 times improvement on the 486, I could get my answers in a single day. I paid a lot of money for my *tricked out* 486, and no one else I knew had a similar machine for another 2 years, but I had a very personal need for its *lightening* speed.

None of my friends did. In fact they thought Word and Excel worked just fine on a 386, and they were right.

Today, if I told you that a nano-display would refresh the computer monitor you are viewing 17 times faster, and that you would be able to see 17 times more colors, you might think, "Who cares?" even though the improvement is significant. If I told you the cost of the new screen would be the same or lower than the current one you are using, you might switch if you had confidence that the company that sold it would be around to service it, build quality, and provide a solid warranty. Those are big "ifs." Told it cost more, I doubt you would switch.

Entirely missing in the paragraph above is the question of "red hot demand" for the fantasy nano-screen. Today, there is no such demand, I am certain (except for a few fanatical *gamers*, animators, and video editors, I would guess). Remember this example when you listen to the breathless claims of stock promoters touting some cool product enhancement (or even new product) enabled by nanotech.

Now look at the lighter side of a minor advance that might have huge, existing market demand. Most golfers hit balls that are difficult to cut or scratch unless you land on gravel, rock, or a cart-path (not uncommon when you play like me). Suppose nanotech supplied a cut and scratch-proof golf ball. What if they could invent a ball that could not be lost? Of course, on an early read-through, Dr. Ruoslahti reminded me that this would be easy to accomplish, requiring only a tiny antenna being implanted in the ball and a simple receiver.) Wouldn't many golfers pay a significant premium? Even *duffers* (pretty much any golfer with a double digit handicap higher than your own) throw away balls with minor imperfections (or use them only when confronted with a water hazard, right?). The math is easy; if I buy twelve balls and throw away three, I would easily pay 20% more per dozen if I did not have to throw away <u>any</u>.

Actually, in 2005 a nanotech company began to manufacture a nanotech golf ball. This ball does not have the characteristics mentioned above. Instead, its core is stabilized by nanoparticles that keep it on a straighter flight-path and with more of the energy from the club contact transferred to enhance distance as well. Basically, the nanotechnology keeps the core from "jiggling" around (like Jell-O) within the thin cover as much as in other balls. At $90/dozen retail, while top of the line Titlelist Pro V 1s go for $45, I do not see much future for the balls (after the initial mystique wears off), but if the performance matches or exceeds, even by a little, the best balls, a good business might develop licensing the IP to Callaway, Maxfli or Titlelist and taking a dime a ball.

Nanotech-enhanced materials will continue to show the earliest financial returns of any nanotech sector for some time. Nanotechnology might not make the products, but it makes products better. Nanotech can make things shinier, harder, more slippery, more flexible, more bacteria resistant, sharper or more conductive of heat and electricity. It can give unique properties to everyday products. Anti-bacterial doorknobs may become commonplace; nanotechnology can make processes more or less combustible, or efficient. Nano-catalysts may speed up specific chemical processes, and perhaps make some processes occur which previously were thought to be impossible or just impossibly expensive

A WINNING TIP FOR MAKING YOUR NANOTECH FORTUNE

Go short on failures to rally on good news. Rumors abound that a company is going to release excellent results on lab work it is doing in combination with a Fortune 100 nanotech powerhouse. The news is even better than expected, and is press released jointly, worldwide. A homerun is anticipated, as the news indicates 10s, possibly 100s of millions of dollars of revenues for the small nanotech company, starting in a couple years and lasting a decade or more as competitors struggle to come up with a good product of their own. Oddly, the stock rallies a percent or two then goes sideways, leaving traders scratching their heads. This is a classic *buy on rumor, sell on news* situation. Short the stock with impunity (of course, carry a buy stop loss just above the recent range); it is going down. The corollary is to *go long on failures to decline on bad news.* This works just as well.

7 AVOID LOSING STRATEGIES

WHO WILL BE THE BIG NANO-LOSERS?

Companies without a clear vision of who their customers are.
—Maximilian M. Schroeck, Ph.D.,
Managing Director, Agilent Ventures

Careless investors.
—Bryan W. Bockhop
Law Firm of Arnall Golden, Gregory

Investors as a group, especially those who do not spend time educating themselves, and invest in anything with 'nano' in the name - and consumer product companies that may become embroiled in product liability litigation, like nanoparticle cosmetic companies getting linked to illnesses.
—Roger Attick, President, CeMines

Mom and pop investors who believe the hype.
—Robert Nolan, NanoMarkets

Proven losing strategies include:

1. **Plunging**
2. **Overtrading**
3. **Buying on Tips**
4. **Failure to do Research or Due Diligence**
5. **Holding on to Losers**
6. *Drinking the Kool-Aid*

In 1997 my company helped raise $24 million for a company that had licensed important Kodak intellectual property related to the *small technology*, OLED (organic light emitting diodes) displays. This technology is and was significant because of lower energy use, lower costs to produce as well as producing a higher quality visual experience for everything from cell phone displays to television.

With my own eyes and ears, I witnessed a smaller than one inch screen with optical enhancement and ear phones produce a full theatre experience of *Star Wars!* It was incredible. I was so glad I had invested my own and my investors' funds in what was clearly going to be a super winner.

As recently as 2005, OLED is still an also-ran, and other *small technologies*, including other OLEDs probably not covered by Kodak patents are growing as well. Furthermore, every year that goes by, the patents become less valuable and the cost of maintaining the licenses goes up.

What happened?

Management did not listen to my company's advice to rapidly co-venture with a major firm and step back to a royalty position. They had visions of manufacturing millions of units per year on their own that we were never able to get out of their heads. Billions that had been spent world-wide on LCD and other technology display manufacturing, production and fabrication plants (*fabs*) were not seen for the huge impediments to development that they very much were.

Getting a huge industry to change to a better technology has been so much "whistling in the wind." Eight years after I saw the future with my own eyes, it still has not arrived.

I had *drunk the OLED Kool-Aid!* Luckily, I had long before kicked the *"follow a nice management team anywhere" Kool-Aid* addiction, and I was able to sell my clients' shares, which were bought in the pre-public market for pennies, into a burst of enthusiasm for the technology at about $6 a share. In 2005, the company's shares still traded hands in the public markets – at around $1.

A Winning Tip for Making Your Nanotech Fortune

Keep your eye on escrow, Rule 144, and regulatory releases of insider and VC stock. Usually 3 to 26 months after a nanotech stock goes public various dates will trigger previously unregistered, restricted or escrowed shares to suddenly become free-trading or available for sale with certain restrictions. While regulations strictly forbid the company from promotion in advance of these dates to facilitate sales, it is uncanny how often good news precedes them. Depending on the size of the release (sometimes it is a significant percentage of the total float) they can put incredible downward pressure or at least a lid on prices for a period of time. *Savvy traders look for great news combined with a huge release to time short sales.*

Avoid the Nano-Hype

Bubble markets, booms and manias have existed in markets almost since the beginning of human commercial history. Whether it was "trons," "tronics," "dot coms" or tulips, investors have been knocked flat hundreds (thousands?) of times. Today, we see more and more companies adding "nano" to their names, even if they have nothing "nano" about them.

While booms get out of hand and lead to inevitable busts that hurt investors, society at large often benefits. Who can deny the productivity gains and all the neat outcomes that we benefit from daily as a result of all the money thrown at the internet and broadband connectivity? When the gold market went wild in the 1980s and money was thrown at any company with "gold" or "mining"

in its name, the result was lower gold prices and major gold discoveries in parts of the world that had never been explored with
modern tools, much less yielded significant production of the yellow metal. The outcome of the petroleum product bull market
that began in 2002 and began to exhibit signs of a mania-like bubble top in 2005 will, I am certain, lead to a tremendous boom in
exploration and new technical advances that will increase supplies
and lower prices in the years that follow to levels unimagined at
the eventual top.

There will be booms and busts and bubbles in *small technology*.
But, unlike commodities-based booms, nanotech represents a very
long-term *growth* story. It will look more like biotech with *rolling*
booms and busts.

Still, you want to avoid, or minimize the impact of the blow-
offs after booms, when the bubble bursts. Following are some
ideas that can help you navigate or avoid these waters entirely.

While I have supported the Canadian Venture Exchange in
the past, think it can be a great place to allow the public to participate in essentially venture capital deals, and have raised money for
companies on the Bulletin Board that went on to success on the
American Stock Exchange, a good dose of cynicism should accom-
pany a review of nanotech companies emanating from either
place. A listing at either, combined with a company name with
"Nano," is a *double whammy*, red flag. Since these stocks are difficult to impossible for all but professionals to short, the best advice
for all but the most astute might be to just ignore them.

The nano-hype will be palpable in the 2007 to 2010 period.
It will manifest in barrages of junk mail and email. I expect to see
TV infomercials as well. Undoubtedly, refugees from the *no money
down real estate seminar* maven world, former self-help gurus, vita-
min and exercise equipment hawkers, multi-level marketing mas-
ters, and even a few so-called spiritual *channelers* will surely be
found doing the rounds at Sheratons and Holiday Inns around the
country: Free entry! (Then their cohorts try to sell you books,
tapes, videos, DVDs, newsletters, magazines... all guaranteed to
ensure that you'll make a fortune in nanotech... "Hey, hasn't that
book been written already?")

Self serving as it sounds, you do not need any of the hype or any of these offerings. Your success and fortune will be more assured if you follow the serious route I propose in this book: paying attention to the experts and focusing on the real science, technology and legitimate fundamental and technical analysis, alone.

In 2005 a nanotech company (with "nanotech" in its name) appeared on the bulletin board trading at $15 to $20 per share. A reverse takeover of a shell in a prosaic, highly non-tech business, the company touted its ownership of some IP being developed by a European university. Anyone with the time to check the company's most recent SEC filing, an 8-K from October 2004, would have been shocked to see that the multiple off-shore entities that sold their "nanotech company" to the shell for 70,000,000 shares with the right to receive 1.9 billion (yes, billion) more! 70,000,000 times $15 is a good week's work; but 1.9 billion times $15 is an awful (might I say "weird") lot of money.

Allow me to remove my tongue from my cheek long enough to say that this is possibly the first big scam of the nanotech age. The business is real. The deals are real. The university and its scientists, and the nanotech IP are all real. What is fraudulent is the market capitalization of the company, which was created out of thin air by savvy stock promoters. They "set" the price to $15. There is no real market. If no one sells the stock down to $14 or 14 cents or 0.14 mils, because no stock exists outside what is owned by the promoters (yes, 95% plus is owned by the promoters, because they set it up that way; it is not a secret; it is all there in the 8-K), then it is "worth" $15.

This is how they are likely to continue from here: They will promote their company over the web, using financial PR, chatting up brokers (and these are the legitimate ways!), and getting placement in financial newsletters. At some point, they will spend about $1 million to direct mail a newsletter promotion to 600,000 to 1.4 million mom and pop investors telling them how the stock could go to $100 and be the next Microsoft. They will put a couple of million shares with a compliant OTC brokerage firm that makes a market in the stock and will be happy to make 20 or 50 cents a share for writing tickets. If you call and buy 100 shares at

$15 or 4,500 shares at $15 or $17 or $23, where they will let the stock drift to draw in the suckers, ahem 'investors,' they just sit back and collect. A 10- or 20-to-1 return on the $1 million spent on this activity is the real business of this company.

They can do this every few months to different mailing lists, too.

Oddly, all these shenanigans are disclosed in fine print in the newsletter itself. The money to do the mailing; the shares paid to the newsletter publisher; the right to sell while promoting readers to buy – it is all laid out in the fine print.

A Winning Tip for Making Your Nanotech Fortune

Float is important. Knowing the total number of shares outstanding and the number that can come out through option and warrant exercise is important for any investor wishing to know the fully diluted market capitalization (read, value) of any company. Few investors, however, look at the *float*, which is more important in the shorter term (two years or less). Take the undiluted number of shares and subtract those held by insiders, VCs, and mutual funds; these are considered to be closely held and "out of the *float*" (which is simply the shares available for trading). In small companies, this number can be 40% or more of the shares outstanding. Here's an example: A company has 16 million shares, 9 million of which are in the float. A Rule 144 deadline frees up 3 million shares. This 33% increase in float is far more negative to the share price than it would appear as an 18% of total shares release. On the other hand, a mutual fund decision to purchase 1 million shares would be more positive than would seem, as it is fully 11% of the float, a huge purchase, which would even trigger a regulatory press release.

Taking The Plunge?

Whenever an investor *plunges* he is no longer investing, nor is he intelligently speculating. He or she is gambling.

Plunging is staking a huge percentage of your total allocation for a particular investing area (i.e., *small technology*) on a single stock, or betting much more than an appropriate allocation on a particular investing area (like putting 40% of your net worth in *small tech*).

To those who say "you must put all of your eggs in one basket, and then watch the basket," I say that is a recipe for disaster. To those who say you will never become rich by investing only a small portion of your wealth in nanotech, I say, "you are right."

It might be sacrilege to say so in a book about nanotech fortunes, but, remember, people get rich by building wealth through their own businesses. In the *Forbes 400* very few arrived due to investing. (And most of those who appear as "investors," indeed became wealthy by investing, but made it onto the list only by *investing for others*.)

Invest enough so that it makes a difference; do not *plunge*.

How much is enough to make a difference? You need to answer that for yourself. Think about it this way. "If I invest $X in this stock and it triples (quintuples, goes up 10 to 1...), will it change my life in some way that matters to me (allow me to go on a better, longer vacation, free me from worry about paying for my daughter's wedding, pay off the mortgage, buy a new couch...)? If the answer is "no" you are not investing enough to cover all the headaches of investing. If, investing $100,000 of your $150,000 savings, you are trying to go from a well-paying 9 to 5 job to retiring before 50 with $10 million, you are plunging (and dreaming).

Everyone who has bought a stock has, at sometime, bought on a particular tip (*As distinct from the kind of common sense or 'good sense' tips highlighted in this book*). No matter what the outcome (almost always bad), buying into a tip this way is always a mistake. I am not talking about using illegal inside information, which should never be done. In most typical stock tip situations, you are hearing about a stock that someone smarter and richer is trying to sell to you, and your tip source is an unwitting dupe. In the best cases, the tipper will be right on the buying, but wrong, or nowhere to be found, on the selling.

The best, honest brokers, investment advisors, analysts and newsletter writers have a natural financial incentive to tell you the truth, and even if they are incorrect, they want you to win. The best advice (as opposed to a *hot tip*) comes from a better, more intelligent, deeper analysis, not from news that is not in the marketplace. Be wary of any advice that begins, "I know some news is coming that others don't know about." If true, it could easily be illegal insider trading. Usually it is not true, in which case you will be one of the losing investors who buy near the end of a rumor, who then fail to *sell on the news*.

Clearly, the corollary to not following tips is to make sure you or your advisor does his or her *due diligence* and research. The hallmark of all of my mutual funds, hedge funds and venture capital funds in nanotech and *small technology* will always be scientific, technical and financial research and due diligence. You are just joining the nano-hypesters if you choose not to do this yourself, or fail to hire a broker or advisor who is not deeply involved. By around 2007/08, I fully expect that (along with the *scamsters*) there will be several significant professional groups or investment houses with excellent *small tech* research capability and offerings.

Overtrading is a losing strategy. Commissions at brokerage firms who aim at traders are now so low that direct costs from overtrading are much less a problem than they once were. However, trading and overtrading have their own hidden costs. It is time-consuming. It wears on the nerves of most folks. The spreads between 'bid' and 'ask' take a serious toll. Assume a stock trades at a relatively small spread of $31.35 X $31.50, and you buy 1000 shares with only a $12 commission. That stock must rise to $33.10 bid (up 5.6%) for you to make just 5% on your money. You lose 5% if the stock just drops to 29.95 bid (down 4.4%). This is a hard headwind to overcome over the long term. Furthermore, the above is nearly a *best-case* example. More often in these relatively illiquid and volatile stocks, the headwind will be much stronger.

Holding onto losing trades is a losing strategy, by definition. Too often I have seen friends fall in love with companies and then see their stocks decline as these companies suffer one problem after another. True, even great companies and stocks have multiple periods of significant declines on their way to investment nirvana. But that is no reason to hold on to losing trades or to stay with declining stocks. This is not straightforward; it is tricky. I am going to say some things that appear contradictory. Please bear with me while I attempt to explain. A Peter Lynch or Warren Buffett can hold on to Coke as it declines from $88 to $38 – they have many other investments, deep insight into the businesses of the companies they hold, and are/were committed to long-term strategies. Except as it applies to *small tech* companies in which you are building a long-term position over a period of a decade or more, like my friend did with Altria, Syntex and Pfizer using a *dollar cost averaging* methodology, you should not hold declining stocks. Admit a mistake and sell your losers somewhere between a 7 and 17% loss, especially on a breakdown below important intermediate or long-term support. You can always buy back in at a later date after the air has cleared. It is much more difficult to get a double after losing 50%, which is what you will need just to breakeven!

8 SECRET TACTICS YOU WILL NEVER HEAR FROM YOUR BROKER

BUY ON MYSTERY; SELL ON HISTORY

The hardest thing for novice investors to understand is why stocks often head down on good news and begin up-trends on bad news. Seeing this happen more than a couple of times is probably more responsible than anything else for driving investors away from fundamental analysis and toward technical analysis. The key is *knowing* whether the news is *anticipated* or not.

A few examples? If droughts have been reported for months in the Ivory Coast, a shortage of cocoa beans would be anticipated; if reported sales of CDMA cell phones are down significantly for two consecutive, very weak quarters, a weak earnings announcement by Qualcomm would be anticipated; likewise, if a small nanotech company is regularly press releasing good results from its new, nano-catalyst for gasoline combustion it was designing for Royal Dutch Petroleum, smart market participants would anticipate that a positive announcement of revenues or a joint venture would be coming from the nanotech company and/or Royal Dutch.

Nothing disappoints like delivering good news when *great* news is expected. A nano-materials company is growing at 10%

per quarter and gives guidance to expect yet another blowout quarter – the quarter proceeds to come in at 9%. Expect the stock to *be taken out and shot.* This company growing at an incredible 46% per year might be susceptible if annual growth slows to 41% (the 9% per quarter). What appears to be pennies or even a single penny is actually a 10.86% decline from the anticipated numbers! Nothing to sneeze at. Even rabid growth is not enough if it disappoints expectations.

Why Your Broker Will Fail You

Can you count on your broker to know that *flash memory* is so inexpensive, that nanotechnology will have a hard time displacing it from all but the most difficult applications even if the nanotechnology can exceed *flash memory's* performance figures by a wide margin technically. A similar situation exists with most competitors to silicon CMOS – it is so cheap and its manufacture so well integrated that it will probably be around for another couple of decades. Will your broker *grok* this, or just promote you into a nanotech deal?

Most brokers are honest, hard working men and women who would love for their clients to make millions. Unfortunately they are not qualified analysts, nor are they paid for the accuracy or profitability of their advice.

Separating Dominos from Papa John's or Coke from Pepsi is hard enough. In high-tech or biotechnology, brokers really cannot be expected to even begin to understand the science and technology, much less be able to ascertain how they apply to the business models of companies or how stock prices are likely to perform when certain corporate or technology development goals are met. Their hearts might be in the right place, but if you are looking for "nanotech help" I am afraid they will fail you.

Live by the Sword; Die by the Sword

If you overtrade, you will be eaten alive by commissions and the spreads between the bids and asks. If you plunge, you will find yourself with two consecutive major losses that destroy your capital and ability to stay in the game. If you buy on tips, you will lose confidence in yourself or lose a friend. If you hold losing trades you will have stocks go to zero. If you fail to do due diligence and research you will end up in the stocks of weak companies with terrible management. "If you live by the sword, you will die by the sword."

USE THE TECHNIQUES THE PROS USE

In 1982 I helped finance a 31 year old entrepreneur without a cent to his name who today is a *Forbes 400* member tagged at $1.1 billion (it is probably triple that amount). By 1988 he was worth $30 to $50 million and I went to Canada to help him run one of his companies. I usually sat directly across from him at his huge desk, and I was there for most of his biggest deals that year. We were the same age and had become friends, so a couple times a week we would head to the nicest hotel in town a few blocks from the office and work out at the gym after a long, hard day at work.

This entrepreneur's lead public company had run from $7 to $16 in about a year, and I was working with large shareholders, mostly mutual fund and European private bank investors. These were days long before Sarbanes-Oxley and Regulation FD which limits *selective disclosure*, and (without violation of then current laws and regulations) a large investor who called and asked the right questions in the right way got better, more timely information than the investing public received by way of shareholder letters and SEC filings. When a mutual fund manager called from San Francisco or New York, or I spent an evening dining with a private banker from Zurich, I would be grilled from beginning to end. Given my background and expertise, combined with my known close relationship with the entrepreneur, I would be expected to be forthcoming with the very most recent news on corporate developments, production, practically weekly earnings and revenues numbers, and merger, acquisition or joint venture deals that were in the making. Of course, some stuff could not be talked about. Some stuff could only be hinted. Some stuff seemed to be communicated by facial expressions and body language.

One rainy afternoon as we crossed a busy city street under his umbrella on our way to the gym, I said "Ed (not his real name), you know the market for your shares is way ahead of itself. Maybe we should tell investors to back off here? They should be able to buy stock 30 - 50% lower in the not too distant future. Basically, your promotional capability alone has it this high at $14; I'm selling my clients' shares while they are continuing to buy based on the good news flow. They may be buying at the top."

At the time I was already a seasoned professional, but his look at me on the other side of the intersection could have stripped bark off a tree. "Darrell, if you EVER think that I will EVER tell anyone, at any time, for any reason (barring an offer from a 'major' at a price I deem fair), to sell shares in my stock, you are just out of your mind!"

We went to the gym, had a good workout, had a great dinner with our wives, and (believe me) that subject NEVER came up again. The moral of the story: The CEO, the key promoter, or the largest shareholder will NEVER give you a reason to sell. You can take that to the bank.

Executives of public companies first and only obligation is to CURRENT, LONG-TERM shareholders. Right thinking CEOs have no interest in traders, speculators or even investors who might hold the stock one, two, three years or more. The cold truth is that they do not and should not care what fates befall those folks. In the CEO's' eyes, those investors who actually put money in the corporate treasury and support the company until it is sold, liquidated or cashed out with the key guy or gal, are the true investors in the company.

The CEOs use high and growing stock valuation to hold and attract key employees, reward supporters, and, most importantly, as a currency to acquire companies, assets, and intellectual property.

If you are an executive (CEO, COO, CIO, or even a mid-level type) in a nanotech company you should be maximizing your own position in terms of stock options and basic compensation and benefits package, and you should align it to performance and service to the true investors in the company. If you are short-sighted you will end up short-changing yourself. If you are unsophisticated in this area, pay for competent advice from a compensation professional to tailor your situation and assure the company is meeting industry standards. You may have significant restrictions on trading your own shares, sharing information about your company with others, or even investing in or shorting shares of related companies. Get the right information, and make sure you clearly understand how you are impacted in your corporate role by Rule 144, Reg FD, Sarbanes-Oxley and the myriad federal, state, and securities laws and regulations which may inform your position.

Being an early (first 10) executive in a private nanotech company that is merged into a GE or IBM or Chevron at a $50 - $200 million valuation is "good work if you can get it," and you could walk away with millions for what will likely be 3 - 6 years of hard efforts. As an executive in the same position, whose company sells or licenses its IP for royalties to a public company with a $5B - $50B market cap within five years you might make a million or two and a couple hundred grand a year for a decade or more; enough for some people to retire. If your nanotech company goes public, and is wildly successful (achieves a market capitalization of at least $1 billion within 7 years of startup), and you are one of the first 50 executive employees, you should be made financially rich beyond your dreams.

These are big stakes. Do not count on a trusted advisor or your corporate attorney, brother-in-law to counsel you. Treat it as an investment. Better to spend $5,000 now to make $7 million in five years instead of $2 million, right? Actually, the basic math easily supports a $5,000 investment in education and negotiating support, now, just to increase that $2 million to $2.5 million. How many chances do we have in life to make a 100:1 return on investment (ROI) in five years? Not *bloody* many.

GETTING DOWNRIGHT CONTRARY

After *Business Week* carried a great article on the future of nanotechnology on its front cover in early 2005, you could hear the collective sigh, the feeling that "at last, we have arrived" emanating from my colleagues in the small technology investing field. "The cover of *Business Week*, what could be more confirming? Finally, the world will know we are here to stay and we are truly *the next big thing*." Over the next few weeks, one nano-pundit after another appeared on CNBC. One would tout his company. Another said there would be six major nanotech IPOs in 2005. A third confirmed that the impact of nanotech on the US economy would exceed a trillion dollars within five years. A fourth intoned that the way to make a fortune was to simply buy many names and hold on for a few years, because this was so clearly the next big thing given that the government was spending billions. A few consumer products with *small tech* improvements were trotted out as a sign of things to come, and sharp MIT grad and resident CNBC humorist, Joe Kernan, tried to dampen the breathless discourse snidely noting reverse takeovers, the pink sheets, and promoters named Guido while observing that the biggest nano companies said to be coming were, in fact, tiny micro-caps. I was targeted for a long interview for Germany's largest selling weekly financial magazine, *Börse Online* (it is best to be compared to *Barron's* in the US), and did the best I could to fight the building nano-hype.

Contrarian that I am, I began to worry. I clearly remember the infamous *Business Week* cover in August 1979 featuring "The Death of Equities" coffin and how that looked from a vantage point 8, 15 or 20 years later. In fact, there have been an impressive series of *wrong calls* both positive and negative seemingly triggered by the *Business Week* cover. It is not as much about being wrong as it has to do with the idea that the cover is picked to sell magazines; topics do not arrive there because there is an educational or instructive need; they arrive because the interest is at a height and the editors become convinced that this cover or title will sell magazines, a subject about which they know a lot.

So, there I was telling anyone who would listen that this is a short term top for nanotech. Be careful. Nanotech will be here for decades, but for 2005 this was more like the proverbial *kiss of death* than the hoped for *clarion call*. More people will know what nanotech is and that it is real, but those suckered into big moves following major press will lose.

True contrarians are those who sell to the new, unwashed masses at times like those. An old friend of mine used to say, "Feed the ducks when they're quacking."

9 ANGELS, VCS, INVESTMENT BANKERS OR THE IPO ENVY GAME

WHEN WILL WE SEE A NANOTECH IPO BOOM?

Maybe 2007-2008 for bio. Maybe 2009-2010 for electronics. But both bulk materials and instrumentation/tools will be dominated by large, already existing companies.
—Maximilian M. Schroeck, Ph.D.,
Managing Director, Agilent Ventures

Tools in 2006-2007. Devices and materials in 2010-2012. 2014 Production and metrology equipment manufacturers, but by then the space will be dominated by large already existing companies.
—Tim Stultz, President, Imago Scientific Instruments

Mark your calendars; 2008-2010. The times will be marked by record levels of capital investment, and be led by a new generation of nano-bio-pharma start-ups and 'spin-off' companies focusing on very early stage cancer detection.
—Roger Attick, President, *CeMines*

2007-2009 as products become real enough to bring to market, and investors become overly bored with the preceding years of flat markets.
—Robert Nolan, NanoMarkets

Angel investors want the companies they invest in to sell shares to VCs at a significantly higher valuation. The VCs want larger companies or investment bankers to take them out at higher yet valuations via mergers and acquisitions (M & A) or IPOs. The companies expect to have made non-dilutive investments in the technology, IP or companies in which they invest, and the public shareholders who buy on the initial public offerings expect to sell to later entering retail investors at yet further valuation increases. *The IPO Envy Game* continues.

The process can absolutely be compared to the manufacturing, wholesaling and retailing of any typical consumer product. Most investors fail to see the process for what it is. Companies are built, sold to wholesalers, who sell them to retailers, who sell them to customers, marking up the price (and hopefully adding value) at each level along the way. Can each of these investors reach their business and investment goals, or is this all gambling, *the greater fool theory*, and nothing but *a moving paper fantasy*?

First, recognize that broker/dealers and investment banks are not investors in the purest sense of the word (even when they take equity, options or warrants as part of their compensation). They perform a business function as distributors of a company's stock to their clients, their distribution network. They are paid for distribution, not for how well their clients do with the stock. Successful VCs might be good early stage (occasionally long-term) investors, but typically they win by building (manufacturing) quality companies, not simply by somehow betting on the right horse.

If value is added at each level, valuations are reasonable at each point, and integrity maintained (big "ifs"), money should be made by each group in succession. However, it often resembles the "building" and marketing of art more than the building and marketing of real estate.

A real-estate speculator buys and develops a lot for $200,000 and builds a small office building for at an additional cost of $1,000,000. He or she later sells it to another investor or user for $1.5 million. Two years later that buyer sells to an investor for $1.8 million. Can that investor make money over the next two years? Maybe; maybe not. However, all things being equal, assuming small increases for inflation in materials, land and contractors, replacement cost after 5 years is probably at least $1.5 million. A new builder would require the usual mark-up for his or her profit and a $1.8 million price-tag is probably assured. Marvin, my real-estate investing father-in-law, always said "the profit is made in the buying, not the selling." You should think the same way as a *small technology* investor.

Compare this concrete, well understood valuation underpinning with that of a work of art.

An oil painting might take an artist a week to paint and have canvas and paint costs of $100. A reasonable valuation at that point might be $1,400 - $1,100 in costs ($1,000 for labor) plus a $300 profit. A wholesaler buys it for that and sells to a retailer for $2,000, and the retailer sells it to the customer for $3,500. In the case of a living, working artist, what are the odds that the price can rise from $3,500 anytime soon? Slim to none. After all, 5 years later the same artist can paint a similar painting (size, by the way, is practically all that counts for living, working artists) for only a few hundred more, even including inflation. The wholesaler will be paying $1800 let us say, instead of $1400. Still well below the $3500 figure.

In the *IPO Envy Game* play with the companies that come closer to the real estate model. If you pay too much, too high a valuation when you buy, you will pay too high a price in lost profit when you sell. If you buy the most beautiful work of art, perfectly rendered, at full (much less excessive) valuation, be prepared to wait an awfully long time to realize a profit, or just be glad to enjoy its beauty. That might be ok with art; with stock certificates it is a real drag.

A WINNING TIP FOR MAKING YOUR NANOTECH FORTUNE

"A stopped clock is right twice a day." This is one of my favorite market sayings. If someone has been saying the bond market is going to crash since 1979, is he or she "right" when and if the bond market should crash in 2006 or 2011? If someone has been predicting gold is going to $1,000 per ounce since

1985, do you congratulate them on their insight if it happens 25 years later? Of course not. There are tens of thousands of seconds in a day. Even a broken clock reads the right time on rare occasions (twice a day, out of those tens of thousands of seconds). The lesson is to lose respect for any prognosticator or professional investor who misses important investment timing by more than a year or two. They are using the wrong premises, by definition. Really, some of them make a good living out of telling folks the same things year after year in an entertaining way. It is good to remember, it is just entertainment, not good investment advice. Of course there is a downside to not following a "stopped clock." (Why, oh why, is there always a downside?) Because "outlier" events (like 100 year floods, being hit on the head by a meteor, etc.) do occur, these folks are right occasionally, and in those rare events it is often spectacular. But in investing, like horseracing and poker, "the race does not always go to the strongest and swiftest, but that is the way to bet." This brings us to *"Fade (go the opposite way, or short) a 'wrong way' Jones."* I had a friend who always told me to buy a stock just before it tanked, and his sell ideas invariably saw the stock rally hard shortly thereafter. A fellow down the hall from me at my San Diego office used to tell me he had just lost a fortune in such and such industry, and had sold at what turned out to be the precise bottom. Then he would pile into another industry only to be down 25% within 3 weeks. Most people ignore these *living barometers*, not I, nor should you. Their input is just as valuable as that of an investor who is always "right." (They are more valuable, because they are more common, for some reason, then people who are "always" right – actually, I do not know anyone who is always right, but many who are "always" wrong.) I know I will get in trouble with the scientists; I have no scientific proof, but I have tremendous anecdotal experience with this phenomenon: I encourage you to have confidence that these "wrong ways" will continue to be, and always will be wrong. You can make a living *fading* these investors. This brings us to my third tip here; *Optimism trumps Pessimism, always.* We should not have unbridled confidence and mere sunny dispositions, but we can, and should have unbridled enthusiasm in the continuing march of humanity toward ever higher levels in every field of endeavor. The world is getting better, not worse. There are depressions, famines, devastating volcanic eruptions, wars, genocide, and market crashes. However, betting on them is a loser's game. In the long run depressions, wars, famines, and every other negative thing ends. But <u>progress is forever</u>. Go with the long term trend. Big investment winners are usually cynics who contend with their enthusiasm for life, and great belief in the future. In nanotech investing it is probably wise to be like the character in the Jackson Browne song, traveling "with my maps and my faith in the distance, moving farther on."

How to Avoid Getting Your Head Handed to You

Some painful loses are inevitable for every investor in nanotechnology. Getting your head handed to you is not inevitable. There are two ways to have your head handed to you; avoid those two things and you will keep your head.

First, as already noted, but its worth emphasizig, do not *plunge*. Nanotechnology is exciting. The extraordinary, exploding profit potential is exciting. Do not let this excitement (or boredom, or anything else) let you invest more in nanotech in total than you can afford to lose, without it impacting your lifestyle in any serious way. If you lose it ALL, it should not mean your daughter cannot go to the college of her choice, or that you will have to cancel that ski vacation to Crested Butte, CO this year (or golf, that is fun there; some folks love mountain biking, but I have a whole sad story about that that I will not go into now: nine words; "unfortunate meeting: fear of heights and 70 foot cliff"). Do not put more into any single company than an amount which if you lost would be more than a month or two of income. Invest enough to make it count. (I still remember **making six times my money in less than a year** in a stock in which I had invested only $1,200. What a bummer. The $7,000 could not significantly impact my lifestyle at the time.) Do not invest enough to make you sweat or lose sleep. Actually, loss of sleep is an excellent indicator that you are plunging. Just lower your position. "Sell down to a sleeping point."

Second, do not let losses run. (Please, let profits run.) Playing golf in Sedona in late 2004 (a beautiful place, everyone should visit), long after the historic high tech train wreck, my assigned partner, a hair salon owner from Scottsdale, asked when I thought *tech was coming back*. Casually asked if he meant things like Cisco and Oracle going back to $80, I was mildly stunned when he said "Yes," that was exactly what he meant. Inquiring if he still held those stocks after buying them in the very late 1990s, the answer came back, "Yes," again. So many novice investors are/were in this situation, probably incorrectly blaming hedge funds and, somewhat correctly, brokerage firms for their situation. This guy had had his head handed to him. It did not need to happen.

Cut losses short. How? Sell. What if you sell and the stock goes up, and you sell at the bottom. So what? That is the cost for NOT having your head handed to you. I am usually unable to tolerate even a 15% decline in a stock. Your tolerance can be a little more or a little less, not much. Whether you use stop loss orders or just get out on a market order, the market is telling a story. The story it is telling when your stock declines is "YOU ARE WRONG!" If you are wrong, you need to sell. Telling the market why it is wrong and you are right is idiotic; it cannot understand you or your pain, does not care, and has no compunction about handing your head to you. Yes, you will miss opportunities, but it is the choice you make to continue to be in the game. My golf buddy for the day could not see that his *opportunity loss* was not the Vitesse or Cisco that was not going up; it was the funds from the sale of those stocks at higher levels at a loss that could have fueled his buying of REITs or energy stocks, truckers, housing stocks or boring, mundane materials companies, all of which soared after 2001 or even after 2003.

Overtrading, relying on bad advice, paying too high commissions, following the hype, failing to place a stop loss, and bad timing are among the things will cause painful losses, or small losses to become great, but, in themselves, are not significant enough sins to cause you to have your head handed to you. Simply follow the two rules in the paragraphs above and you will avoid that feared fate.

10 Promoters, Newsletter Writers, Crooks & Scoundrels

REVEAL ONE AREA OF NANOTECHNOLOGY BEING PROMOTED BY OTHERS THAT YOU BELIEVE IS EITHER SCIENCE FICTION, OR SO FAR IN THE FUTURE THAT RETURNS LIE BEYOND MOST INVESTORS' LONG-TERM.

Molecular computing based on bottom up structures is still science fiction.
—Maximilian M. Schroeck, Ph.D.,
Agilent Ventures

Some of the hype surrounding scalable, highly intelligent cellular MEMs technology is real cowboy stuff. Investors will get trampled.—
—Roger Attick, *CeMines*

Self assembling nano-robots are science fiction.
—Bryan W. Bockhop, Arnall Golden, Gregory

We have already spent some time on hype, science fiction and scams. We have examined how unscrupulous newsletter writers use email and regular junk mail to implore unsuspecting retail investors to jump into worthless stocks, encouraging them to buy pieces of paper from crooked insiders for thousands of dollars.

Some promoters are not crooks or scoundrels, but unwitting dupes. They might be honest, but not smart or sophisticated. If they have outgoing sales personalities, are "hale fellows, well met," and can *shoot the bull* with a few key nanotech phrases or buzz-words thrown in for good measure, they can be used by the truly criminal to "move stock" or "dump paper." You can spot these characters, because they are never supported by serious, credible scientists. Lack of a deeply involved director or executive with a strong scientific background is a big red flag. Make sure the scientist is not simply on board for figurehead involvement. They should have key man participation in the company.

You might think, because I talk about it so much, that I believe that *small tech* and nanotech are going to be especially fruitful areas for the scoundrels and denizens that populate the micro-cap, pink sheet and bulletin board worlds. You would be right. It is as easy to understand why that is as this: It would be difficult to pull the wool over an investor's eyes about which hamburger is better (McDonalds or Burger King); less difficult to do so about which personal audio MP3 player is better (iPod or Samsung YP109GS); even less difficult to confuse an investor as to which ACE inhibitor is better (Prinivil or Capoten); and, oh, how easy can it can it be to confuse one about which nanotech solution to the computer memory question is likely to succeed (electron-based spintronics or MRAM)? – go figure.

Yep, this is going to be an attractive place for crooks, because the *pickings* are going to be so easy.

11

MODELING THE WINNERS

OR "IN THE LAND OF THE BLIND, THE ONE-EYED MAN IS KING"

AS A GROUP, WHO WILL BE THE BIGGEST WINNERS IN NANOTECH, AND WHY?

Venture capitalists, they'll ride the bubble wave and exit early. Founders of companies, they cash out with the VCs. Universities; they'll get tremendous research and grant funding.
—**Robert Nolan**, Principal, NanoMarkets

Except for the scientists reading this, you and I are not in any lines to get nanotech research grants. Except for the entrepreneurs, venture capitalists and Angel investors among you, most readers will not be very early stage investors in *small tech* company stock. You are unlikely to hold penny, dime or quarter shares.

Given that the biggest winners in the rolling nanotech booms will be the folks listed above, how will you be able to model them to join them in the winners circle?

You can begin by identifying the winning groups as they develop. Some VCs, investment banks and analysts will develop followings because they do what they do very well. This will also hold true in nanotechnology, and while you will be unable to position yourself at the same prices that they do, your will be able to follow them into candidate stocks that are more likely to be winners.

This is a bit like knowing about what and where the top real estate investor in your town or city is investing. You may not be able to buy 1,800 acres at the edge of town, but you may be able to pick up a valuable 30 acres nearby that will increase substantially when the *smart money* land moves.

You can profit handsomely from following *smart money*.

By 2007 - 2008 it should be clear who the early, *smart money*, investment leaders are; you can model them by acquiring shares in companies in which they have a stake. The caveat is to not buy blindly. Pay attention to valuation and your entry level. Furthermore, you need to know how the group you are modeling plays the game. Will they sell on the earliest release of their shares from regulatory restrictions? Will they sell a small part and hold the balance for at least a year or more? Once you understand a bit about their reasons for investing, usual holding timeframe and *modus operandi*, you can participate with the leaders. Just stay out of their way and don't allow them to get in yours.

Will you be paying $12 for something for which they paid $1 or $7? Yes, quite often. Not to fear, if you've done your homework. It is not unlike buying the thirty acres above for $10,000 per acre a year after the large, shrewd investor (who, by the way, is a professional who spends every waking minute studying the local real estate market) paid $1,800 per acre for his or hers.

You are not going to care when Toll Brothers or Beazer pays you $35,000 per acre 2 years later (Please take the point of this story. It might be hard to relate to if you are from Ohio; it happens all the time in California.)!

As a *small tech* investment writer myself, it might be self-serving to say so, but sharp analysts, that you enjoy reading, in whom you trust, who can demonstrate success can be followed with certain caveats. Demonstrated success has nothing to do with breathless claims in advertising. It is carried in each issue where the price of entry and the current price are listed. Letters that don't carry their track record, warts and all, should be avoided. Also, beware of any letter writer (or any analyst or broker for that matter) who does not tell you, in advance, how you and he or she will know when they're wrong. It can be technical: "We will sell should the stock break down below $19.55/share." It can be news based: "We'll *lose* our shares if the company cannot announce that the nano-encapsulated formulation has entered Phase II studies by January 20th?" It can be fundamental: "The Company must exceed the middle of the range of its earnings guidance for the quarter of 20 to 24 cents per share, or we'll be sellers."

If you want to model what the winners above are *actually doing* to achieve their success, there are no shortcuts. The only way to be precisely like a successful, full-time pro is to become one.

After reading this book and studying the information in the appendix, you may decide to do just that.

A WINNING TIP FOR MAKING YOUR NANOTECH FORTUNE

Stock prices do not rise in the face of growing revenues and earnings; stock prices rise as *the rate of growth of revenues and earnings* increases. If you are unfamiliar with this notion, reread and consider the preceding sentence. It is not merely a "distinction without a difference." Price/earnings ratios decline just for this reason. If a company is growing at 23% per year for 3 years, and earns $0.36 per share, then announces *guidance* to earn $0.41 the next year, you can rest assured the stock will decline. Increasing earnings more than 10% seems like a good thing, but in the harsh world of *the market* this will be seen as *significant decline* in the *rate* of growth. The inverse also works. Accelerating the earnings and revenues rate of growth will be rewarded.

12 TRADING NANOTECH STOCKS FOR SHORT-TERM PROFIT

TRUMP CARDS FOR FUNDAMENTALISTS

Being a fundamentally-based, short-term trader is a rarity, as the two are nearly mutually exclusive. However, whether you are trading with the trend or counter to it, certain fundamental news events can be traded with or against for short-term profits.

After incredibly bad news kills a stock (the kind that drives prices down 25% or more in a single day) there is, among bulls, a strong desire to buy the stock too soon. If you find yourself among them, fight the urge. Expect the stock to be lower, probably significantly, 3 to 5 months later. If you are still bullish after four months, look for a place to buy for a rally lasting 3 to 10 weeks. This rebound will not likely get anywhere near the previous high, but could be rewarding. Carry a stop loss just below the most recent low (as long as it is an amount you are comfortable losing should you be wrong) and you should be in a profitable, short-term, *long* position.

If you find the urge too great, and must buy sooner, wait for a three day high to be made followed by another declining day. If you must, buy on a *stop* just above that three day high, and carry a *stop loss* just below the recently made low. At worst, your risk will be contained to less than 5% of your cost, and at best you will have a sharp, 3 to 18 day rally from which to profit.

Simply reverse/invert the above process if you are bearish, and great news drives a stock up 25% or more in a single day.

Important, unexpected news is a fundamental that trumps any technical pattern or analysis. In early 2005 two very negative completely separate FDA actions hit *small tech* companies, Elan and Advanced Magnetics, for a loop. Advance lost 75% of its value in 2 weeks, including a one day drop of more than 60%, and Elan lost about 90% in less than 2 months, including two one-day drops of about 65% each! Prior to the drops Elan had a fairly nondescript, mildly bearish technical pattern, but Advanced Magnetics had a super-bullish chart, the only negative being a severely short-term overbought reading, that, in and of itself would have indicated a roughly 10 - 20% decline over a 1 week to 1 month period, followed by a continuation of the uptrend at a lower rate of growth.

Totally unexpected negative news rendered all of this technical analysis moot. Unexpected positive news has the same impact; but to the upside, and *technicals* be damned.

TRUMP CARDS FOR TECHNICIANS

Fundamentalists are often shocked when good news fails to take a stock higher. Often a technical pattern is controlling and the culprit. This isn't mysticism. In this case, the pattern is simply a way of visualizing the place where sellers have put their sell limit orders. Imagine this: A stock was heavily bought around $20 per share and dropped to $12 dollars over the next year. Many of those who bought at $20 get it in their heads to sell if they can get back to breakeven; around $20/share. Not so strangely, there are many limit sell orders on the books in the $19 to $21 range. That story is manifested in a chart as *resistance* at $20. Not hard to imagine so far? Now, with the stock rallying to the $18.50 area, tremendously bullish news is announced that should make the stock go up 20% or more, because 3,000,000 shares are expected to be purchased on the news and the stock normally trades

150,000 shares/day... etc. In this case the technicals trump the fundamentals – there are 2.5 million shares for sale between $19 and $21 and the stock gets to only $20.50 to $21.25 before weakening again.

See, it's not mystical, not voodoo, not totally subjective. Technical analysis simply focuses on and tries to measure the supply and demand for and levels of support and resistance for the shares themselves; not supply and demand for the company's products, or revenues and earnings for the company. Technical analysts assume (with the exception of the "trump" cards referenced above) that the best information is already "in" the market, and that it has already been analyzed and valued by the best (fundamentalist) minds in the business.

SHORT SELLERS: DEALING WITH THEM; BEING ONE YOURSELF

Sometimes professional short-sellers will tear apart a company that you like. Be careful. They might be right.

Just as professional touts can *bull* a stock, pro *short artists* can drive shares down with an onslaught of negative press and bad-mouthing. A few of these types perform an exceptional public service by alerting investors and authorities to scams and accounting frauds as well as inflated earnings or undisclosed self-dealing. Pay particular attention to these, especially if you are long on a stock they mention and you receive new input.

Remember, just like the recommender of a stock who promotes old news, these *shorters* are also sometimes promoting negative news that has been in the market for sometime, perhaps driving prices down for months. If you really know the company's story, this might be a signal to step up to the plate.

If – despite all my caveats – you still want to short stocks, do it this way:

1. Short securities that are overvalued *and* overbought, that have already begun to decline (Meaning: Only short stocks that are in 11 week <u>downtrends</u>, that are trading at infinite or insane

multiples to earnings, and whose most recent three-month high was at a one-year or more high.)

2. Short stocks that have a *fatal flaw* such as poor management, a poor business model, a secondary or tertiary – or, better yet, even worse position in the space.

3. Have a low-risk entry point. In other words, know where you are wrong on the stock and place a buy stop loss order there. Be sure the amount you are risking is small relative to the amount you hope to gain.

4. Consult a tax advisor, but keep in mind that treatment for short sales is different. Remember to cover your short, and your plan should be much shorter term for shorts than long. My experience is that most successful shorts should be covered in days or weeks, not months.

A Winning Tip for Making Your Nanotech Fortune

The best timeframe for short-term trading and short selling is 6 to 10 days to 6 to 10 weeks. Day trading is a loser for all but full-time pros, and you're not *short-term-trading* if you are holding positions for 4 - 6 months. *Never give back a large quickly made profit.* You buy a stock at $12 hoping it can go to $17 in 2 to 3 months. Within a week it is at $14 or $15.25; I think it's crazy to allow that trade to turn into anything but a good profit. Letting it turn into a loss is a sin. I can hear you now, "But what if I'm stopped out with a $1.50 gain and then it goes to $17 in a month or two?" My first response is: "Too bad; find something important to get upset about." May second response is simply this: **"You can always re-enter a trade."** With the low commissions available you should never be afraid to re-enter a trade, higher or lower, if your conviction is still there and you are presented with a low-risk entry point.

13 Playing the Inevitable Busts

The best way to play busts for investors will be to heavily short from the top, and covering completely and going long at the inevitable bottom. "Good work, if you can get it."

You will be doing quite well if you are out of nanotech stocks or have only a small position during these sometimes sudden and always massive declines that for decades will characterize *small tech* equities from time to time.

The signs of a top are signaled by key technical patterns, followed by a confirming collapse below important short-term, then intermediate term support. For those not so inclined, mass psychology gives a very good reading as well.

Let's discuss that first. Remember, the first sign of a bust is the final stage of a boom. That means we are looking for a top. All tops look the same. At gold mining, biotech, petroleum and internet tops, folks who have no special knowledge or interest in the fields are buying heavily and telling their neighbors and relatives to follow suit. TV and radio are full of never-heard-of-analysts and touts promoting this stock or that. IPOs double or triple on the first day of trading. Your gardener gives you a stock tip or your cabbie tells you how they just made $5,000 on a flyer.

"Wait," you say. "All that happened in 1997 and the internet top didn't come until three years later. Your model is not specific enough to be helpful." Well, think back to your specific recollections. I think you'll find that while the market was indeed exploding in 1997, you didn't start hearing about your neighbor's or gardener's stock options, or how he just made a big score in Qualcomm, or one-day profits in Yahoo until 1999. Had you started looking for the exits then, the collapse below intermediate support in the first half of 2000 would have been your trigger to say "goodbye" to the high-flying tech and internet market.

So a booming market, even an insanely booming market alone is not enough to mark a top. You have to hear the noise coming from silly places. **Then look for a breakdown below the previous intermediate low.** (Remember, bull markets are typified by rising highs and rising lows.) A break below the previous intermediate low breaks that trend and is your signal to exit.

Standing aside with no long positions is a perfectly good way to play the inevitable busts. If you're more sophisticated and a more active trader you might consider shorting the more grossly overvalued stocks. Remember; if you are long (in a cash account), you can only lose what you invest. Theoretically, however, you can lose an infinite amount if you're short. So, in case you turn out to be wrong, short with stop loss order protection, and be aware that occasionally stocks gap up well above the stops you place, inflicting you with more severe losses than you expect.

Also, for most people, shorting is a loser's game. Think of this relationship. If a shorted stock goes to zero, you double your money; make 100%. That's the very best you can do. On the other hand, if you buy a stock you can theoretically make an infinite amount on your money, and, while infinite has never happened, and such returns are not every day occurrences, 800%, 2,200% and even 34,000% returns have been made in stocks over time from the long side.

FLIES IN THE OINTMENT

This is the longest chapter in the book.

For good reason: As of 2005 (and I expect for at least a dozen years beyond), there are a lot of "flies in the ointment," things that can negatively influence nanotech and your investments, and being aware of them can keep you out of a lot of trouble. Below are some of the most critical understandings you can have as a sophisticated small tech investor over the next decade or more:

Patents often expire before a product makes it to market. This happens far more often than one would expect. When control is lost, profit opportunities are lost. As mentioned before, time from science to technology to product to market is quite long. This is another reason for startups to partner with powerful companies early.

Entrepreneurs in the field are untested. That's an understatement. In 2005, many are downright "green." At the earliest, I do not expect to see even a dozen proven business leaders in the space until 2006-2008.

Solid business models and a real *value proposition* are rare in nanotech business plans. I see more technologies in search of markets, science projects masquerading as commercial technologies, potential products misaimed at the wrong market, interesting technologies without a "hot" or addressable market, and companies that are unable to provide a compelling reason why the customer must buy than you would believe. Not "hot" market: the market for elementary school paste. Not "addressable" market: people who don't wear shoes. Neither "hot" nor "addressable" market: the market of people who want a better butter knife. You would be amazed at the number of "plans" that are nothing but a mere list of opportunities.

Scalability is a major hurdle most companies have not adequately addressed. Just because you can do it once in a lab, just because you can make a thousand prototypes, just because you can make 1,000 tons in a month, does not mean you can scale up to the levels that industry demands. I heard an Intel exec once say that if you couldn't build a billion connections, a billion times, in a short period of time, with an extremely low error rate, he wasn't interested.

Development at major companies is quite far along. Don't forget, while your micro-cap is toiling away at a new gizmo that disinfects polluted water, ten, fifteen or fifty blue chips are working on similar technologies. Worse, they may actually hold the controlling IP, or be willing to litigate aggressively enough to drive your micro-cap out of the market or even out of business.

Patents can be reverse engineered. Biotech and pharmaceutical scientists are often incredulous that the change in a single molecule or the addition of a carbon atom or molecule can eviscerate the basis of a challenge. Depend on the major companies being all-business, impersonal and ruthless and you won't be disappointed.

Not enough attention is paid to the "pollution" that occurs at the nanoscale (i.e., radio waves interfere with nanocomputers). Physics, biology and chemistry that "work" in a clean room laboratory under ideal conditions may not perform as advertised in the real world. In addition, there are seemingly arbitrary atomic scale and quantum forces that may not be immediately detectable by anyone but a specialist, which can play havoc on the road to a technology and product development.

Advocates of nanomedicine sometimes forget that the liver has an unfortunate, not at all trivial "tendency" to remove nanoparticles from the bloodstream before they can do anything. The liver has to be "fooled" by a variety of tactics, all of which may not work for a specific particle and its load. The human body's own natural defense mechanisms are sometimes a bigger hurdle than the FDA approval process.

Very few people/scientists are trained in the interdisciplinary aspects of nanotech. For all those scientists (and the ranks of nanoscientists grows in leaps and bounds every few months) and business people who grasp their discipline and technology quite well, there are relatively few for whom "nanotechnology is a state of mind." Cross-pollination and training in physics, electrical engineering, chemistry and biology are virtually required to really "get" the nanotech realm, and while growing dramatically, these trained and practiced individuals are still a small group.

Packaging is a major issue. Think about the MEMs component of a larger device or instrument that you can actually see with the naked eye. The MEMs might have a nanotechnology component. How does a company package the MEMs product? How about the nano-product? What does the package look like? Who makes it? How does it protect? How is it thrown away or recycled? Ask your local nano-entreprenuer these questions; you might get blank stares.

Small things are not frictionless. When 60 atom carbon spheres rub against 60 atom carbon spheres or when fluids wend through super-tiny channels, there can be "erosion" and there can be the quantum equivalent of forces we experience as stickiness. These are potential monkey wrenches thrown into the development process. Smart companies will use these types of forces and the "problems" they cause to invent new, even more interesting products that turn proverbial "lemons into lemonade."

Great IP doesn't always win. There are many deeply entrenched technologies. Cheaper, faster, stronger won't be enough. CMOS is the "poster-child" technology that is usually referenced. The argument follows these lines: we have billions invested; there is no pressing market need to change; we see 10-20 more years of future technology development without reaching a nanotech solution. *There may be a $300 Billion market for nanotech products by 2008 as expected; let's hope it's not 300 billion $1 markets!* This facetious comment is not wholly laughable. I heard a pitch recently about a nanotech process that makes washers used in the oil drilling industry last longer and do their job better. I heard that about $30 million worth of these washers are sold annually. How much could a material additive be worth? Perhaps 6% of the total? That's $1.8 million per year (for the total market!). How much would a royalty be worth? 8% of that? $145,000 per year in revenues?! OK earnings? Why be in that business? Why chase a small market? This is a potentially major issue for many *small tech* startups.

Being essentially commodities (nanoparticle manufacturers, for example), many nano-products may, unfortunately, produce nano-profits. So many nanotech companies' products cost $5,000 per gram and cost only $100 to produce! Unfortunately, last year it was $15,000 per gram, and in three years it may be only $75 per gram! That's not a business. It's not even a good hobby. Commodities businesses whether potatoes (Simplot), PCs (Dell), or nanoparticles (who knows?) eventually drive out all but the most efficient producer/s, and net profits severely erode over time.

A financing paradox exists. Required early-stage investments can be too large for early-stage investors, while returns are too low for late-stage investors because returns are so far away. This paradox makes financing *small tech* difficult using the current accepted model. I am exploring alternatives including some combination of incubator and merchant banking models (similar to the old style *mining houses*) because so few business models and plans for nanotech deals *cut the mustard* or make sense for the standard Angel, VC, M&A or IPO route.

Except for tools, instruments and materials, most products are still years away (expect steadily rising growth, but no product explosion until the 2008-2018 timeframe). Some very interesting consumer products and medical diagnostic plays are also "ready for primetime" now, but most products being developed by other "fast track" companies will not be market-ready (assuming a great joint venture partner; not exactly the safest assumption) until 2008 - 2012.

Debilitating IP wars are inevitable. As soon as someone starts to make serious money from nanotech during 2007 - 2015, there will be an absolute explosion of patent litigation. So many overlapping patents exist that disputes will be rampant. The whole "industry" will likely suffer severe developmental delay as the winners and losers are sorted out. Most disputes will be settled by cash or cross-licensing or royalties, but most of the winners will be the large, established companies with deep pockets such as IBM, DuPont, and GE.

Politically motivated, agenda-charged, non-scientific, environmental extremists and other Luddites will negatively impact the scientific and business development of nanotechnology. Hopefully public education and science will win in the end. As I've said before, there are serious environmental issues related to nanotechnology, but self-assembling nanobots and "grey goo" are not among them. They are pure science fiction. Scientists, entrepreneurs and governments as well as the *free market* influence of insurance companies are all in line to keep the use and manufacture of *small tech* products safe, and their impact on the environment minimized. The scissors in your drawer can be used to kill someone, and in every breath you breathe there are nanoparticles of soot or auto exhaust-related particulates, whatever.

This brings us to another "fly." Insurance companies might not insure "nano" companies. Due to lack of understanding and in-house scientific expertise, insurers may balk at underwriting real nano-related risks. This would not be inconsequential for a company or group of companies operating in a particular technical area, and could derail development of more than one worthwhile project.

Scientists and nano workers may not make the best business managers. This seems to be the case now, and it is unlikely that many professional managers will be attracted to the space until at least serious financings or revenues have been occurring with some dependability; probably by 2008 - 2010.

Patents are just one piece of the IP protection puzzle, a puzzle that includes branding, customer relationships, trademarks, copyrights, know-how, and trade secrets. If only it were merely about patents, our analysis tasks would be simpler. However, protection of these other facets is essential to protecting a special knowledge, process, and business. Clearly, a company can have all of the patent protection in the world but lose a customer who has soured on the relationship, or lose the most important part of their IP when the "secret sauce" of an important process walks out the door in the form of a production line manager with the trade secret in his head.

One should always remember *Biotech's Dismal Bottom Line*: From a *Wall Street Journal* article by David P. Hamilton of May 20, 2004: "Since the first biotechnology company went public a quarter century ago, stock market investors have put somewhere close to $100 billion into the industry. The results so far: More than a hundred new drugs and vaccines, several hundred million people helped by biotech medicines – and cumulative net losses of more than $40 billion for the industry's public companies." On the plus side, the article goes on to say that while biotech stock fortunes have been illusive, Amgen did have an 11 to 1 run over one short, eight-month period.

Finally, on a sadder note, much of nanotech is "much ado about nothing." Sometimes a worthless technology might have 20 patents on it. Some very complex sounding technologies do very mundane things; sometimes quite inefficiently, at that.

WALLS OF WORRY AND SLOPES OF HOPE, REDUX

Be vigilant for signs of worry and hope. They will be your best indicators for the future direction of *small tech* stocks. When the proverbial *flies in the ointment* of the previous chapter dominate the headlines and inform investor opinion while stocks stay steady or firm, you're on safe ground; the bull will run. When nanotech investors start talking about *hoped for* mergers or higher earnings, really *necessary* acquisitions or FDA approvals, needed or essential target dates to be met, or investors hoping share prices get stronger, be afraid – the bear is growling.

14 SELL THEM PICKS & SHOVELS

Frankly, 'nanotech' is a frame of mind. Nanotechnology, MEMs, microfluidics: they're all part of the same toolset.
—**Evelyn Hu, Ph.D.**, Physicist and Engineer
Member, SAB: The Nanotech Company

When prospectors appeared at mining camps in the Old West, savvy merchants already had picks, shovels, sluices and pans for placer mining available for sale. In a gold rush town there would be hundreds or thousands of buyers and the only ones who made money in these rushes, as it usually turned out, were the merchants selling the picks and shovels to the miners.

All enterprises require *tools of the trade*. Carpenters need hammers and nails, barbers need scissors and combs, stock traders need Bloomberg machines and phones, scientists need microscopes and beakers.

The tools needed to build businesses based on products from the micro or nanoscale have to be incredibly precise and expensive. Clean rooms for avoiding contamination can cost millions.

Atomic Force Microscopes and other tools for visualization cost a hundred thousand and much more. Incredibly tiny forces must be measured by instruments sometimes so expensive that only government or university labs can afford them. Supersensitive scales are needed. Lasers, rare gases, heavy metals, x-rays, MRIs, complete laboratories, instruments that can move individual molecules or atoms, and spectrographic tools (instruments used to determine the masses of atoms or molecules, in which a beam of charged particles is passed through an electromagnetic field that separates particles of different masses. The resulting distribution or spectrum of masses is recorded on a photographic plate – everyone should have one of these) are all costly.

Cost doesn't matter.

These (and this is by no means an exhaustive list) are the tools of the nanotech trade. They aren't just useful. They're essential.

Some of the first companies to make serious profits from the nanotech booms are and will be these *pick and shovel* makers.

An important winning strategy is to invest in these companies at reasonable valuations.

Peter Hebert, the bright chief of Lux Research and Josh Wolfe's partner and Co-Founder of Lux Capital, had some interesting things to say in 2004 about what nanotech investments he found attractive:

"On the private side of things, we're looking to invest in companies that control the IP critical to integrating nanotechnology into the industrial food chain. We really do see today as a unique opportunity to invest in the materials building blocks for decades to come. We're also keen on market-specific opportunities. We like nanotech's intersection with biotechnology, with applications addressing markets like orthopedics and regenerative medicine. We think nanoscale advances in electronics and semiconductors offer tremendous opportunities ? particularly if the economics of manufacturing them can be down-shifted using the power of biology and Mother Nature. And considering the massive demand, supply constraints, and social pressure, it's hard to miss if you can deliver low-cost functionality in alternative energy (Easier said then done, of course!). On the pub-

*lic end of the equation, from down here we think the instrumenta-
tion providers look very attractive. We believe the nanotech build-
out represents a solid growth business for the next several years... .
By these companies' current valuations, we suspect investors don't
grasp this reality."*

The Nanotech Patent Thicket

Scientists in an emerging field like nanotechnology face a
delicate balancing act. The U.S. Patent and Trade (USPTO)
Office can take years to get up to speed on relevant issues in a
rapidly changing technology. Ideally, innovative companies
should be granted reasonable rights to a new technique or
material, without getting such broad protection that innovation is stifled elsewhere. During the USPTO learning process
overly broad patents are often issued, and companies and scientists need effective coping strategies. Just as in mining, with
the buzz of claim activity in the hot areas of research, there are
naturally a greater number of overlapping patents. The Patent
Office is making good progress in limiting overly broad
patents. They are making it easier to challenge patents (without formal litigation).

There are also strategies available to those willing to invest in
their IP portfolios that provide protection in the event of a
"patent attack."

WHEN FILING FOR PATENTS

When applying for a patent, scientists need to be aware
that there are likely to be a large number of potentially related patents that have already been filed. There may be patents
already granted that are related to a material you may be
applying in some new way. For example, in nanotechnology,
there are people who are exploring the antimicrobial properties of silver nanocrystals. Even if they have their own method
of producing silver nanocrystals, they would themselves still
need to ascertain whether someone has a patent that covers

the silver nanocrystals. People often forget that when a competitor has a patent on a product, such as silver nanocrystals, that claim excludes anyone from using silver nanocrystals for any purpose without permission. In patent parlance, this is known as a "freedom-to-operate" problem.

Product claims, such as a hypothetical product claim covering all silver nanocrystals, have broad exclusionary powers. They block all uses of the product, even those invented in the future by others. For example, if you have invented a method of using silver nanocrystals to kill microbes, you may encounter one or more previous product patents that block you from using certain types of silver nanocrystals in your method. Accordingly, you could also be faced with a situation in which you need to get a license from the underlying owner of the basic product patent that covers silver nanocrystals.

People often refer to these situations as "patent thickets," or patent entanglements, a conflicting snarl of legal issues that can trap entrepreneurs.

This doesn't mean you shouldn't seek to patent the use of as many new ways of using a product as you can – those patents will be valuable in their own right. They may, for example, have longer patent terms than the previous patent on the product, depending on the date of filing. For example there are some carbon nanotube patents that are close to expiration right now.

But people are just beginning to tap the end uses of carbon nanotubes, and many of these new applications for carbon nanotubes are just now being filed as patent applications. Under our current system, a patent will last 20 years from its filing date (21 years if you file a "provisional" application first). But you still need to look closely to determine if other people have a patent still in force that may need to be licensed.

THE BEST OFFENSE IS A STRONG DEFENSE

The best strategy is to pursue broad patents yourself, while being cautious to include as many narrower (more defensible) claims as possible in your patent. In that way, you create as much leverage as you can to deal with these emerging "patent thickets." For example, if two competitors each have their own patent which blocks the other's product from being launched the stage is set for a cross-license in which they license each other so that they can both launch their respective products. But if one of the two competitors has no applicable patents, then that competitor has no leverage with which to drive the other competitor to grant a license. So the more potentially blocking patents you have working for you, the more leverage you will have available to you to push competitors to grant you the license you need or else deter them from asserting their patents against your products.

CHALLENGING A PATENT

If an inventor believes a patent was granted improperly, it is possible to challenge it without resorting to litigation, which can be extremely expensive. For most innovative young companies, litigation is too expensive and too much of a drain on resources, so it is just not an option. In the U.S., we have a system for challenging patents that is called reexamination. In the rest of the world, this procedure is known as opposition. But our system of reexamination in the U.S. is limited and only allows you to challenge a patent on very narrow grounds.

To illustrate one set of conditions where reexamination might be a useful option, suppose that a competitor has an overly broad patent in which only one very broad claim is blocking your product. Yet you are aware of a journal article (published several years prior to the filing date of this patent) which clearly discloses every single feature contained in the overly broad claim. In this scenario, reexamination may be a useful option that would allow you to submit the journal article to the USPTO, who would then take a second look at the patent in light of the new "prior art" you submitted. If they agree with your arguments, they would hold the overly broad claim unpatentable and it would be removed from the patent. Then you would be free to sell your product.

OTHER CHANGES UNDERWAY

The USPTO just announced the creation of a nanotechnology classification (called "Class 977"), which will help in the following ways:

- Facilitate the searching of "prior art" related to Nanotechnology.
- Function as a collection of issued U.S. patents and published pre-grant patent applications relating to nanotechnology across the technology centers, and
- Assist in the development of an expanded, more comprehensive Nanotechnology Crossreference Art Collection classification schedule.

This is a first step toward developing a more sophisticated classification system which, in the future, may include various subclasses to further group related nanotechnology applications together. The danger at present is that an inexperienced examiner may not be aware of all the "prior art" that limits the scope of a nanotechnology application, which could lead to issuance of an overly broad claim. Also, in the future, there is hope that the USPTO will be able to identify particular groups of nanotechnology patent applications to make sure they are directed to those examiners within the USPTO who have the most experience handling such applications.

Another way to improve quality would be the creation of a nanotechnology examining group within the USPTO. The USPTO does not yet have a separate group of patent examiners for nanotechnology, such as the group that exists for biotechnology. Creating a nanotech examination group would require a system that allows the USPTO to identify discreet sectors of nanotech, as mentioned above, so that these cases can be grouped together and sent to an examiner who has the best background to handle that particular group of nanotech cases.

Creating a nanotechnology group would be difficult because nanotech is spread across so many different types of science, but the USPTO can begin to organize certain areas where there are large numbers of applications such as nanowires, carbon nanotubes, and different types of nanocrystals.

The USPTO faces other challenges, including the annual diversion of user fees for unrelated spending programs by Congress. In other words, a large chunk of all the fees generated when patents are filed are not returned to the USPTO every year. This makes it hard for the USPTO to hire new examiners in critical areas such as nanotechnology or devote adequate resources to initiatives like the classification system discussed above.

While improvements have been made in our patent system, it is a challenge to properly calibrate the power of patents and ensure that patents are thoroughly and properly reviewed at the USPTO. Since 2004, reports have issued from the FTC and other agencies calling for still more reforms to achieve a better balance between innovation and competition. In the current environment, it is important for aspiring nanotechnology start-ups to seek broad claims while at the same time including narrower, more defensible claims in every application. This is the best way to make it through the patent thicket.

—**Stephen B. Maebius**, Partner, Foley & Lardner
Leader, Nanotechnology Practice
Member, Corporate Development Advisory Board
The Nanotech Company, LLC

15 SIX STEPS TO A NANOTECH FORTUNE

n early 2005, mutual fund manager Thiemo Lang wrote an interesting column for *Small Times* which asked and answered whether an investor was better served by focusing on material suppliers, process enablers, manufacturing companies, IP powerhouses or the producers of "micro- and nano-refined" end products. (Answer: Diversify.) He also asked whether there should be a focus on existing mid- and large-cap stocks or on new revolutionary entrants. (Answer: Diversify.)

He noted that most micro- and nanotech innovations were aiming to improve existing products in established markets. Even if they could promise vastly superior technology and performance, new entrants acting as suppliers would be unlikely to penetrate mass markets and displace incumbents. Winning customers without a history of demonstrated reliability as well as great economics proves extremely difficult at best.

Most important, Lang said, was a careful analysis of how a company's product or technology is integrated into existing value chains. Since many small-tech companies do not have direct access customers, they are dependent on the success of their partners.

Finally, Lang made the point that, for existing markets, start-ups would have more success applying a license and royalty-based business model. While leaving them a smaller piece of the pie, he postulated, "it would liberate them from the execution risks of investing in mass production facilities."

So, You Want to Go Public? IPO Hurdles: How to Handle Them and Make the Cut

There's no doubt public investors are becoming more curious about nanotechnology. Nearly everyone our firm speaks to wants to know more about its potential. The education process can be arduous; starting with the notion this is not so much an industry as it is something people "do." And by the way, today those people seem to be calling themselves anything but "nanotechnologists"!

What do professional investors know about nanotechnology? In 2005, they don't seem to know much more than the general public. Most of their information comes from popular media, and only a handful of investment research shops have decided to introduce nanotechnology to their clients.

Let's say a nanotech management or its investors decide to tap the public markets for equity. What are minimum "standards" for "going public"?

First, the question is not really whether it's possible. It is. Importantly, how a company goes public differentiates strategies and requirements. If management and the board are determined to take a company public – it can almost certainly be done.

There's almost *always* an investment banker somewhere willing to accept the challenge and opportunity. Standards differ, but, generally, if there's a deal to be done – there's a banker ready to do it. The same would apply to the sales arms of these banks. If there's a market for a security – they will sell it. This is Economics 101. If there's a buyer – at a profitable price – a seller materializes.

Assuming the risks are disclosed, there's a huge range of appetites for risk among the professional and retail investing public.

Of course, there are some procedural and legal issues to work through, but they are not particularly onerous for a company with audited results. For example, listing requirement hurdles are low for companies in business two or more years. A NASDAQ National Market listing does require a $75 million market capitalization with $20 million in public float, but that's only if there are no profits and no stockholder's equity! If a company actually has positive book value the requirements get a lot easier. With $1 million in net income, for example, a company is almost a no-brainer for a national listing. Don't qualify for a national listing? Slews of companies – in fact the vast majority – go public on the Over the Counter Bulletin Board or NASDAQ Small Cap Market.

The IPO's we read about in the papers are just the tip of the iceberg. Thousands of small companies go public every year.

The key question is what the management or VCs want to accomplish. A visible and liquid listing becomes very important, for example, if investors are not going to be "cashing out" on the transaction (and, for sure, investors are very wary of investors selling major stakes in a public offering). One of the unfortunate effects of the complete de-linkage between institutional research and investment banking has been the abandonment of trading and researching small cap companies. More and more companies' stocks trade in "limbo" with little or no trading and sponsorship. This is rarely what a quality company would want from a public offering.

If a company's aspiration is still to go public with a national or respected boutique or regional investment bank firm, the standards for making it through their commitment and marketing committees obviously rise. These investment banks are listening to their institutional clients who, generally, have been shouting loud and clear that IPO candidates should have proven business plans with product revenues, a path to profitability, and world-class technology.

Bankers and investors also pay attention to the existing investors in the company. There's validation if the venture capitalists (if there are any at all) are a highly regarded group.

Such backing helps build investment banker confidence in the company, helping ensure that it has been guided correctly and that its books and practices are "on the up and up." Those buying the public equity will also look to see if there are VCs in the investor base holding on to their stock. Any VC with a strong track record of bringing companies public, staying in past the lock-up period and selling much higher than the IPO price is admired by an institutional investor.

Is it possible to go from either corporate or "Angel" investing directly to the public marketplace? Yes, but the chances of getting a high-profile bank involved are always enhanced when there's been at least one round of strong venture capital funding.

At my firm, our mandate is to partner with "The Stars of Tomorrow – Today." Good advice for anyone. How do we find these stars? Sometimes accounting results fail to tell the entire story. Early stage companies might be "on the cusp" of becoming profitable or, in some cases, just recording product revenue. So we use some subjective criteria such as our "4Ps": People, Products, Potential, and Predictability. We acknowledge that at the earlier stages of a company's development it is more difficult to predict its future. However, the people, products, and potential are generally there from the start to be evaluated.

So who is the real arbiter of value? Who raises and lowers the "hurdles" to going public? We would contend it is the professional investor. He or she moves these hurdles up and down dramatically with "market conditions" or, more accurately, according to sentiment. Sentiment seems to almost entirely correlate with trailing returns in the NAS-DAQ market, where nearly all new companies tend to dwell. If that sounds like performance chases performance, well, there you have it. When NASDAQ is on the rise, the hurdles go down and companies sprint to market.

Hurdles certainly rise when the NASDAQ is in the doldrums.

Still, in any market condition there's an appetite for at least some new companies, particularly those with established businesses, great growth prospects, and something distinctive to sell. The weaker the NASDAQ, the less appetite for what many call "science projects," although "life science" projects seem to be somewhat of an exception; maybe it's all the aging *baby boomers*.

Of course, a Google would have come public in nearly any market, but the story for nanotechnology is different, as we found in 2004. Nanosys, a nanotechnology company with an impressive IP platform and partnerships, attempted a public offering in early summer 2004. Despite cautionary language in its prospectus as to the eventuality of any revenues, venture capitalists and their investment bankers had confidently priced the equity value of the company at more than $350 million. Alas, either due to worsening "market conditions" or to a last minute *reality check* by investors, the offering was pulled from the market. For the next 3 quarters, at least, not a single nanotechnology company filed an S-1 to "go public".

In our opinion, nanotechnology management and its investors should think carefully before accessing the public markets. There are certainly more stringent responsibilities of having public equity. Just consider that Sarbanes-Oxley reporting can cost a small company $1 million in incremental expenses. In a public market, this could shave significant dollars from market value. Stock option expensing drags down the bottom line and valuation. Finally, due to the pitfalls of potential personal exposure, assembling a Board of Directors for a public company has become ever more difficult. We still suspect, however, that despite the challenges, most nanotech and other *small tech* CEOs place "going public" as one of their core goals.

Perhaps as a result of the higher hurdles and the Market's returning focus on value, we note that more nanotechnology companies are venture capital funded for a longer period prior to going public. Some of these have seen $30 million or more in capital raises – normally in the range one would expect from the primary portion of an IPO. These venture rounds should satiate the appetite for capital for many of these private companies until at least well into 2006.

> Our advice to these private, emerging growth stars is to be "ready" to go public when those hurdles are low, but to have a real "story" to tell and the numbers to "back it up."
>
> **—By Stuart Pulvirent**
> Partner and Sr. Research Analyst, Life Sciences & Nanotechnology, ThinkEquity Partners, LLC

FOR PRIVATE AND PUBLIC NANOTECH COMPANIES

You run a nanotech company and want to make a fortune for yourself and your shareholders. Let me tell you the secret. Align yourself with the top people you can find in the field. Get to know and work with the top nano-knowledgeable IP, corporate and securities attorneys, accountants, VCs, Angels, investment bankers, brokers, analysts, scientific advisors, investor relations and financial PR firms. Don't settle for less, and continuously pursue relationships with the highest-caliber, most ethical people you are able to find. By doing this simple thing, you will be ahead of 99% of all other nanotech companies, because most everyone else is pursuing some shortcut. Once you're in the top 1%, you have to bring your and your company's best game. Presumably, you've hired the best employees, you've got the best board of directors and scientists for the development of your business and technology, and you're working with the best advisory and professional support group. Now, get the most money and the best terms you can to support the mission, and make sure that it is not wasted.

Take care of your investors and they will take care of you. As you always under-promise and over-perform, while continuously *exceeding* your performance hash marks, the market will reward you and your happy shareholders with a regular increasing valuation.

Maybe it is easier said than done? How does one always under-promise and over-perform? One does it by intentionally under-promising. It is not lying to say you expect revenues to exceed $0.13 per share if you actually expect them to exceed $0.15 per share. The difference in "the love" you will feel depending on which style you chose, when you actually come in with a $0.16 number, will be huge. You had better beat your number by a penny. You are a demigod if you beat it by 20%; a god if you beat it by 10% or more month in and month out. No one will accuse you of intentionally low-balling your number (for years, anyway); you will be credited with being "conservative."

That's all there is to it. Nothing more. You don't need the best technology. You do not need a better mousetrap. As noted, I often tell entrepreneurs who come to me seeking advice, relationships with my ultimate nanotech rolodex of professional contacts or funding, "McDonald's does not make the best hamburger sandwich in the world; Microsoft does not have the best operating system in the world." Business and investment success are tied to a different set of values than success in science or technology. Confuse them at your peril. I've talked to dozens of geophysicists who talked themselves out of investing in profit-exploding gold mining stocks, and quite a few biologists and biotech execs who over-thought the potential for problems in particular biotech startups and missed 1,000% profits.

If you are associated with a serious *small tech* company, and are not making the appropriate professional contacts you need in your own backyard, contact my company or a professional firm listed in the appendix to this book that will see to it that you get further along toward your goals. Expect that your relationship will help get Angel groups, VCs, broker dealers and retail investors further along in their goals of making their **Nanotech Fortunes** much sooner as well.

For Nanotech Executives and Entrepreneurs

> ### Nanobusiness Balancing Act: The Importance of Management is Often Underestimated
>
> As the event director of several nanotechnology conferences over the course of the last decade, I have been in the position to watch hundreds of nanotech companies spring up.

Many have died out already; some continue to limp along, still waiting for their big break. But for the potential investor in nanotech, there's an important lesson to be learned from the handful of nanotech companies that have grown into successful businesses. While the technology behind a business is critical, the human element that a company brings to the table when trying to access capital is equally important. *Experienced management* is the most important element that someone considering an investment in a nanotech company should look for.

Take a step back for a moment from all of the hype and breathlessness about new technologies. Let's agree that nanotechnology is absolutely the foundation of the next technological and business revolution. Let's remember that we're talking about investing ? so we need to be a little rational. If you think critically, you will realize that by the time a nanotech company is about to come to the market for capital, *its technology has already been vetted*. Pundits, analysts and stock-pickers seem to waste a great deal of energy deciding whether a technology will work. Let them. You should focus on management.

One of the real perks of my job has been getting to know the people in the nanotech field. I also ran conferences for *Red Herring* for a number of years. During that time, I came to realize that behind the brilliant scientific minds and PhDs, we're really just dealing with people and despite the obvious technical brilliance of most people in nanotech, the limits of human capacity eventually come into play. Most mortals simply do not have the range to be both a visionary scientist and an elite corporate executive capable of pushing a business toward success in this hyper-competitive environment. Don't get me wrong – I really enjoy the people I meet. However, I don't think it's disparaging to say that most do not have either the marketing savvy or the polished personae necessary to navigate the intense scrutiny of this Sarbanes-Oxley/Reg FD era.

Our new technologies are amazing. Yet many of them are *similar* – maybe not to scientists – but to the consumer who will only see the end result or experience the benefit. The way the products are *marketed* will ultimately determine whether a company is successful. Here we can learn a lesson from the internet boom which showcased so many great new technological advances. But a closer look shows that the companies that thrived, with the possible exception of Google, were not the renegade companies that bucked the way business was done. Instead, they were the eBays and Yahoos of the world that took an innovative new product and used savvy marketing tactics to differentiate them from the pack. One of the best ways I know to help ensure the marketing success of a nanotech company is to hire on an experienced pro, preferably one from a *Fortune 100* company who has handled the pressures and been through the rigors of capturing market share from determined competitors. A great example of a nanotechnology company hiring the proper management team is the fabric innovations company Nano-Tex. Donn Tice, CEO of Nano-Tex is a former Procter & Gamble brand manager for the Folger's coffee line, among other high-profile products. When Nano-Tex squares off in the marketplace against other similarly placed companies with technology of equal quality, but led by scientists, who would you put your money on to build a brand image and capture market share?

This rule of thumb applies further down the corporate ladder as well. Public companies today endure unparalleled scrutiny from Wall Street, investors, and the SEC. Just as with any other publicly traded company, experienced, poised leadership at the CEO and CFO levels is one of the key ingredients to meeting shareholder expectations and holding up under the scrutiny. This is a completely different ballgame than building a great piece of technology. Most would call it an evil, albeit a necessary one. I've learned from my nanotech friends that science can be a deeply personal experience, and that creating a technology and bringing it to fruition as a workable product is an indescribable moment of pride. But I've seen companies with fantastic technology get into real trouble because the creator let that pride get in the way of bringing in an experienced management team. Realistically, though, the nanotech crowd really should take a look around the rest of American business.

Granted, Bill Gates, the ultimate techno-geek, does a fantastic job with Microsoft, but he is the exception to the rule – the proverbial diamond in the rough.

After five years I have yet to meet the Bill Gates of Nanotechnology.

I've got plenty of anecdotes about the characters that run in the nanotech realm. Again, I'm fond of many of them, but there is a *laissez faire* air about them, as we witnessed in the freewheeling internet days – and we know what that leads to! A perfect example is the exchange I witnessed recently on the tradeshow floor between a young creator of a promising technology and a group of potential investors. After a productive conversation where the enthusiastic scientist detailed the virtues of his product to a clearly impressed group, he went on to invite the whole crew over to a local gentlemen's club! Again, would the CEO of GE, P&G, or Ford do such a thing – at least publicly? Would you think twice about investing with this company?

Want more? These give startling insight into the relative lack of business savvy at work in nanotechnology circa 2005. In the rush to secure funding someone's labor of love can lead to awfully strange behavior. For example a Ph.D. from a start-up called me once a week for a month to beg for a free attendee pass to a conference I was running. She explained that her company had received a round-one SBIR (Small Business Innovation Research program grant for early stage funding), but that they had little money left. Over the course of our numerous conversations, it became apparent to me that she had no "business sense." Against my better judgment, I relented the day before the conference and agreed to let her attend for an afternoon at no charge. The moment she arrived, she asked me to introduce her to Josh Wolfe of the *Forbes/Wolfe Nanotech Report* and Lux Capital, but I was reluctant. As soon as Josh finished his keynote speech, the woman nudged me towards him, but before I could make a proper introduction, she pushed me aside, pulled out her proposal and said, "Josh, I have an unbelievable deal for you. You've got to read this now!" Josh calmly introduced himself and told her he would read the proposal, but the woman was wildly insistent. "No, you have to read this now! I need $50,000 by Friday and you can only get this deal today." It was Wednesday, and, not surprisingly, the woman's tactics didn't go over very well.

When seeking funding, nanotech startups often do not have a sound "pitch" strategy. The nanotech conference that we run features a "pitch room" where startups can meet potential investors and try to line up capital. After one particularly interesting pitch, I opened the room to questions. Naturally, the assembled group wanted to know how much capital the company was seeking. The presenter looked confused, and after a pause, stated that he did not know how much money he was trying to raise!

Another great pitch room anecdote really gets to the heart of just how little knowledge some nanotech companies have when it comes to business. An obviously bright young scientist led off the morning with an intriguing presentation to the audience. During the question session, he proceeded to tell the stunned room that he was not seeking capital and was not interested in securing any investment. This young man was followed by a succession of five other companies, all of whom inexplicably stated *emphatically* that they were not trying to raise money (despite the fact that they were eager to address the "pitch room"). When the last company exited the floor, I pulled the presenter aside and asked him why his company wasn't looking for capital. "Well, we were all talking in the hallway before the pitch session," he began, "and the first guy that presented today was telling us that his PR rep told him to tell the investors that he wasn't looking for any money, because to do otherwise would make the company look desperate. We all thought that sounded like pretty good advice."

Finally, in considering a nanotech investment, don't be too impressed by the level of someone's education. There are plenty of brilliant scientists whose love for the invention blocks out basic considerations like whether there is a market for the product. I was introduced to one such person through a friend in the industry. During our first meeting, it was obvious that the man had a brilliant scientific mind, and the degrees to match. He also had a product that sounded like it would be cutting edge. After some discussion, he asked me to read and comment on his written proposal. Two things stood out. First, after wading through a horrendously written piece of techno-babble that very few investors would be able to understand, I realized the proposal made no mention of the potential market for his product. Second, he was pitching his product and business as involved in nanotech, but insisted on using the phrase "Nano Technology" throughout his proposal. It was fairly obvious that his passion for the technology he had created prevented him from taking any constructive criticism. After telling me I had no idea what I was talking about, he went on a long diatribe about the "fact" that nanotechnology was actually two words. He then told me that he had no idea what the potential market for his product was, and didn't really care. It would simply just sell. With that, he hung up the phone.

If you only take two things away from my words as a potential investor in nanotech companies, I would hope that they would be the following: strive to find companies with sound technologies, but with equally sound management, as marketing and effective leadership will eventually be the keys to profitability. Second, if you are going to take a chance on an unproven leadership group with great technology, go out and meet them face-to-face before making a decision. Many of these companies present their wares regularly at conferences or tradeshows and are more than happy to talk to potential investors. Getting to know the leadership is really the only way you'll know if you are investing in a company that will be able to manage the "nanobusiness balancing act."

—**Vincent Caprio**, Event Director of The NanoBusiness Alliance's Annual Conference and The Emerging Technologies Conference in association with *MIT's Technology Review Magazine*.

To set the landscape: With large, mature companies there are few surprises; they are well-analyzed by bright people and they are well-understood.

Small companies?

They are largely unknown. They are mysterious, and there can be many surprises.

Oddly, the cost of pure research and early stage development is really quite small compared to engineering and developing a commercial product from a technology. Startups and small companies sometimes completely miss that point. In biotech, while it might take $10 to $50 million and 3 - 7 years to identify a potential drug or treatment, it can take another dozen or more years and hundreds of millions of dollars to bring a drug to market. More often than most would guess, after $150 million or more has been spent, the product is doomed by the FDA or leapfrogged by a better drug or treatment. More often than admitted, patents expire before the product can earn a penny in the marketplace. In mining, one can usually get a good feel through exploration that a given property is worthy of developing in a serious way with the expenditure of only about $5 million. Full development through finance feasibility and the building of a mine might take another 6 or 7 years and several hundred million. For startup and early-stage nanotech and *small tech* companies the dollar numbers, timeframes and odds for success (and ability to maintain the benefits of their IP estate) are equally, if not more, daunting.

How a company crosses this "Valley of Death" from science to technology and on to a developed product and the marketplace is probably the single most important thing for the entrepreneurs of *small tech* companies to grasp.

When David Met Goliath—The Art of Corporate Partnering for Nanotechnology Startups

Strategic partnerships can greatly benefit large and small companies alike. The rapid growth of my former startup SouthWest NanoTechnologies, Inc. ("SWeNT") can be attributed, in part, to an early partnership with ConocoPhillips ("COP") and a subsequent partnership with a Fortune 100 semiconductor company. Using a technique similar to that described in this article, a previous startup of mine was successfully sold to DuPont ("DD"). This was widely regarded as the first Fortune 500 acquisition in nanotech. In previous assignments, I've developed entrepreneurial partnerships from the other side of the table, as a university technology transfer associate, and before that with a global energy company. In all cases there was a recurring theme: organizations will partner to extend their reach, and, if successful, will create an entity whose value is greater than the sum of its parts.

If you are involved with a startup company, where do you begin? After all, corporate partnering means very different things to different organizations. In a general sense it involves a variety of collaborative opportunities: technology and/or manufacturing collaborations; co-marketing and distribution; mergers and acquisitions ("M&A"); direct investment; preferred vendor arrangements; and/or sharing of "soft resources" (which may include market data, product stewardship guidance, informal business advice, etc.). If you are a startup company, an equally important issue is how to avoid being taken advantage of while still delivering value to your partner. This article should provide guidance in corporate partnering to the nanotechnology entrepreneur with very limited resources, a great idea and a will to succeed.

Technology commercialization is a risky proposition any way you slice it. Several nanotech companies involve long-term propositions that do not fit the traditional five-year exit window required by a typical venture capitalist. The good news is that several multinational companies now have Corporate Venture Capital ("CVC") groups, which are not solely driven by a financial return, but also by strategic alignment with a startup. For a large organization, partnering early and often is a great way to reduce the risk of developing and/or accessing promising business opportunities. The startup company may choose to partner for one or more of the following reasons:

1. Financial support with the relatively long-term perspective of a corporate partner and/or investor;

2. Vast industry knowledge;

3. Access to key markets and customers;

4. Instant legitimacy and recognition;

5. And perhaps most importantly, acceleration of a product's time-to-market.

The downside of partnering should also be considered carefully; although, with careful planning and creative thinking, the downside can often be managed. Considerations might include the following:

1. Existing and future Intellectual Property ("IP") rights should be addressed VERY carefully;

2. Corporate partners will likely want exclusivity in certain markets, for some defined period of time;

3. Large corporations typically move slowly, and big company dynamics almost always result in big bureaucracy;

4. Startups may become dependent on the partner's continued involvement which can result in additional pressure around predetermined milestones;

5. Loss of the startup's autonomy and control of its own destiny, if the company misses its milestones or gives up too much during the negotiation process; and perhaps most importantly,

6. Risk of losing or seriously diluting the startup's financial windfall in the event of a successful exit.

I. WHAT'S IN IT FOR LARGE COMPANIES?

It is often said that entrenched chemical, pharmaceutical and semiconductor companies will benefit most from a successful nanotech industry (though I will hesitate to call it an industry just yet). Overall, this may be true, but the entrepreneurs and early stakeholders have assumed a great risk and will expect to be compensated accordingly when this transition occurs. One way to extend the reach of a multinational corporation is by working with small, nimble startups for the following reasons:

1. Savings on R&D, coupled with shortened development timeframes via the reduction of overhead and internal controls;

2. R&D and product synergies with existing product lines, which can expand market reach and IP estates;

3. New revenue via royalty streams, contract manufacturing, direct sales and/or appreciation of equity;

4. Access to high-growth markets may provide a first-mover advantage; and

5. New business relationships.

6. The downside for a large corporation is somewhat different and must be managed in an entirely different manner. This includes the following:

   • Potential culture clash with a startup company's employees and management;
   • Capital, brand and personal reputation are at risk;

- Opportunity cost of deploying capital to an external R&D effort;
- "NIH" or "Not Invented Here" Syndrome which results from employees' desires to value internal developments over external technology acquisitions, making startup technology collaborations difficult to integrate; and
- Conflicts of interest with existing product lines and their management, existing partners and/or portfolio companies. This is often further amplified by the frequent "turf battles" that occur in a large organization.

II. THE PROCESS

How does one initiate a corporate partnership? There are several ways of accomplishing such, and the process will vary from company to company; but the following method has worked for me:

STEP 1: MAKE A LIST OF IDEAL PARTNERS

Assemble an internal team with technical and business talent. Having a great networker as a co-lead for your partnership team can accelerate the process. Start by looking for prospects with a track record of working with startup companies. Many large organizations have internal CVC funds, suggesting that they are generally well-equipped to work with startup companies. Look for complementary product lines that might benefit from collaborating with your company. Often times this is a sub-system manufacturer, rather than the Original Equipment Manufacturer ("OEM"). By way of example, if you are selling automotive paint additives, approach paint manufacturers rather than Ford or GM. Research the prospect companies by reading press releases and articles, and learn about their stated growth objectives. These may be financial, technical, geographic or otherwise. Align your pitch with those objectives, and be sure to contact multiple partnership candidates in each product segment. You might want to advise your prospect that you're also talking to their competition, but do so in a very subtle manner, and only after they have shown initial interest.

STEP 2: IDENTIFY AND CONTACT TECHNICAL AND BUSINESS CHAMPIONS WITHIN THE TARGET ORGANIZATION

In large corporations, the quickest route to a partnership is often via a referral from internal R&D or business personnel. This may occur when a need has already been identified for your unique capabilities or technology. If you can't find an internal contact directly, the next best alternative is to ask a colleague for a referral, and/or cultivate relationships by attending related industry conferences. Seek out titles such as Research Fellow, Business or Corporate Development Manager, Technology Assessment Manager, Extramural or External R&D Advisor, or R&D Manager. The most difficult method is to contact the company directly without a referral, which is sometimes referred to as "cold-calling." Locate the proper technical or business contact via news articles, peer-reviewed scientific journals, or by using the company's website. If you can't obtain a phone number or email address via Google, simply call the company switchboard during normal business hours and ask. This technique works even with companies that have 100,000+ employees. If your idea is compelling, they will listen.

STEP 3: DEMONSTRATE VALUE TO THE PROSPECT

Contact your champion; briefly introduce your technology to generate interest; and send your literature and a sample. After the initial call, your goals are 1) to have them evaluate your sample quickly; 2) to assemble a deal team with the 4 - 5 people that can assess the importance of collaborating with your company; and 3) to arrange a meeting, as below. At this point, their deal team will consist mostly of technical personnel; though, try to insist on one or two businesspeople, which will accelerate a consensus. Remember that you are fighting two battles; one in the lab (technical viability) and one in the boardroom (economic viability). Without the prospect's technical and business talent working together, your deal will be very politely put on the shelf with all of the other great ideas. Don't oversell the fact that you are in "nanotech." Where you see a vast business opportunity, your prospect may only see a bolt-on addition to their product line. ALWAYS ask for a two-way confidentiality agreement at this point, with a term of at least five years. You may also want to include provisions for sample evaluation in that agreement, or ask for a separate *Materials Transfer Agreement*. These set guidelines for evaluation, arrangements for disposal and handling and often provide some protection against reverse-engineering of your product.

STEP 4: VISIT THEM IN PERSON

Once you've demonstrated some initial technical and economic value to the prospect, push for a meeting at their location or yours. If at their location, try to include the prospect's entire deal team, as described above. This is where you begin the hard sell, i.e., how you will make money together. A few ways to accomplish this in order of increasing difficulty include the following:

1. New Revenue Opportunities – especially where product synergies exist;

2. Cost Savings – cost-cutting initiatives that may significantly impact existing product lines;

3. Other – providing environmental, safety, marketing, or other secondary benefits.

It is absolutely crucial that you "dollarize" the benefit of your product or service. By way of example, imagine that you are selling carbon fiber, and that your prospect currently uses carbon black to dissipate 10 units of heat per minute. If your $10/lb carbon nanotubes dissipate 10 units of heat per minute, and they are currently buying a $2 carbon black to dissipate 1 unit of heat per minute, their effective cost is $20. You've just saved the prospect $10 per widget. If you are a few years away from a product, show them your timeline for achieving the $10 cost basis. Equally important, you must propose a few options for working together. Are you looking for sponsored research funding (sometimes referred to as Non-Recoverable Engineering or "NRE" funding)? Direct investment? Joint development? Preferential pricing? Ask them how they would prefer to work together, and do your best to be flexible. If there is a quick and easy deal to be made (even if you have to accept a small portion of what you were seeking), start simple and close the easy deal first. You can always press for more collaboration later. Agree on a few action items with due dates, then strive to complete yours as quickly as possible.

One caveat: Never talk about a deal before it is done. Entrepreneurs are typically headstrong and like to advertise the fact that they are working with Company X on a joint development deal. Resist the urge to discuss your pending collaboration with outside investors, colleagues, the media or anyone else. Negotiations can fall apart at any time, especially in high-risk technology deals. If the prospect learns of your indiscretion, your deal is in jeopardy. Honor your confidentiality agreement, and you will preserve your reputation if things don't work out. In many instances, my companies were turned down several times before we were able to close a deal with a particular company. If you play your cards right, you should be able to contact them at a later time.

STEP 5: BRAZEN IT THROUGH

Now is the time to iron out terms and push for a contract, noting that nobody was ever fired for saying "no" to a new project. Remember that a big company is often laden with big bureaucracy, so be patient. If you can, involve an attorney only after the basic ground rules for your collaboration have been agreed upon. Try to clamp down on excessive "lawyering" on both sides, which slows everyone down. However, I urge you to be very cautious with your intellectual property arrangement. I have not discussed IP herein, and will only suggest that you hire very experienced counsel to protect your long-term interests.

How long will the entire process take? If the prospect has already identified a need for your product, deals can close very rapidly. Depending on the complexity of your deal, it might take 1-3 months from initial contact to closing. More often the process will take 6 - 12 months, so again, be patient. Another caveat: never let a deal die by failing to pay attention to it. Send a friendly reminder if you don't hear from them after a few weeks.

STEP 6: MANAGING THE PARTNERSHIP

I won't spend much time on this topic, as it warrants another article in its own right. Hopefully, you have developed a win-win arrangement with your partner, and both parties will benefit greatly from the collaboration. Don't worry if both parties aren't entirely happy with the deal – this is often a good sign. Communicate the obligations of your contract to all pertinent employees, and make them accountable for their portion of the deal. Try to secure early wins by meeting your agreed-upon milestones ahead of schedule. Remember that your partner is not your friend, and your champions have their own people to answer to internally.

III. CONCLUSION

Technology commercialization is not easy. If it were, everyone would be doing it. However, where there is risk and uncertainty, where there is hard work and serendipity, entrepreneurs will find a way to create lasting institutions.

Entrepreneurs and executives from other far flung fields are needed to drive the *small tech* revolution, and while busts will necessarily appear from time to time, the inevitable long-term boom in nano will ensure that marketing VPs from Apple, tech commercialization experts from Intel, *biz dev* (business development) pros from Disney, and many others will find their fortunes and futures in nanotech.

My advice to you is to orient yourself this way now, and plan your early escape to the commercial world of nanotechnology. Top executives and entrepreneurs who enter the field before 2010 could achieve the same financial and career success that many early stage (1990) internet or biotech (1985) execs achieved.

Thoroughly familiarize yourself with the state of the technology, business and state of investment. Then get good advice on options, compensation and equity packages. Dive in. The water's fine.

—By Mike Moradi, Venture Development Associates, LLC

FOR NANOSCIENTISTS AND NANOTECHNOLOGISTS

The Holy Grail of nanotechnology is the discovery of a nanosystem where binding is converted into work.
—Erkki Ruoslahti

Dr. Ruoslahti explained to me that proteins already do this. However, in the process they create molecules that are immuno-genic (a bad thing).

Scientists, along the path to "The Holy Grail" there are many interesting goals and targets. I would not presume to give you any advice on "winning" or "success" in your chosen field. If you are reading this book, whether you are a physicist, chemist, biologist, material scientist or biomedical engineer you probably already perceive yourself as a *nanoscientist*.

By their nature, great scientists, like great artists, pursue goals that are internally driven. I am not going to tell you to get out there and start making money.

However, if you are oriented that way, or are already working in a commercial setting, I would encourage you to do three straightforward things: get professional advice to understand and maximize your interest in any IP for which you or your team is responsible; focus as much as possible on *low-hanging fruit* (science with a quick roadmap to product and commercialization such as one that solves a problem that is unsolvable except by the application of *small science or technology*, or one that so greatly improves quality or efficiency of an existing product at such a low cost that it will be nearly irresistible in the market); seek equity whenever and wherever appropriate.

Often scientists and technologists are ill-prepared for the peculiar challenges of the marketplace. Seek competent professional and legal advice.

FOR NANOTECH PROFESSIONAL SERVICES FIRMS

Patent attorneys are the obvious first movers in a space like nanotechnology. Only partly tongue-in-cheek, perhaps patent litigators are the likely second movers in the space.

In addition, certainly corporate attorneys, securities attorneys, CPAs, technology commercialization specialists and other professional firms have many reasons to establish and promote *small tech* practices.

The patent business is rampant and the *thickets* and overlapping claims ensure that litigation is in the offing. Some key carbon nanotube patents (there are hundreds in total), for example, reside at Fortune 100 companies, some with established small companies and some at startups. One company was already involved in 5,000 disputes as long ago as 2004.

As M & A, partnerships, IPO, fund and other securities work increases, securities and corporate attorneys that develop an expertise and visibility in the space will reap accelerating fees.

As of 2005 the largest, most well-known, national law and accounting firms had developed or were developing this in-house expertise and practice. The real opportunity is for mid-sized, regional firms, especially those located in entrepreneurial or academic hotbeds, to do the same.

FOR ANGELS

Angel and VC nanotech investments 1997 - 2003 – black hole of dead money, or fortunate to be so early?

Mostly dead money, with the exceptions of solid-state materials and tools. IP-rich start-ups targeting the development of nano-enablers complementary to existing technologies will have the best chances to produce investor returns.
—**Maximilian M. Schroeck, Ph.D.,** Agilent Ventures

Wealthy individuals should seriously consider the Angel route.

If you are fortunate enough to have a liquid net worth in excess of $3 million and earnings of $300,000 or more per year in 2005 dollars, you have opportunities to participate in investments and speculations in nanotechnology start-ups that are not open to the general public. As a so-called accredited investor, you can do your own research ("due diligence"), and invest privately alongside company scientists and executives, and their friends and relatives. Or, by providing funds to an Angel group, venture capital or private equity fund, you may participate in ground-floor investments, managed by professionals who have the time and expertise to perform a high level of due diligence.

The biggest Angel investor in the world in nanotechnology is Jim Von Ehr, who at last count had invested $47 million of his own money into nanotech startups (much into Zyvex, his own very interesting company).

What's the killer product in 10 years? You know, I shy away from telling people what the product is in 10 years. I turn the question around and say, "So, what's the most important thing you'll need in 10 years? Can you tell me?" Go back to 1994 and say, "What do you think the most important thing in 2004 is going to be?" The Internet probably wouldn't have been on the list. Very few people even knew that the Internet was there. To have said, "I don't like my megabyte-per-second broadband. I want 100-megabyte-per-second broadband," would have been science fiction in 1994.
—**James Von Ehr**

Lone Angel investors in high-tech industries are typically wealthy individuals with strong background and contacts in the related industry and/or science. (Think of a biochemist hired by Amgen in 1983 who retired at the age of 47 in 1999 with $30 million in stock, tons of biotech knowledge and industry contacts with nothing better to do than to invest a quarter to a third of that in a field he loves. Taking a chance of finding the next Amgen and adding a zero to his or her net worth could be quite gratifying. Now, add the Internet and stock option booms of the mid 1990s, and you can multiply their number by 10,000!) These 10,000 or so individuals are usually well known in the academic circles in which they live and do business. So, for example, biotech Angels in San Diego are very well known by biologists, chemists and medical researchers at the University of California at San Diego, The Burnham Institute, Salk, and Scripps. Angels interested in cutting-edge computer technology in the Boston suburbs are well known to Harvard and MIT professors oriented that way.

These lone wolfs are fairly rare. If you have the funds and skill set, you should definitely consider deeply surveying the nanotech and "small tech" landscape (a great place to start is and the resources acknowledged in the appendix at the end of this book), and becoming one yourself. If you are willing to pay the dues, I believe you will find your competition limited. If you are scared off this concept, and prefer to bounce your ideas off a like-minded group, you should consider joining or starting an Angel group in your own town or city.

If you live in San Diego, San Francisco, Chicago or Boston (among others) with their strong universities, institutional infrastructure, and financial sophistication, you will probably want to join an existing group. However, any town with a strong scientific university nearby is a candidate for an Angel group oriented toward nanotech. There is every reason to expect Albany, Durham, Austin, and Cleveland to generate significant nano-activity over the next 10 - 15 years.

That being said, maybe I am prejudiced but I believe California and, specifically, San Diego, where I make my home, will be the hottest hotbed for Angel-action in *small tech*.

San Diego is already a worldwide leader in IT, wireless and biotech. There is much reason to believe that a convergence of these important three industries is the point at which nanotechnology will find its highest commercial and human progress expression.

FOR VENTURE CAPITALISTS

Imagine machines so small that they are imperceptible to the human eye. Machines that are so small, gravity and inertia cease to be important, and where atomic forces and surface science dominate instead.
—ABB Ltd. Website

ABB scientists say materials can be re-engineered atom by atom, to offer an explosion in performance that will lead to radical changes in industry and the world around us.
—ABB Ltd. Website

Nanotechnology will change the very foundations of cancer diagnosis, treatment, and prevention.
—U.S. Department of Health and Human Services NIH,
National Cancer Institute pamphlet:
Going Small for Big Advances: Using Nanotechnology to Advance Cancer Diagnosis, Prevention and Treatment

If you are a VC and are not already taking a serious look at nanotech and *small technology* startups, the above three quotes alone should be enough to light a fire under you. If you are a VC already into the whole *nano* thing, I can't say too much more except to get competent scientific advice and watch valuations

A representative of the Korean government asked me a few questions in 2004. Following is the exchange:

Darrell, what are your current views on the state of nanotech investment by venture capital firms in America? What do they think about the future of nanotechnology and the prospects for investment? How and how much do they invest? What's their likely future view on same?

DB: VCs have been investing less and less in Nanotech start-ups from 2000 - 2004. However, that trend appears to have ended. While no one is rushing to invest in technologies without appropriate business models, several key events should invigorate the sector by 2006 - 2008. A commercial movie with a nanotech theme (albeit potentially unfavorable), *Prey*, is due out in 2006.

Angels are investing up to the first $3 million (individually, $50,000 to $1,000,000). VCs are coming in with the next $3 to $50 million (individual firms $300,000 to $5 million). Buyouts and joint ventures with major companies are the likely exit strategies for the time being, but I foresee a real IPO boom in nanotech stocks in the U.S. sometime between 2006 and 2008. At that time properly positioned nanotech companies, both U.S. and foreign, will find public markets in the U.S., possibly even if they are not close to commercializing their technology (For an example, see the U.S. biotech industry since 1982).

Many uninformed VCs will lose money or have very long timeframes to *liquidity events* in nanotech names, but the more astute and well-timed investments in companies that recognize the importance of marketing themselves, as well as good science and technology, should pay off very well, indeed.

What are the current technological developments in each field?

DB: With the help of the scientists with whom I work closely, I can tell you that computing companies such as IBM have been developing high density memory storage devices using magnetism at the nanoscale, and that other major companies have been developing nanoscale lithography for chip production. Other research has been developed on Single Electron Transistors in University labs. This is a technology in which the flow of single electrons can be controlled from a source to a drain. Quantum dots have been researched as possible computing devices, completely changing the power of binary code. And nanowires and nanotubes will be used in on-chip circuitry.

In biology, while quantum dots have been tested in animals as photo-luminescent tracking devices for non-surgical characterization of diseases or organ problems, we do not think this is a viable approach, since semiconducting materials are toxic. The quantum dots are targeted to specific enzymes in the body and produce photo-luminescent properties when charged. Companies have developed similar, safer particles to track and collect particles in the body. Further, DNA has been speculated as a nanotool for self-assembly and organization of nanotubes and molecular binding. In addition, there are good nanoparticle drug and gene delivery systems that are moving along through the pipeline.

In materials, much work has been done in the area of creating bulk nanocrystaline materials since these would provide stronger materials with better properties. Some techniques for this include ECAP (equal channel angular processing), or spinodal decomposition. Much work has been done by material scientists in the growth of carbon nanotubes. The majority of the current work is done on developing organized uniform nanotubes for practical use. Carbon nanotubes have even been incorporated in the refinement microscopy techniques such as Atomic Force Microscopy. Carbon nanotubes have also recently been manipulated to have uses in solar cell energy generation.

In optics, nanowire lasers have been produced with the emphasis of the research done by Dr. Pedong Yang, of the University of California at Berkley. Thin film technology has been incorporated into the development of LCD screens.

Darrell, what about so-called new technologies? Can you speak about each by field?

DB: In materials we're seeing, among other things, antibacterial coatings and fire retardant additives. In bio, nanoparticulate drug delivery and lab-on-a-chip are hot areas attracting research and financing. In electronics, Magnetic RAM (MRAM), LCD backlighting, thin-film solar cells and carbon nanotube transistors are getting play."

The caveat with the above and all talk of developments in nanotechnology and the rest of *small tech* is that new, often dramatic developments are literally happening weekly, if not daily. By the time you read this all of the above could/will be extremely dated; it will certainly be superseded.

FOR ANALYSTS

In the collective opinion of the committee of scientists, engineers and technology professionals convened in January 1999 by the [U.S. Government's] Interagency Working Group on Nanoscience, Engineering and Technology (IWGN), "The total societal impact of nanotechnology is expected to be much greater than that of the silicon integrated circuit because the technology is applicable in many more fields than just electronics."

—*Nanotechnology: Shaping the World Atom By Atom*
a publication of the US government's National Science and Technology Council Committee on Technology

As a high-tech *buy or sell-side* (fund side or broker side) analyst, note the above quotation carefully. If true, perhaps you should be considering a career focus change to nanotechnology?

For the sake of balance, it is fair to argue that nanotechnology, micro-technology, MEMs and micro-fluidics represent too tiny (no pun intended) a market capitalization and fee generating potential to change career tracks. It is also fair to argue that most of the best so-called nanotech companies will not be labeled as "nanotech" at all, but will, instead, be called "bio-medical," "electronics," "display technology," "computer memory" or "basic materials" companies. But, especially if you are younger or looking for an *edge* or point of differentiation, a switch to a *small tech* focus should advance your career while generating increasing publicity and income to your firm. As an early mover you and your company will benefit from seeing the best deals earlier, and enjoy increasing deal flow as the pace of M & A and IPOs explodes between 2007 and 2015.

I can make no stronger case than to add the final paragraph in the government pamphlet quoted above.

It no longer seems a question of whether nanotechnology will become a reality. The big questions are how important and transfor-

mative nanotechnology will become. Will it become affordable, who will be the leaders, and how can it be used to make the world a better place? – questions that will, in time, be answered.

FOR INVESTMENT BANKS

Investment banks have from 2005 - 2010 to become leaders in *small technology*. I believe that those that do will win big in the decades to follow. M & A and IPO fees that are miniscule now, won't be so laughable in 2008 - 2010, and will be downright juicy in the following 5 to 10 years.

I especially encourage regional firms with 200 - 500 brokers to strongly consider moving in this direction and hiring appropriate analysts. I feel like the man in *The Graduate* who said one word to the Dustin Hoffman character about his future career, "Plastics!"

My two words to smaller investment banks: *"Small technology!"*

Modern Portfolio Theory: An Asset Allocator's Approach to Nanotech

Nanotechnology may fire your imagination and get your blood racing, but you certainly shouldn't buy every nanotech story, stock or private placement that comes down the pike.

Even with all the promise that nanotechnology holds, there are plenty of bad and mediocre investment "opportunities."

Using *Modern Portfolio Theory* as a starting point, there are two reasonable, alternative approaches to investing in nanotech companies. One starts with a dispassionate view of how an investment like nanotechnology would fit into an existing portfolio. The second would take a traditional approach through an investment banking firm or broker.

With the first approach, step one would be to decide how much to invest; the second step would be to determine how to implement the investment, and in the third step, one would ascertain how to monitor investment performance.

The economic and commercial impacts of nanotechnology are just beginning to make themselves felt. While many companies and individuals are making headway in the development of new technologies, many of the opportunities are either in private placements or in newly-funded deals. Today many companies are being funded without clear evidence that they have a product or technology to be delivered.

With the somewhat chaotic development of a new industry as a backdrop, an investment into nanotechnology should be viewed as a *sector investment*. The sub-asset class that nanotechnology represents, and its associated attributes, including some illiquidity, will cause it in early stages to behave much like a private equity investment. In that light you have to consider the appropriate amount of your portfolio that should be committed to such an asset sub-class. Most advisors would consider 5% to 10% of a portfolio as a maximum commitment to a sub-asset class of this nature, assuming that the investment itself is broadly diversified within the sub-asset class. *The resultant portfolio can be optimized with asset allocation models and subjected to scenario analyses with Monte-Carlo or other probability tools.* This is a fancy way of saying that when you add nanotech stocks to your portfolio it's wise to look at how a variety of economic variables might affect the performance of the portfolio as a whole, and make sure you are truly diversified.

Looking at an extreme situation might help you with this point. You wouldn't want to put 10% of your money in nanotech stocks, be 20% short bonds, have no cash, 20% in other technology stocks, and 30% in non-tech, small-cap, growth stocks and 20% short utilities. This would be a clear recipe for disaster. It seems like a diversified portfolio, but examine it carefully. Several of the positions are highly correlated and offer no true diversification. Without properly testing your portfolio, your situation might be flirting with disaster.

Assumptions in models for your sub-asset class returns should fit in between that of small-cap investing and that of emerging equity markets. A premium should be attached to this sector over and above what broad market returns may be because of the inefficiency (lots of volatility, lots of illiquidity, and "slippage" – big spreads between bid and ask) of the market.

Knowledge of early-stage and mid-stage investing can provide you with significant advantages. Knowledge of the technology and the potential for business utilization and delivery will be critical. In his Letter to Shareholders in 1997, Warren Buffett stated, "What an investor needs is the ability to evaluate selected businesses."

With many equity sub-asset classes, actual security selection becomes less important in an efficient market. However, nanotechnology, as a new industry sector, will be largely cloaked in hyperbole, marketing and just plain ignorance. As information becomes murkier or more difficult to evaluate, **security selection becomes the single most contributing factor to returns.**

While nanotechnology investing looks like a top-down proposition, the *bottom-up* emphasis inherent in security selection becomes even more critical to add value, whether in the form of additional return or in controlling risk from negative security selection. A long/short discipline or strategy can further reduce risks. Should a portfolio manager take a more active approach with management teams of the companies, good long investment research can support insights into those companies which may not make the grade, providing additional opportunities to enhance portfolio returns. A commitment to short strategies also allows the manager to step away from the sector when many companies may look significantly overvalued.

Prudent investors should look for an investment manager to research, diversify and to oversee the resultant portfolio. What to buy, what to sell, when to buy, when to sell, are all functions of a professional money manager. Being that nanotechnology is in its infancy as an investing sub-asset class, you will have to rely on a manager's background of success in similar investments and endeavors. Traditional research, reliance on industry experts, and key scientists all help in evaluating nanotech investments.

Benchmarks to measure performance against include small-cap, emerging market and growth stock indices, as well as sector-specific benchmarks like *The Nanotech Company Index of Small-Technology Stocks.*

The second alternative to investing in this asset class would be to work with a Financial Adviser/Broker who focuses on nanotech, and has access to analysts who are able to research and follow nanotechnology investments. Your confidence in the knowledge, ethics and capabilities of any broker you work with is paramount. As in any disciplined approach to investing there must be a conscious effort to create appropriate diversification in building your own portfolio of nanotech companies. If your broker is the sole source of ideas, be diligent in evaluating proposed individual companies by reviewing supporting information that should support the basis of the recommendation. Use common sense to test each company's story for reasonable valuations, reasonable expectations and a realistic time frame to deliver. When an emerging technology sector becomes popular and the stocks are making news, be wary of the crowd of names driven by a potential swarm of promoters who can catch even good brokers off guard. Given the vast resources available thru online search, we have excellent tools to check and balance the information and ideas presented.

In conclusion, whether you employ your capital for nanotechnology through the services of a fund manager or work with a knowledgeable broker, enjoy the experience of participating in one of the most important emerging technology trends and investment opportunities in our lifetime.

—Richard Goldstein, Sr. VP – Investments, Moors & Cabot
—Thomas Yanari, Vice President, Envestnet

FOR BROKERS

As a former brokerage and investment banking executive, I can honestly say I have never seen better opportunities to gain competitive advantages like those offered today in nanotechnology.

Small, regional, nanotech-focused brokerage firms and stockbrokers who become nanotech experts will make a killing in the coming booms that occur with regularity over the next 20 to 30 years. To begin to become an expert in the field, you should study this book, subscribe and have your clients subscribe to my nanotech newsletters, visit nanotechnology.com regularly, and spend about 150 hours sampling the smorgasbord of nano/financial information provided in the appendix at the end of the book.

As your firm's analysts and brokers specialize in nanotech, you will achieve a cachet in your region and respect that cannot possibly be achieved by focusing on mining, financials, energy, utilities, wireless, autos, consumer products, defense or any other industry group. As you build vibrant, interesting relationships with local scientists, engineers, and entrepreneurs, your analysts and brokers will "catch the fever." They will get excited, and excited salespeople mean *exciting* fees and commissions.

As my friends Richard Goldstein, Thomas Yanari and the unnamed investment banking VP detailed above and below have pointed out, you do not have to be a genius or a scientist. If you are enthusiastic about helping others to change the world for the better, while making a fortune, you can employ geniuses and scientists, make them part of the team and partners in your growth. At the least, you are invited to contact me directly.

You owe it to your career to consider that nanotechnology could be you or your firm's ticket to exceptional revenue growth for years and decades to come. This is no internet fad.

Who is Nanotechnology for? How a Broker Can Become an Expert

I do not have an advanced degree in chemistry, or a lab with a dozen Ph.D.s. I am not CEO of a nanotechnology company, nor am I a CNBC pundit. I started my journey with a successful Wall Street career and a large client base, but without experience in nanotech or any idea that client interest might develop. I didn't know anything about the companies or the universities doing research or anything else "nano." I just began with a curiosity about this exciting, new scientific concept, and a desire to catch on to the next big, interesting industry that might provide profits for my clients.

In the two or three years that I have pursued my nanotechnology practice, I have come to believe that this may be the most important thing happening in America today. Everyone who has an interest in the world around them should be aware of what is happening in the *nano game*. Nano isn't just important to scientists, or venture capitalists, or the media. Whether you have a scientific background or not, if you have an interest in your local economy, if you went or are going to college, if you care about keeping America safe and strong, if you are concerned about the environment, or if you just want to make a lot of money, I believe nanotech is for you.

In this short article I hope to pass along a few of the reasons I believe nanotech is so important to just about everyone, and a couple of suggestions to help you become a "nano-success"

Many people look to nanotechnology for scientific advances that can enable products and technologies that can only be imagined today. New companies that are using nanotech and patenting their science have the potential to become tomorrow's business leaders. Today's tech market leaders are companies that, in many cases, didn't exist ten or twenty years ago and are using technology that only existed in the imagination of their founders a decade ago. If we go back twenty years and look at the market leaders of that time, we will see that many of them were based on technology that didn't exist ten years before that.

It is clear that those who identify market-changing technology, and build solid businesses around them, have the chance to become the next hugely successful companies. We all hope to find the next Microsoft or Google early, and nanotech is clearly a possible source of tomorrow's corporate success stories. If you are interested in making money, then nanotech is for you.

Nanotechnology also has an extremely important role in the economic development efforts of a number of states and counties. While the San Francisco Bay area and the greater Boston area continue to be the places where new tech companies make their homes, other communities are spending heavily to attract and retain scientific talent to their locales. Upstate New York, the greater Cleveland area, Chicago, and Albuquerque come to mind as areas that have developed strong presences in the world of nanotech. I am from Upstate New York, near Albany, and am very excited to see my home town starting to become a vibrant economic center once again after decades of decline. Nanotech has a further promise for many other "old economy" areas of America. Most of these old economies are commodity-based, industrial, chemical, textile and manufacturing type towns. Nanotech is already having a substantial impact on these basic industries and promises more in the future. The communities that encourage nanotech companies to do business have the potential to see jobs created, not destroyed, skilled labor in demand instead of moving to a third world country, housing prices and tax bases increasing rather than decreasing. If you are interested in seeing your local economy growing and creating high paying jobs, then nanotech is for you.

Nanotech is also playing an extremely important role in our national security. I work in New York City. I was in New York on September 11 and during the anthrax attacks. I know that I am not the only New Yorker to fear another attack on our city. Whether chemical, biological, nuclear or conventional, I fear that another attack on our city is very possible. I see advances in nanotechnologies as an important step in detecting and stopping such attacks. I see the potential for nano-enabled devices to stop devastating weapons from appearing at our shipping and freight hubs. I see nano-coatings on buildings preventing the spread of airborne diseases or chemicals. I see nano-enabled equipment helping our first responders in emergencies. If you are interested in keeping America safe and fighting terrorism, then nanotech is for you.

Nanotechnology will continue to be an important feature in the growth of many of our best colleges and universities. There are half a dozen "centers of excellence" designated by the government as major hubs of nanotech research, but this is only a part of the story. Many other universities are starting and expanding their nanotech efforts, as are a number of community colleges and even high schools and junior highs. California recently named a 40-person "blue ribbon" panel, chaired by two terrific statewide leaders, Steve Westly and Mike Honda. When I saw the other panelists chosen, I was impressed by their academic credentials and their focus on education. They are not just from elite universities but, importantly, represent the strong state schools and community colleges as well. California's elected leaders understand that the number one factor for an entrepreneur in choosing where to locate their company is access to skilled workers. If you have children that hope to go to college and be able to compete for jobs in the 21st century marketplace then nanotech is for you.

If you are in the military, nanotech is for you. If you play competitive sports, nanotech is for you. If you are in the medical field, nanotech is for you. If you drive a car, own a home, eat food, or care about the environment … .

The key to making money in nanotech as a stockbroker is to be an "expert" in the field and make contact with others who are similarly oriented. A few thoughts:

1. Be an expert. Read a lot. There are half a dozen websites, half a dozen blogs and half a dozen publications that can keep you well-informed on the important news in the field. Darrell has kindly listed all the important sources in the appendix of this book (but most important is his free eDigest of international nanotech news, *The Best of the NanoWeek and nanotechnology.com*). Learn the terminology. Get to know where the money is going and who is making news.

2. Identify people that you can help. Know who in your community or field of interest are the players making

things happen in nanotech, and make it your business to know them. Call your local elected officials or college and let them know of your interest in nanotechnology. Plug into the community that you want to pursue. Go to nanotech conferences and seminars. Visit local companies that are doing nanotech.

3. Market your expertise. People don't know that you are an expert unless you tell them and show them. Nanotechnology is such a new field that in 2005 knowing just a little puts you ahead of 99%. Knowing a lot is a powerful tool. Put people together if you think they can be helpful to each other. Share contacts with others. Create a circle of knowledge and, with you in the center, enlarge the circle for everyone's benefit. People will come to you if they know that you can help them.

4. Look for opportunities. As you become known in your circle of business associates as someone who is helpful they will start to come to you for help. Be prepared to pursue the opportunities presented to you. If there is a new company that is being formed in your area, get to know the founders. If there is a professor at your local school that is well-known, help them when they are starting something new. Ask people what you can do to help.

5. Do not be afraid to fail. Many of the companies working on nano-products are going to fail. You may not be able to help every entrepreneur. You might not get into the ground floor the first time.

6. Maintain an excellent reputation. The nano community is a small one (no pun intended). If you establish a relationship with someone who is doing good work, ask for referrals. Build your network. Everyone is connected in this field. "Google" people. Find the connections. People do business with me because I do a good job for them, but also

because they know that by dealing with me they enter into a network of like-minded and compelling executives who can add value to their business interests. A carefully cultivated reputation throughout my career continues to be my greatest asset in my nanotechnology efforts.

I buy and sell stocks and bonds for a living for myself and others, and have been doing this for fifteen years. Three years ago I didn't know the first thing about nanotechnology. In a short period of time I have been able to develop an expertise and a reputation as a reliable source of investment intelligence about nanotechnology, and as a useful person to know for nanotech CEOs as they seek to grow their companies. Whether your interests are on Wall Street or Main Street, the field is wide open for you to develop your expertise, really grow your business, and help write the chapter in the amazing book that will lead to your own Nanotech Fortunes.

—An Unnamed Vice President-Investments at a Major NYSE Member Firm

FOR INVESTORS

"(The Company)… has built a body of specialized knowledge in chemical etching and electro-discharge machining of features in silicon, and various electro-optics topics, including miniature photomultiplier design and fabrication, new photocathode materials, and new miniature dynode designs."

Huh? Now you know why I depend on scientists.

If you use discount brokers, and make all of your own investment decisions, bear with me for a moment while I explain the art of choosing a broker. I would advise you to read along for now; you should be open to the possibility that you are going to need extra help in nanotech.

A good broker, while hard to find, should be a valued partner in the search for significant, long-term investments in nanotech and other *small tech* stocks.

Now, I was a broker once and I've managed brokers and some of my best friends are brokers. In fact, current nanotech advances have 'proven' that brokers are the brightest people on the planet.

A fellow I know heard about this newly developed science and wanted to have the brain transplant he had always wanted and somehow thought nanotech would enable. He inquired of his surgeon to recommend some truly smart brains for his transplant.

"Well, chemistry teacher brains are a bargain at $6,000 per ounce; I'd recommend them," said the doctor.

"That's about as much as I can afford," said my friend, "but, just out of curiosity, what brains are more expensive than them?"

"Well, nuclear physicist brains are more than twice that! $12,500 per ounce, and you can hardly get them anymore, what with Feynman and all, and his influence on this darn nanotechnology field. Damn shame, too, because they are really a good value – all things considered."

"Hey, what about nanoscientist brains? I'll bet they're pretty good. Are they a bargain, too?" asked my friend, no fool he.

"Actually, nanoscientist brains are *hot* right now; I'm doing a transplant for a multi-millionaire tomorrow, and he's paying $45,000 per ounce for the nanoscientist brains. You know they are really incredibly sharp, these nanoscientists; blooming geniuses actually."

"Wow," said my stunned buddy, "That's way out of my range. I can't imagine there would be any more expensive brains than those, right?"

"Well, actually, the most expensive brains by far are stockbroker brains. They are $600,000 **per gram**!"

"What? How can that be?" asked my friend, reeling with disorientation by this point. "I never imagined stockbroker brains would be anywhere near the top, much less the most expensive brains in the world."

The doctor straightened his tie, adjusted his glasses, lowered his gaze, and looked at his patient in dead seriousness. "Do you have any idea how many stockbrokers it takes to get a gram of brains?"

Yes, stockbrokers are easy targets (please no hard feelings; I was a stockbroker once; feel free to use this joke – I stole it – and replace brokers with your own profession of choice), but finding a good one (and they are out there) can accelerate and expand your nanotech fortune.

This is how to find a broker.

First, eliminate any broker without a minimum of six continuous years as a broker. Sorry, even brilliant new brokers have not seen "anything." It is true that a 15-year career could be nothing more than one year's experience 15 times, but you should be able to feel the professionalism and knowledge of a truly good broker. To some degree this is a matter of salesmanship (make no mistake: all great brokers are great salesman), but great brokers are great because they ask questions and make sure they are actually helping their clients achieve goals that their clients actually have.

All things being equal, yes, I would prefer a broker with 20 years experience to one with 15 and one with 15 years to one with 8. My empirical experience leads me to believe that brokers who begin in their 20s and stay with it (instead of becoming venture capitalists, fund managers, analysts, or asset acquisition experts) usually hit their stride around 30 - 32; have one major mess-up/failure in their 30s (hubris?); then get back on track, at the top of their game, somewhere between age 42 and 46. The most successful brokers retire wealthy, with their clients' lot in life dramatically improved, between 52 and 58 years of age, to a home in Aspen or Montecito or a new career as an Angel, VC, or hedge fund manager.

Second, eliminate any broker with a serious disciplinary action on his or her NASD or SEC record, and any broker who works for a firm or a branch that has been disciplined for a serious breach of ethics in the last 5 years. Of course, perfectly fine firms like Merrill Lynch and Wachovia Securities suffer many disciplinary actions if only because of their size alone. I am not referring to that type of action. And even excellent brokers are occasionally sued by unscrupulous clients or make technical errors related to securities regulations for which they might have a small fine ($1,000 or less) or suspension (one month or less). However, from time to time large firms are disciplined for activity that is illegal or for unconscionable business practices, or an otherwise fine broker has multiple infractions or a single serious one, and you should make it your practice to avoid those firms, and individuals.

For small firms, be tough. Do not have an account with a broker or firm that has ongoing or serious regulatory problems.

Third, find a specialist. When I had my natural resource practice, I was devoted to it. It was a matter of pride that other brokers called me for my opinion when they were recommending mining shares to their clients. I made it a point that no one would know more about new projects, new discoveries or new financings than I did. I meticulously read all of the important newsletters and periodicals, and called on my rolodex of industry contacts constantly. Your *small tech* broker should be a *small tech* broker. Period. Life is too short to deal with masqueraders and dilettantes. This is not to say that you should expect your broker to be a scientist, or even that he or she should be able to "remember high school chemistry." However, he or she should be completely tied into the nanotech world (reading, attending seminars and industry conferences, perhaps speaking and writing on the subject from a lay point of view, and especially aligning with a scientist or group that can ensure he separates science from science fiction).

Fourth, deal with someone you like and who respects the way you work. If you want to talk to your broker weekly, and enjoy "give-and-take" of ideas, find a broker who likes that way of working as well. On the other hand, you will find it trying, at best, if your broker calls you every time he wants to present an investment idea, but you want him to handle things on a limited power of attorney basis with little or no input from you. This is a matter of personal style. Make sure you and your broker are on the same wavelength.

By the way, jokes about stockbroker brains aside, you should respect your stockbroker's mind. He or she should be bright and articulate; you should find your broker's insights sharp and shrewd. He or she should think like tough-minded businesspeople think. Cheerleaders need not apply.

A word of advice on dealing with your broker with regard to commissions: consider the commissions to be payment for services rendered; not the cost of executing a trade. If all you want is trade execution, use a discount firm. I do. If you want the advice and help of a professional, be prepared to pay for it. That said, negotiate a fair price. If you demand 30 minutes a week of your broker's time and you only do $200 a month in commissions, you are asking too much, or your broker is not providing a truly valuable service (truly exceptional brokers do not work that cheap). On the other hand, if you pay $1,500 a month in commissions and just check in for a 10-minute update every couple of weeks, you are doing yourself a disservice by not negotiating a sharply reduced rate. Here is all you need to say: "Carrie, I think you're great, and I really value your help with these nanotech issues. I know some people would take your advice and execute 200 shares with you, and then do 3,000 shares at some discount broker. I don't want to do that; how can we make this arrangement work better?" If this sounds like it reflects your situation, send me a note if this tactic does not save you at least 25-35%, immediately.

Ron Barron, one of the great long-term investors of the last quarter century, has built a great record by 1) Buying into very long-term trends based on nearly immovable 10- to 30-year demographics (like homeland security, adult education services, health care and housing) and 2) Buying individual stocks only after they have been sold-off by investors focused on the short-term. In the January 10, 2005 issue of *Barron's* he had some excellent words of advice for investors which I quote below. They have tremendous import for all "small tech" investors:

"Investors are focused on what's happening next quarter. They all want to buy at the same time. They want to sell at the same time. But if you are knowledgeable about a business and an industry and are willing to take a contrary position, that gives you a great opportunity. And this happens across the board in stock after stock, industry after industry.... One other point. The tremendous growth in hedge funds and other short-term-focused investors benefits our approach of trying to buy things at good prices. The focus on quarter-to-quarter performance has accentuated the volatility of many of the stocks we own, and given us more opportunity to buy things cheaply. **Stocks are increasingly depressed for short-term reasons.**" (my bold, underline)

Now that you have a great broker or have decided to invest on your own (and not use a fund manager's services like my own) by using a discount firm, what are your ***winning strategies*** as a long-term, *small tech* investor? Remember, as a non-specialist, non-professional, you are going to put no more than 5% - 15% of your total investment capital into "small tech" shares.

Winning Strategy #1: Identify four to ten true, nanotech growth companies and *dollar cost average*, every quarter over a period of 10 - 20 years. This is the most difficult strategy because, unlike the two strategies below, it demands both investment knowledge and discipline. While we expect rolling bull and bear markets in nanotech stocks lasting decades, with extended periods of 20-70% declines followed by similar length rallies of 150 - 350%, *dollar cost averaging* over the long term should pay off *in spades*.

The problem is that to take this route you have to attempt to identify the Microsofts, Starbucks, Wal-Marts, eBays, Cokes, Applied Materials and Amgens of nanotech. You must find companies with scalable business models and great managements capable of persistently growing earnings (such as rarely if ever missing two consecutive quarters) at a significant rate (like 15%+ compounded annually) for 20 years or more. These companies are extremely rare. They are hard to identify in their 5th year as a public company; even more difficult before that.

However, with diligence and intelligence (genius not needed) you can find them. You only need to find 3 to 6 of them. Following are the key features of a true growth company: While they regularly meet and exceed their numbers every quarter, they build and plan for the long-term; they think 10 to 20 years into the future. How do you know? They tell you in their annual reports and shareholder letters. They hire the best, and pay up for high IQ. True growth companies are #1 in the world (or a very competitive #2) in every single business in which they compete, or they exit or sell the business. They completely dominate their markets. They meet the same or better fate when they expand internationally. They are obsessive about serving their customers. Their stocks push higher and higher and higher with brief periods of backsliding; just about all the time.

This last point gives average investors headaches. When a stock doubles, triples or goes up 700% most investors want to take their profits off the table, and assume that "what goes up must come down," "oak trees don't grow to the sky," "bulls make money, bears make money and pigs never do" and other such stuff that absolutely applies to most equities, all cyclical stocks, and yet DO NOT APPLY WHATSOEVER TO TRUE GROWTH STOCKS.

You cannot get from 0 to 120 miles per hour without going 75 miles an hour. You cannot get a 10,000% return without going through a 700% return. If you take the time and have the investor smarts, many of the youngest of you should make 60 to 100 times your money or more over the next 20 to 30 years.

Winning Strategy #2: Buy a diversified basket of 20 to 40 *small tech* stocks or an ETF (should one come to exist) near three year lows and sell near four year highs. This is the second most difficult strategy because it requires discipline and confidence, and you will suffer occasional losses. This strategy takes its cue from the saying "when the gun goes off, all the turkeys will fly."

Assuming rolling booms and busts (or even not assuming them), investors will see 3-year lows and 4-year highs from time to time. No prediction capability needed, you will see the lows and highs made in 20/20 hindsight. Using this *winning strategy* you should regularly make a significant portion of the largest up-move in any 3 to 6 year period. You will be out of the market much of the time.

Exchange traded funds (ETFs like the QQQQ for the NAS-DAQ 100) could be established for *small tech* or nanotech equities. In 2005, my staff at **www.nanotechnology.com** uncovered 148 international, publicly traded *small tech* equities with a total market capitalization in excess of $195 billion. We expect the number of companies to grow in excess of 10% per year for many years while the average one of these stocks increases in value by 15% compounded per year. An ETF made up of investments in these shares would be expected to grow at the same rate. Twice the rate of average equity performance for the past 75 years, or 16 - 21% compounded annually, would not be unusual over the long-term for a high growth, high tech space like nanotechnology.

Winning Strategy #3: *Dollar cost average* into a diversified basket or ETF and build for 10 - 40 years. In this scenario you do not sell; you do not let the big 1- to 3-year declines shake you out of the market. You buy the same dollar amount of the basket or ETF (or mutual fund if The Nanotech Company, LLC manages one) every month or quarter, no matter the price. By buying the same dollar amount, say $2,000, you will be buying more shares when prices are low and fewer when prices are high. This arithmetically lowers your average cost, which, invariably pays off over the long-term quite nicely assuming an overall rise in prices. With those assumptions, your performance will beat buying the same number of shares (as opposed to the same dollar amount) by a country mile.

FOR SPECULATORS

Do not underestimate the power of a single unexpected piece of good or bad news or a single analyst report to drive the market direction of a nanotech stock for days or weeks. The anti-analyst sentiment of the very early days of this century are over, or forgotten. In late 2004, a single analyst report shot an already overpriced, household tech name up more than 20% in a few days. A few weeks before, a negative FDA input crashed a biotech stock 75% in one day.

Remember the "gold causes cancer; gold cures cancer" rule. Do not *plunge* or *put all of your eggs in one basket*. A 40% one-day drop in a stock that is only 10% of your trading portfolio only constitutes a 4% decline of the whole. This is a terrible enough result, but not the end of the world.

While leveraged *matched pair* trading (think: buying $20,000 worth of Ford and simultaneously shorting $20,000 worth of GM) is a great way to speculate and mimic professional traders; it will be an unavailable strategy in nanotech (or even the more broadly defined, *small tech*) for years, until there are dozens of large, publicly traded, competing nanotech companies.

However, a leveraged *long/short* strategy could work for nimble speculators now. Many public *small tech* companies are doomed to fail before 2010 (how many stocks with $100 million market caps and nothing to show for it in 2005 can exist?); they have grossly overpriced stocks, and there are already some dominant companies beginning to emerge, especially among relatively older companies whose products are already selling well. While high P/E ratios appear commonly among this group, at least there is an E to go along with the P. Almost all of the "shortables" have no E whatsoever, in fact they usually have no R (revenues!).

In this strategy one uses margin (or not) to sell short 50% of the dollar value of the portfolio while *going long* the same amount. (think: long $1 million total of IBM, Amgen and AIG while going short $1 million total of Chevron, Qualcomm, Morgan Stanley, Claire Stores and Clorox). One's goal is that if the market stays flat the longs rise a bit; if the market goes up, the longs go up a greater percentage than the shorts; and if the market goes down, the longs go down a lower percentage than the shorts.

Of course, in speculator dreamland, the longs go straight up and the shorts (*dogs* that they are) sink like a stone.

Properly constructed and applied, with excellent stock-picking, this type of strategy can regularly return 10 - 15% per year *independent* of the direction of the market, or even the direction of nanotech or *small tech* stocks as a group. (Disclosure: I manage a hedge fund for institutions, family offices, and sophisticated investors that pursues this strategy.)

"Wait!" I can hear you asking, "Can't I make a fortune trading nanotech shares?" Of course you can, but it will be difficult.

Let me give you the bad news first; then I will let you in on the two best ways to speculate for huge gains in nanotechnology stocks.

The Bad News: This book is not one of those *feel good* infomercials about option or currency-trading that you see on television more and more these days. Professional traders and speculators roar with delight (and disgust) when they see the wool being pulled over the public's eyes about the ease of making money trading.

Pros trade systems and methods with tremendous discipline. Some hit *singles and doubles* and regularly make 15 - 30% annually with a ratio of 3 or 4 winners for every 8 - 10 trades, while others *swing for the fences*, happy to make 1 or 2 huge profits for every 10 trades, while closing the other 9 or 10 trades with only small losses. The second group tends to have wild swings, losing 20% or more in a single month or quarter only to come back with some years up 65% or more and occasional losing years.

There HAVE been a few (extremely few) legitimate traders who have made 35%+ compounded returns, with a significant amount of starting capital, over a period of close to a decade or more. One or two lucky trades or turning $20,000 into $300,000 in one year in options or futures do not count – that is called "luck" – $1,000 into $150,000 (ahem) in cattle futures in a single year is called "the biggest outlier ever" or "public gullibility".

Anyone who claims they can take $10,000 and make 1% in a day (or even 0.5%), and repeat that day after day is a liar. At that rate, in a mere three years your $10,000 would have bulged to over $200 million! Nothing close to that has EVER been done. So if you want to trade professionally, do it full-time, and become great at it, you have your work cut out for you. It is a fascinating journey, but certainly not for everyone. The pro traders reading this would be well-served by using their already honed skills, my tips in this book, and their knowledge that until 2009 at least they will have *easy pickings* and little serious competition at the table in these under-researched, illiquid shares.

The Good News: For a longer term investor/speculator there are two winning strategies: *The Rifle* and *The Shotgun* approaches. As their names imply *The Shotgun* takes advantage of the adage, "When the gun goes off, all the turkeys will fly." *The Rifle* reflects the old saw, "Put all your eggs in one basket, and then watch the basket." There are secrets to having these strategies work profitably for you and making your nanotech fortune.

For *The Shotgun*: You will buy a portfolio of *small tech* stocks across the broadest range of disciplines, but a truly limited level of corporate development. You will not want to mimic a nanotech index, or, by the time you read this, there may be an ETF (Exchange Traded Fund) you can buy or sell like an individual stock. Speculators: Do not waste your time with that. You will have to have start-up medical device makers, materials companies, computer memory companies, agricultural products suppliers, among others in your *Shotgun* portfolio; have a minimum of 15 companies represented (25 - 35 is fine). Put equal dollars into each. Emphasize the most speculative, highly leveraged stocks that trade at least $300,000 worth of stock per day, and have market caps between $15 and $150 million. Counterintuitively, pick the stocks that are furthest from revenues, much less earnings. Now, *here is the key*: there are only two times to acquire this type portfolio and only three times to liquidate.

Acquire at these strategic winning points:

1. Sometimes 4 to 12 months after the nanotech indices have made 18 month *lows*, a clear, multi-month trading range will form, and begin to evidence a slight, but clear, upward tilt. When and only when that pattern is in evidence, buy on the break-out above that range.

2. Sometimes 1 to 4 months after the nanotech indices have made one year *highs*, a clear, multi-week trading range will form, and begin to evidence a tightening of the range *and* a very clear upward bias. When and only when that pattern is in evidence, buy on the breakout above that range.

Liquidate at any strategic point below that occurs first:

1. Any breakdown to a new 18 month low.

2. Any overall loss of 8% from the entry point.

3. Any loss of 8% at any time after a 200% gain is reached.

For *The Rifle* approach, you will focus on only 3 - 6 companies that you believe will be the true blue chips of *small tech*, and *dollar cost average* into them in an aggressive way. After a 12- to 18- month decline in *small tech* stocks, you will divide your specuative funds for this play into 12 equal parts and place 1/12th into this group each month for one year. You will sell on any 8% loss of the total of the funds you set aside for this speculation, or any loss of 8% after a 200% gain is made, or any breakdown to a new 18-month low after the first 6 months of this exercise, whichever comes first.

16 BEYOND NANOTECH

While the business and products of nanotechnology will dominate the financial landscape for decades, eventually another paradigm will hold sway. Nanotech is mostly the outgrowth of the pure science of Einstein near the beginning of the 20th century, through Feynman in the middle of the century to work by folks at IBM and elsewhere in the 1970s and '80s.

From roughly 1980 to 2005, the subatomic world, the world of wormholes, string theory, black holes and quarks has fascinated some of the world's brightest minds, in the same way the beginnings of nanoscience did from 1960 - 1990.

It is hard to believe. Not only are some of these "particles" smaller than atoms – some are *thousands* of times smaller!

Nanotechnology will rule from around 2010 until, at least, sometime between 2040 and 2080. For those of us who are around, in the vague future starting between 2035 and 2125, that subatomic world beyond nanotech will begin to drive the economy. There will be no shortage of ways to make money, **and a very strange place it will be.**

Beyond the infinitesimally small, humankind may well "return" to the infinitesimally large. If the right genius scientist learns to change a property within an atom that, in turn, changes a property within every other atom in the universe, perhaps that property will imbue human life on Earth with peace and immortality. Maybe the possibility that such a person might arrive on the scene one day is something upon which scientists, Hassidic rabbis, yogis, Buddhist monks, and fundamentalist Christians can all agree.

A brief, final note: In 1976, a short time before my partner and I built the largest regional discount brokerage firm in D.C., I formed another firm with two other partners. Just as we had anticipated the burgeoning discount brokerage field, before Schwab or Quick & Reilly even had a D.C. office, my new partnership focused on what we called "one-stop financial services." We saw the services provided multi-millionaires (quite a bit of money in those days) by certain "white shoe" brokerage firms, and felt we could do the same for the upper-middle-class. The typical well-off, but not rich, investor in those days did his or her banking, stock brokerage, life, health, home, auto and liability insurance, real estate, borrowing, estate planning, trusts, mortgage, commodities, and collectables at different places with different professionals. Our concept, and it was later picked up by everyone from Merrill Lynch to Citigroup, was that it would be simpler for one trusted professional team to provide an extremely high level of personalized service to investors with less than large fortunes: a mini-multi-family office concept if you will.

We were a success almost from the first day, attracting the foremost toy inventor of those days (remember *Electronic Battleship*), a couple of *trust fund babies*, a "rich uncle" or two, and a small real estate investor trying to get to the next level. We networked furiously, and *technology transferred* to trusted outside professionals when the expertise required was outside Allan's (legal and corporate), Justin's (real estate and negotiation) or mine (equities, futures and insurance). When one of the *trust fund babies,* a young army captain with a growing family came to us – we'll call him Rick Edmonds – one of the first things we determined was that he needed an estate plan.

After we took down his balance sheet and life-planning issues input, we presented the information to our estate planning associate, Harold, and had a meeting with him in our Bethesda, MD office before we presented, along with him, to our captain. Harold sat down in a large chair in front of a small coffee table, while my partners and I sat (a little to a lot lower) together, on a small couch on the other side of the coffee table. Harold let out a big sigh, clasped his hands together on his lap and expelled, "When this Rick Edmonds guy dies, he's gonna have real problems!"

Allan looked at me, I looked at Allan, we both looked at Justin who was staring at both of us, and we all (except Harold) burst out laughing. We got control of ourselves quickly, but Harold's ridiculously absurd statement that made a kind of sense on some weird level of financial understanding we each possessed, triggered an insight and that riotous laugh.

Today, I am absorbed in accelerating the growth of *small tech* companies and helping investors. For me, that meeting is a reminder about what is really important in life. Had Captain Edmonds been there, he would have laughed too.

In 1976 it was "one-stop financial services" years ahead of the crowd. In 1978 it was discount stock brokerage (my firm in Washington, D.C. was a discounter within a year of their regulatory acceptance and prior to Schwab even having a D.C. office; well before even 3% of the investing public had ever used a discount broker). In 1980 (I started *The Prospector* in 1981) it was precious metals mining investing (participating in the financing of a dozen of the most successful mining companies of the last 30 years). In 1982 it was oil and gas in time for the boom. In 1988 I left mining (at an auspicious moment). In 1995 I got back in for the short-lived mid-1990s reinvestment frenzy, and heavily into natural gas in 1997 (helping establish companies that eventually created nearly $5 billion in equity). I built and managed a hedge and private equity fund in 1996. I got investors into the Internet in 1997 and out in 2000 (earning them 81% on their money along the way).

The bottom line: For some reason I tend to read the tealeaves in advance of the crowd. Look back at the years that followed after my major moves. I have a history of anticipating major financial trends. This is not to say I cannot make a mistake; I do not claim to be any kind of genius, but I have never had a stronger intuition (and they have been pretty certain feelings in the past) than I have now about the future of nanotechnology and investing in *small tech*.

To elaborate for a moment: Very few financial professionals know more about the mining and oil and gas businesses and cycles. From 2002 into 2005, gold, silver, oil, and gas have been in major bull markets. While I was buying Devon, Chevron, Apache, Newmont, and many others for my accounts, I was focused on building my nanotech business. Aware it was coming, I chose to basically *sit out* the strongest natural resource bull market in 20 years, because nanotechnology has so much more potential. Precious metals and energy are going to top for years to come in 2005 to 2006, and as if in a mirror image, *Big Pharma* will probably bottom in 2005 or 2006 for years to come. However, nanotech and *small technology* stocks are going to dominate the financial landscape in a way that very few emerging industries or market segments have ever done. Look for those rolling booms and busts for 20 to 50 years or more.

Now, that is a long-term, upward curve from which to profit. Watch out for the inevitable bumps and slides. This is a moving train. Get on for the ride of your life.

Appendix

Tools & Resources
for Your
Nanotech Fortune

Famous People in the Nanotech World

Phaedon Avouris: Currently focused on molecular electronics and carbon nanotubes, Avouris heads the nanotech team at IBM.

Pulickel Ajayan: Research interests focused on the synthesis of nanostructures. One of the pioneers in carbon nanotubes; demonstrated possibilities for using them for fabricating nanowires, composites, and novel ceramic fibers.

Angela Belcher: Emerging as one of today's most exciting scientists, Belcher specializes in biomimicry, the study and use of "Mother Nature's Blue-Print" at MIT. Her mentor was Evelyn Hu, a prominent physicist and engineer who sits on the SAB of The Nanotech Company.

Sangeeta Bhatia: An SAB member of The Nanotech Company and MIT professor. Strong nanotech work in medical engineering and medical physics and current research in the development of novel biological micro-electro-mechanical systems (BioMEMS).

Gerd Binnig: Binning is a joint recipient of the Nobel Prize for his work with Heinrich Rohrer in scanning tunneling microscopy. He is a research member at IBM's Zurich Research Laboratory.

Larry Bock: Co-founder and CEO of Nanosys, Inc., and has successfully launched more than eleven biotech companies. Criticized from some quarters for "looking out for #1," he has a proven capability for building companies, and teaming incredibly talented scientists.

K. Eric Drexler: Eric Drexler is an MIT trained theoretical researcher focused on the development and impact of emerging nanotechnologies. He is best known for his description of the physical principles of molecular manufacturing systems, a subject of much critical debate. In the "religion" of nanotechnology, he represents/leads the most far-out, largely marginalized believers in self-assembling molecular machines, a specific *inorganic* concept discredited by most respected scientists. I (and MANY other nanotech folk) read his book, *Engines of Creation*, in the late 1980s, was fascinated, and hooked for life on a fascination with nanotechnology.

Don Eigler: As an IBM researcher, Dr. Eigler has demonstrated the ability to manipulate individual atoms with extreme precision. He has developed a variety of nanotechnologies including single atom electrical switches, and "quantum corral" electron traps.

Stephen Empedocles: Co-founder and Director of Business Development at Nanosys, Inc. Stephen Empedocles is a scientist involved in the study of nanomaterials and the commercialization of nanotechnology.

Richard P. Feynman: Considered one of the greatest theoretical physicists of the twentieth century, Feynman gave birth to the world of nanotechnology in 1959 with his groundbreaking talk, "There's Plenty of Room at the Bottom." A very special book on his life, *Genius: The Life and Science of Richard Feynman*, by James Gleick, is fascinating reading.

Reza Ghadiri: Professor at The Scripps Research Institute and winner of the Feynman Prize in Nanotechnology, his research involves de novo design of synthetic proteins and enzymes; self-assembling peptide nanotubes and biomaterials; design of novel biosensors; self-replicating molecular systems and self-organized chemical networks; and molecular computation. He is a member of The Nanotech Company's SAB.

James Heath: Heath is a Professor of Chemistry at CalTech with an established reputation in molecular electronics.

Evelyn Hu: Physicist member of the National Academy of Engineering. Now on sabbatical from UCSB; working with protégé Angela Belcher (see above) at start-up Cambrios; recognized for nanofabrication techniques to facilitate the study of superconducting and semiconducting devices and circuits; and an SAB member of The Nanotech Company.

Sumio Iijima: Dr. Iijima discovered carbon nanotubes in 1991, and has since become a leading researcher in the international circle of scientists working on the development and study of nanotubes. Since carbon nanotubes are just about the bricks of the nanotech world, this is a storied accomplishment.

Steve Jurvetson: Jurvetson is a venture capitalist who has become a leading investor in nanotechnology. Steve, among the most brilliant extemporaneous speakers you will ever hear, is one of the earliest and *loudest* proponents of nanotechnology: his unbridled enthusiasm has been criticized, and the story has yet to be written on whether he was *too* early, or in the sweetest sweet spot.

Harry Kroto: Sir Harry Kroto was jointly awarded the Nobel Laureate for his discovery of C60 Buckyballs. The work was done with Richard Smalley (see below) and Robert Curl. Along with quantum dots and nanotubes, Buckyballs or Fullerenes form the *trinity* of nanoparticles.

Ray Kurzweil: Recipient of the National Medal of Technology in 1999, Ray Kurweil is respected as one of the most prominent inventors and entrepreneurs in today's technology markets. He is an outspoken proponent of the fusion between human and machine intelligence. I saw Ray speak as a _hologram_ from somewhere in Asia at a nano-conference in Texas in 2001. He can make the future sound more incredible than any movie, and make it seem only weeks, not decades, away.

Charles Lieber: Charles Lieber holds the Mark Hyman Chair of Chemistry at Harvard University and has done extensive work in the study of nanowires, nanodots, and nanotubes. He is also a co-founder of Nanosys.

Stephen Maebius: Nanotech patent attorney extraordinaire and leader of the Nanotechnology Industry Team at Foley & Lardner. He serves on the advisory board of the NanoBusiness Alliance and the Corporate Development Advisory Board of The Nanotech Company. He is the editor-in-chief of the *Nanotechnology Law & Business Journal*, and is credited with having filed the most nanotech patents.

Ralph Merkle: Dr. Merkle, an extensively published, controversial, Stanford trained, established scientist with a focus on computational nanotechnology, is a research scientist with Zyvex Corporation. He has chaired several Foresight Conferences on Nanotechnolgy, and was co-recipient of the Feynman Prize in 1998 for work in Nanotechnology Theory. Not to be sacrilegious, but think John the Baptist to Drexler's Jesus.

Chad Mirkin: As the 2002 Feynman Prize recipient Chad Mirkin has launched three nanotech startups (Nanophase, Nanosphere, and NanoInk), and is a Professor of Chemistry and Director of the Institute of Nanotechnology, and Center for Nanofabrication and Molecular Self-Assembly at Northwestern. Chad is recognized as a true leading light in nanotech, and his lab is one of the most productive in the nation.

F. Mark Modzelewski: Mark, the co-founder and first Executive Director of the NanoBusiness Alliance, now works for Lux Research in NYC.

Hari Manoharan: Young Stanford physics professor with skyrocketing nano-career focusing on nanoassembly using atomic and molecular manipulation. According to scientists on the frontier of nano, a couple of Manoharan's more spectacular achievements qualify as "a technical tour de force, an elegant piece of work."

Edward Moran: The head of Deloitte & Touche's Nanotech Industry Practice, co-founder of the NanoBusiness Alliance, and one of the emerging industry's most respected speakers. Ed chairs the Corporate Development Advisory Board of The Nanotech Company, LLC.

Cherry Murray: Deputy Director for Science & Technology at Lawrence Livermore National Laboratory, and winner of the American Physical Society's prestigious George Pake Prize for 2005 for fundamental studies in surface and scattering physics, this former senior vice president of Bell Labs Research is also a member of the National Academy of Sciences, the National Academy of Engineering, the American Academy of Arts and Sciences. In 2002, *Discover Magazine* named her one of the "50 Most Important Women in Science."

Mihail C. Roco: Dr. Roco is the Senior Advisor for Nanotechnology at the National Science Foundation. He also chairs the National Science and Technology Council's subcommittee on nanoscale science. He is the U.S. government's number one name in nanotechnology, and probably knows more about what is going on in nanotech labs and corporations around the world than anyone else.

Hinrich Rohrer: Rohrer is a joint recipient of the Nobel Prize for his work with Gerd Binning in scanning tunneling microscopy. He is a retired research scientist from IBM.

Erkki Ruoslahti: Distinguished Professor and former CEO of The Burnham Institute, Dr. Ruoslahti is the 2005 winner of the internationally prestigious Japan Prize given for scientific achievement that benefits humankind in a significant way. Co-founder and Chairman of the Scientific Advisory Board (SAB) of The Nanotech Company, LLC, he is a member of the National Academy of Sciences, Institute of Medicine, and the National Academy of Arts and Sciences. Ruoslahti is a leading scientist in the extracellular matrix and tumor biology fields, discoverer of the RGD cell adhesion motif and the founder of three biotech companies. He has developed a vascular targeting technology and is applying this technology into nanomedicine.

Richard E. Smalley: Dr. Smalley received the Nobel Prize in 1996 for the discovery of fullerenes and is head of the Center for Nanoscale Science and Technology at Rice University. He is focused on the viable integration of single-walled carbon nanotubes into commercialized technologies. Smalley is one of the most famous names in the history of nano. He is a very busy man, striving for a second Nobel, which may arrive in 2009 - 2015 if his prodigious work continues.

Sam Stupp: Stupp is a leading light in nanotech and Professor of Chemistry at Northwestern University studying the regeneration of bone, heart, and nerve tissue through nanoscale science.

Nathan Tinker: Co-Founder of The NanoBusiness Alliance and one of the most respected, insightful "catbird seat sitters" on the whole nanotech phenomenon. Known as an effective nanotech-conference speaker advocate, his rolodex of contacts is legendary. He works closely with The Nanotech Company, LLC, and we hope to be able to announce soon his appointment as a Senior Director of our firm.

James Von Ehr II: Von Ehr is a respected leader within the nanotech industry with strong commitment to the development of nanotechnology in Texas. He is founder and Chief Executive Officer of Zyvex Corporation, specializing in nanotechnology tool development. On the "downside," he occasionally is painted as a supporter of the Foresight Foundation *religion*. Jim has invested more of his own money ($47 million at last count) in nanotechnology than any other human being.

John Walker: Sir John Walker along with biochemist Paul Boyer was jointly awarded the Nobel Prize for Chemistry in 1997. The work involved a study of the enzymatic process involved in the production of energy-storage molecules.

George M. Whitesides: Dr Whitesides, one of the world's most respected scientists, is the Mallinckrodt Professor of Chemistry at Harvard University. He is best known for his study of self-assembling chemical compounds, and is a member of the National Academy of Sciences and the American Academy of Arts and Sciences. In 2001/02 he was associated with The Nanotech Company's predecessor SAB; we miss that association, but he is very busy with his science.

Stan Williams: As Director of Quantum Science Research at Hewlett-Packard, Williams leads HP Labs' nanostructure research.

Josh Wolfe: Josh Wolfe is a co-founder and Managing Partner of Lux Capital, a VC firm focused on investments in nanotechnology. He is also author of the monthly *Forbes/Wolfe Nanotech Report* and a sought-after and articulate spokesperson for the emerging nanotech world.

THE MOST INTERESTING NANOTECH-RELATED BOOKS FOR NON-SCIENTIST INVESTORS (ALL OF THESE BOOKS ARE AVAILABLE AT WWW.NANOTECHNOLOGY.COM)

<u>**Engines of Creation: The Coming Era of Nanotechnology,**</u> K.Erik Drexler, 1986. Many scientists, nanotech executives, and venture capitalists point to this controversial book as what first sparked their interest in nanotechnology. It is provocative, mind-

expanding, and a great "read." However, recently, its unrealistic notions about self-assembling molecular machines and other futuristic musings have brought its author nothing but strong criticism from the scientific community.

Introduction to Nanotechnology. C.P. Poole and F.J. Owens, 2003, John Wiley & Sons. This book provides an introduction to the subject of nanotechnology on a level that allows researchers outside of this field to begin a technical understanding of this very technical world. A general understanding of the science related to the subject is necessary for the understanding of this text. For scientists and engineers only.

Nanotechnology, edited by, B.C. Crandall, 1996, MIT Press. An introduction to nanotechnology is provided; however the focus of this book is a compilation of possible future applications in nanotechnology. From "cosmetic nanosurgery" to "invisible suits", this is an attempt to provide a time machine into the future of nanotechnology.

Nanotechnology: A Gentle Introduction to the Next Big Idea. M. Ratner and D. Ratner, 2003, Prentice Hall. The Ratner father/son team has presented an up-to-date, comprehensive, overview of nanotechnology and its applications. The non-scientist should expect to understand 80% of the subject matter presented. For a technically complete, yet comparatively non-technical explanation of nanotechnology, this is a good starting point.

The Investor's Guide to Nanotechnology & Micromachines, by G. Fishbine, 2002, John Wiley & Sons. The strength of this book lies in its ability to direct investors to growing trends in nanotechnology. This is more "nanotech 101" for investor-types, than a book about successful investing.

The Next Big Thing is Really Small. J. Uldrich with D. Newberry, 2003, Crown Business. This is a business-oriented overview of the emerging nanotech world. With very little technical information presented, this is an easy-to-read, comprehensive window into the financial dynamics of today's nanotech industry.

Understanding Nanotechnology, from the editors of *Scientific American*, 2002, Byron Preiss Visual. This is a concise yet comprehensive description of nanotechnology and the applications of nanotechnology for the scientist who didn't receive a graduate degree in engineering. The all-star team of co-authors have made nanotech somewhat understandable to the rest of us.

Nanocosm: Nanotechnology and the Big Changes Coming from the Inconceivably Small. William Illsey Atkinson, 2003, Amacom. This is an entertainingly written diatribe against Drexler, written by a non-scientist, like myself, but seemingly without a tough scientific editor. Like Drexler, take it all with a "pound of salt" and it's a worthwhile, though not definitive, read.

THE MOST INFORMATIVE NANOTECH NEWSLETTERS (ALL AVAILABLE AT WWW.NANOTECHNOLOGY.COM)

The Best of the Nano Week. **Free** e-digest of international *small technology* news. The letter saves you countless hours of research, as The Nanotech Company scientists and financial execs review more than 130 small tech press releases and articles each week to find you the 8-12 that are the most important. Then, we not only provide a short intro and link to the article, but give you our unique and usually controversial *take* on the news from our scientific, technical and business perspectives. (See the Archive of past issues and order on) – Complimentary to all **Nanotech Fortunes** readers.

Forbes/Wolfe Nanotech Report. VC and nanotech booster-extraordinaire Josh Wolfe's take on emerging nanotechnology, nanoscience developing in universities, national labs and emerging and publicly traded companies. An excellent, well-written resource for those interested in the serious, sci/tech side of things. More on financings and technology being developed than a stock market, stock pick type letter.

The **Small Tech** *Prospector.* My personal favorite. E-mail based. Investment and speculative **long and short calls** on more than 150 publicly traded *small-technology*-related international companies. Semiconductor, microelectronics, nanotech, microfluidics, opto-electric, laser and MEMs companies are covered. The author is unafraid of short-term trading opportunities and offers specific, hopefully profit-exploding recommendations. Scams and hypes are definitely called out. $139/year – Special discount: Only $89 first year for **Nanotech Fortunes** readers! (Order online at www.nanotechnology.com)

The Best Nanotech Websites

http://www.nanoapex.com/ A bland website, yet one that gets the job done. Most stories, divided into scientific and business news, are press releases or mirrored from other print and Internet media.

http://www.nano.org.uk An excellent British site intended to foster, develop, and promote all aspects of science and nanotechnology.

http://www.nanobusiness.org/ The NanoBusiness Alliance is an industry group, shouldering the responsibilities of promoting nanotech and lobbying Washington.

http://www.nanotechnology.com The Nanotech Company, LLC's website. As Managing Director, I guess I'm biased: we are the best in the world. **Free subscription** to the international eDigest of nanotechnology and "small technology" news, *The Best of the NanoWeek*, is available on site, as well as *The* Small Tech *Prospector* ($139 - $89 special intro price for *Nanotech Fortune* readers). The deepest, most valuable insights on the web for investors, nano-execs and scientists alike.

http://www.nanotechweb.org Published by the Institute of Physics in the UK, the news on this site is mostly original, generally including interviews with the authors of scientific studies. Definite scientific achievements slant. Great place to visit.

http://www.nanotechwire.com Difficult to figure how they make any money, but this is an interesting, informative site, especially with regard to its monthly calendar of nanotech events worldwide that never fails to uncover the smallest, exotic, most esoteric nano-conferences out there.

http://www.nanovip.com/ Contains a thorough listing of nanotech companies, categorized by industry. The site also allows you to add your company/site to the index.

http://nsti.org The Nanoscience and Technology Institute (NSTI) is on top of the game. Billing themselves as a nanotech consultancy, their main activity so far has been holding an excellent yearly business-focused nanotech conference.

http://pubs.acs.org/journals/nalefd/index.html Home site of *Nano Letters*, a premiere scientific journal geared specifically for nanotechnology research. Published by the American Chemical Society (ACS), accessing full articles requires a subscription.

http://www.smalltimes.com A very well-produced site with mostly original news stories on small (micro, MEMS, and nano) technologies. The site covers most nanotech developments, with a bias towards the business side, and categorizes the stories well. They also produce a glossy magazine (Subscribe – it's free) and boast a small tech index.

ACADEMIC/GOVERNMENT LABS

http://www.cchem.berkeley.edu/~pagrp/
Paul Alivisatos – UC Berkeley
This guy was nano before nano was cool. "Mr. Cluster" was a founding scientist at Quantum Dot Corp, and also a member of the Nanosys SAB.

http://www.chem.northwestern.edu/~mkngrp/
Chad Mirkin – Northwestern University
Responsible for breakthroughs in directed nanoscale assembly and

dip-pen nanolithography. Mirkin startups have included Nanosphere and Nanoink.

http://www.cnf.cornell.edu/
Cornell Nanoscale Science and Technology Facility
This is the facility that produced the "nanoguitar" in 1997, and then followed it up with a playable version in 2003.

http://www.cnsi.ucla.edu/
California NanoSystems Institute
An institute that includes a diverse group of nanoscientists from UCLA and UCSB. The group is directed by Evelyn Hu, a member of The Nanotech Company, LLC and **SAB.**

http://cnst.rice.edu/
Center for Nanoscale Science and Technology –
Rice University
A loosely connected center that includes a diverse group of nanoscientists, including Jennifer West, Naomi Halas (of nanoshells fame), Vicki Colvin (environmental) and Richard Smalley (buckyballs).

http://www.hgc.cornell.edu/index.html
Harold Craighead – Cornell University
A pioneer in single molecule physics, Craighead founded Nanofluidics, a company hoping to sequence DNA by watching single bases as they are added to a growing strand by polymerase.

http://www.masstech.org/nano/index.htm
Massachusetts is one of the most high-profile nanotechnology states, boasts a central website for its nanotech initiative. It gives a good overview of the state's efforts, both in academic labs and industry.

http://www.nano.gov/
US National Nanotechnology Initiative
The website for the US National Nanotechnology Initiative is a

good source of basic nanotech information. Following links from the homepage, one finds a listing of NNI centers and funding opportunities for academics and startups.

http://nano.med.umich.edu/
Center for Biologic Nanotechnology – University of Michigan

A hotbed for dendrimer research, the center is directed by James Baker. Their focus is on targeting and drug delivery using these unique branching molecules.

http://www.nano.washington.edu/index.asp
Center for Nanotechnology – University of Washington

Out of the university of Allan Hoffman and Buddy Ratner comes a nanotech center with a focus on bio-inspired materials. It shares a close connection with nearby Pacific Northwest National Labs (PNNL), and is a member of the NSF nanotech infrastructure network.

http://www.scripps.edu/chem/ghadiri/group.html
Reza Ghadiri – Scripps

Feynman Nanotechnology prize winner and member of our SAB, Reza Ghadiri's lab at Scripps is renowned for his work with peptide nanotubes.

http://seemanlab4.chem.nyu.edu/homepage.html
Ned Seeman – NYU

NYU's Ned Seeman told me he has actually only been working on the same chemistry/crystallography problem for 23 years. Now he finds himself suddenly a nanoscientist. He's ok with it though. His fascinating work – using synthetic DNA as a backbone for building nanostructures – is featured.

THE IMPORTANT NANO CONFERENCES

http://www.chemistry.org
ACS National Meeting

Though definitely aimed at scientific and academic audiences, we had to include this one. Every time the ACS meeting comes around, the news is filled with new nanoscale innovations. While it may not be the place to learn about the next nano-darling, it is the place to find the science to start your own.

http://www.ianano.org/
NanoWorld Expo

One of the few general interest nano conference held in the U.S., but with an international focus. The long list of speakers has a slight science focus, but the technical details will certainly be toned down and will be of interest to investors.

http://www.ibfconferences.com/ibf/index.asp

IBF – International Business Forum does an excellent job at the very high-end conference for the professional investing community, and their Annual Nanotech Investing Forum in Rancho Mirage, CA, proves a networking bonanza for those who can afford it.

http://www.infocastinc.com/NNI/nnihome.htm
National Nanotechnology Initiative (NNI) Conference

Sponsored and attended by numerous government agencies (NIH, NSF, DOD, NASA, etc), this conference has been a key intersection between government's nanotech initiative and the marketplace.

http://www.nanoevent.com

An annual event held by the NanoBusiness Alliance, an industry group responsible for producing white papers and lobbying congress. This is an excellent conference for literally anyone interested in nanotechnology and nanotech investing.

http://www.nsti.org
NTSI

NSTI puts on a good show – and has done so since 2002. Their conference and trade show is packed with a broad range of technology, startup and investment talks/exhibits.

Other conferences:

ASME Annual Integrated Nanosystems Conference & Showcase
A focus on state-of-the art devices and systems, nanoscale phenomena, and nanomanufacturing.
http://www.asmeconferences.org

ASME Nano Training Bootcamp
Specifically organized to offer a detailed and tutorial-based account of advances and fundamentals of nanoscience.
http://www.asmeconferences.org

DOE NanoSummit
The Department of Energy's conference on nanotechnology.
https://public.ornl.gov/conf

The Nano Summit Research Conference
A forum for medical, natural science and engineering researchers and students in Texas.
http://www.nanotechfoundation.org/WWO.html

THE 25 MOST IMPORTANT SMALL TECH PUBLIC COMPANIES

PUBLIC HEAVYWEIGHTS:

The ABB Group (ABB)
ABB is working on reengineering materials at the atomic scale and integrating IT (information technology) and communications with micromechanical structures (MEMs).
www.abb.com

Accelrys (ACCL)
Accelrys provides software for pharmaceutical, chemical and material research. Their patented software makes it possible to model complex scenarios of atomistic, mesoscale, and crystallization issues on the PC.
http://www.accelrys.com

Agilent (A)
"All of our businesses are seeking higher speeds of measurement at

lower cost, and I strongly believe that nanobiotechnology will be an increasingly key field in our future."
—**Darlene Solomon**, Director of Life Science Technologies Lab

ASML (ASML)
A partner with IBM in the $400 million center in Albany.

Ansys (ANSS)
Heavily involved in MEMs and Microsystems.

BASF (BF)
Interested in functional surfaces ? for instance, with self-cleaning properties or special moistening properties ? and in discovering new procedures, products and systems

Cabot (CBT)
Aerogel, their unique form of highly porous silica (nanoparticle), is known as light weight and exceptional insulating solid. They also develop a family of hydrophobic silica aerogels and something called Nanogel, a translucent aerogel with thermal protection, high quality diffused light and sound reduction for the construction market, as well as carbon black, an old material that is arguably nano.

Coherent (COHR)
Developing lasers for use in micromachining processes where the laser is pulsing at femtoseconds (!) (one thousandth of a nanosecond – yikes!). In the lab they can drill super tiny holes in silicon with this method likely to be useful for something.

Corning (GLW)
This old line company is heavily involved in all aspects of *small technology* in everything from bio to optical applications.

Dupont (DD)
Dupont is creating field emission flat panel displays with CNT technologies. Researchers are also pioneering new methods of CNT organization with the use of DNA.
http://www.dupont.com

General Electric Co. (GE)
The Global Research Program at GE develops nanomaterials and CNT technologies with the hope of replacing silicon as a critical chip material.

General Motors Co. (GM)
GM has begun to integrate materials such as nanoscale clay into its manufacturing line for reinforcement or development of lighter, safer, and more efficient automotive components.
http://www.gm.com

Hewlett Packard (HPQ)
HP is currently developing molecular memory and logic chips with the hope of becoming the premier provider of nanoscaled processors. Such processors would be small enough to find applications in materials ranging from fibers in a shirt, to the delivery vessels of medicines.
http://www.hp.com

IBM (IBM)
IBM researchers are experimenting with self-assembly to create molecular patterns which could act as stencils for chip circuitry. IBM is the worldwide leader in nanotech IP.
http://www.ibm.com

Intel (INTC)
Intel has turned to the self-assembly properties of gate materials on silicone wafers for the integration of nanoscaled transistors in chip manufacturing.
http://www.intel.com

Lucent Technologies (LU)
Bell Labs (part of Lucent Tech.) with mPhase is involved in the development of nanotechnology-based power cell technology. Lucent researchers have also been involved in nanodevices such as self-assembled DNA motorized tweezers.
http://www.lucent.com

FEI (FEIC)

FEI creates analytical tools for the study of materials at the sub-micron level. This is achieved through charged particle beam systems which can characterize and manipulate atomic scaled systems.

http://www.feic.com

Flamel Technologies (FLML)

Flamel Technologies is a French company specializing in the delivery of acute, time controlled therapy with their "micro pump" technology.

http://www.flamel-technologies.fr

mPhase Technologies (XDSL)

MPhase Technologies develops telecommunications and nanotechnology solutions. Current collaborations on power cell research with Lucent Technologies show promising breakthroughs in the efficiency and shelf life of novel batteries.

http://www.mphasetech.com

Motorola (MOT)

Work with carbon nanotubes, molecular electronics, and micro fuel cells is all part of a significant portfolio of *small tech* initiatives at this technology leader.

Nanogen (NGEN)

Nanogen is focused on the design and commercialization of molecular diagnostic tests for the medical community and clinical researchers. As of 2005 we agree that they have begun to develop true nanotech products.

http://www.nanogen.com

Nanophase Technologies (NANX)

This is a company which explores various material processing techniques to prepare bulk nanocrystalline materials with the use of highly controlled surface chemistries.

http://www.nanophase.com

Texas Instruments (TXN)

DLP display technology was invented here. If it has to do with semiconductors, wireless or information technology, TI is a true leader in *small technology* IP.

Veeco Instruments (VECO)

Veeco provides a large range of process equipment and analytical tools for semiconductors and metrology research. They may be best known as leaders in the development of scanning probe microscopy tools such as AFM.
http://www.veeco.com

Xerox (XRX)

Cutting edge research continues at their PARC Center. Work in nanotechnology and microsystems; replacing mechanics of copiers and printers with microelectromechanical devices (MEMs). Seeking ways to make paper smarter; develop new forms of data displays; novel ways that paper can carry more information: technologies beyond paper that will support ubiquitous ultra-low-cost displays (electronic paper).

FOLLOWING ARE SOME SMALLER PUBLIC COMPANIES THAT ARE EXHIBITING PRESENCE IN THE EMERGING SMALL TECH AREA.

Altair Nanotechnologies, Inc. is developing a technology platform for manufacturing a wide variety of nanomaterials and nano-based products. The company's materials are being developed for potential applications in fuel cells, solar cells, advanced energy storage devices (batteries), thermal spray coatings, cosmetics and material protection.

BioSante Pharmaceuticals, Inc. is a development-stage biopharmaceutical company that is developing hormone therapy products to treat men and women. The Company is also developing a proprietary calcium phosphate, nanoparticulate-based platform technology (CAP) for vaccine adjuvants or immune system boosters and drug delivery systems.

NVE Corporation develops and sells devices using spintronics which utilizes electron spin rather than electron charge to acquire, store and transmit information. It is also a licensor of magnetic random access memory technology (MRAM), which has potential in electronic memory.

JMAR Technologies, Inc. develops advanced lasers, laser-produced plasma sources and x-ray lithography steppers for semiconductor fabrication.

Immunicon Corp. develops and commercializes proprietary cell-based research and diagnostic products with a focus on cancer. They use patented magnetic nanoparticles called ferrofluids, in systems to collect and analyze rare cells from blood.

Private Startup Companies:

Advanced Diamond Technologies
ADT commercializes patented techniques for making thin films of nanocrystalline diamond.
http://www.thindiamond.com

Angstrovision
This is a company focused on developing high-precision imaging technologies for nanoscale metrology and 3D imaging.
http://www.angstrovision.com

Argonide
Argonide offers and develops custom-made nanopowders with high burning rates in propellant combustion.
http://www.argonide.com

BioForce Nanosciences
Nanoarray technologies for solid-phase, high-throughput biomolecular analysis
http://www.bioforcenano.com/

Csixty
Working on development of biopharmaceutical applications of fullerenes (buckyballs)
http://www.csixty.com/

Carbon Nanotechnologies
Produces carbon nanotubes (Buckytubes) in large scale (100lb/day). Has signed a slew of collaborations and filed many patents. Trying to solve precision problems with manufacturing and yield. Since the properties of buckytubes can differ wildly depending on their exact geometry, this is a significant problem that limits the use of the material.
www.cnanotech.com

Dendritic Nanotechnologies
Carbon-based technology useful for pharmaceuticals, cosmetics, energy storage, etc.
http://dnanotech.com/

Discera
Discera creates wireless solutions with nanotechnology through the development of integrated microcomponents.
http://www.discera.com

Evident Technologies
Semiconductor nanocrystals (quantum dots) for biomedical research applications.
www.evidenttech.com

Fluidigm
Fluidigm is best known for the development of patented nano-valve technologies enabling free interface diffusion (FID) within nanoscale geometries.
http://www.fluidigm.com

Kionix
Kionix is involved in high-performance MEMS inertial sensors for

high-volume automotive and consumer electronics markets.
http://www.kionix.com

Konarka Technologies

Konarka uses photovoltaic cells (PVCs) from nanosized particles of titanium dioxide to create plastics that use solar power to run electrical devices.
http://www.konarkatech.com

Molecular Imprints

Nano-imprint lithography for electronics applications
http://molecularimprints.com

NanoBio

Biopharmaceutical company with patented antimicrobial nanoemulsion technology
http://www.nanobio.com/

NanoCrystal Technologies

NanoCrystal Technologies is involved in the research of quantum confined atoms and the luminescent properties of such materials.
http://www.nanocrystals.com

NanoCure

Targeted drug delivery using dendrimers for cancer therapeutics
Currently funded by government grants
http://www.nanocure.com/

Nanodynamics

A leading manufacturer of nanomaterials. Famous for the nano-golf ball.
http://www.nanodynamics.com/

Nanofilm

Nanofilm develops and commercializes ultra-thin nanofilms for transparent materials such as eyewear or swimming goggles.
http://www.nanofilm.cc

NanoInk
NanoInk develops lithography tools which can convert an AFM into a dip-pen nanolithography machine.
http://www.nanoink-inc.com

Nanomix
Nanomix develops nanoelectronic sensors that integrate CNTs with silicon microstructures.
http://www.nano.com

Nano Opto
Nano Opto applies nano-optic and nano-manufacturing technologies to design and fabricate components for optical systems and networking.
http://www.nanoopto.com

Nanosolar
Printed thin-film solar cells, communications, displays, etc.
http://www.nanosolar.com

Nanosphere
Clinical genetic diagnostics equipment based on DNA coated gold nanoparticles
http://www.nanosphere-inc.com

Nanosys
Nanosys is currently developing commercial gas sensors using nanowire technologies, yet the company has interests in many nanotechnology applications and a significant IP portfolio.
http://www.nanosysinc.com

Nano-Tex
This company develops advanced material technologies to create, improve, and revolutionize fabrics and other textiles at the molecular level.
http://www.nano-tex.com

NanoWave
NanoWave develops instruments for ultrahigh precision position measurement and control using scanning probe technology.
http://www.nanowave.com

Nantero
Highly regarded, well-funded company using carbon nanotubes for next-generation of semiconductor devices. Developing NRAM (high density nonvolatile Random Access Memory).
http://www.nantero.com/

NeoPhotonics is commercializing nanomaterials-based active and passive integrated planar optical components, and completed an equity funding round of $25 million.
http://www.neophotonics.com/

NTera
NTera is a European company developing a variety of patented nanomaterials for display screen technologies.
Based in Dublin, Ireland
http://www.ntera.com

Quantum Dot
Trying to develop quantum dot solutions for drug delivery problems and medical imaging techniques.
http://www.qdots.com

Versilant Nanotechnologies
Versilant is involved in the development of nanomaterials and nanotechnologies for advanced automotive, avionic and aerospace applications, with specific interests in CNT technologies.
http://www.versilant.com

Zettacore
Zettacore is developing novel solutions in the research and development of moloecular memory in circuit design.
http://www.zettacore.com

Zyvex

Zyvex Co. is a molecular nanotechnology company exploring both the "top down" and "bottom up" approach to the development of MEMS and NEMS.

http://www.zyvex.com

THE LEADING NANOTECH RESEARCH UNIVERSITIES

Brown University
• Nano & Micromechanics Laboratory
  http://en732c.engin.brown.edu/

California Institute of Technology (Caltech)
• Materials and Process Simulation Center
  http://www.wag.caltech.edu/
• Roukes Group-explorations with Three-Dimensional Nano-structures in Physics, Engineering and Biology
  http://www.its.caltech.edu/~nano/home.html
• Solid State Device Physics (SSDP) Research Group-Department of Applied Physics
  http://www.ssdp.caltech.edu/ssdp/

Carnegie Mellon University
• Carnegie Mellon University Buckyball Project
  http://neon.mems.cmu.edu/bucky/Home_Page.html

Columbia University
• Center for Electronic Transport in Molecular Nanostructures
  http://www.cise.columbia.edu/nsec/index_nonphp.html
• NANOWEB - Nanotechnology Resources at Columbia University
  http://www.columbia.edu/cu/osi/nanoindex.html

Cornell University
• Nanofabrication Facility. Part of the National Nanofabrication Users Network (NNUN)
  http://www.cnf.cornell.edu/

- Alliance for Nanomedical Technologies
  http://www.research.cornell.edu/anmt/
- Center for Nanoscale Systems in Information Technology
  http://www.cns.cornell.edu/
- Nanobiotechnology Center
  http://www.nbtc.cornell.edu/
- Applied Physics - Nanoscience and Nanotechnology
  http://www.aep.cornell.edu/eng10_page.cfm?webpageID=20

Duke University
- Nanoscience Group
  http://www.phy.duke.edu/research/nano/
- Eom Research Group, Thin Films Laboratory
  http://www.duke.edu/~eom/research.html
(GO DUKE! – can't help it. I'm an alum.)

Georgia Institute of Technology
- Nanoscience Group
  http://www.nanoscience.gatech.edu/zlwang/
- Nanotechnology and Microfluidics
  http://www.che.gatech.edu/Research/nanotech.htm
- Nanostructure Research Laboratory
  http://www.physics.gatech.edu/research/whetten/
- Nanostructure Optoelectronics Group
  http://www.ee.gatech.edu/research/nanostructure_optoelectronics/

Harvard University
- Nanoscale Science and Engineering Center – Science of Nanoscale Systems and their Device Applications
  http://www.nsec.harvard.edu/
- George M. Whitesides Research Group
  http://gmwgroup.harvard.edu/domino/html/webpage/homepage2.nsf
- Hongkun Park – Physics and Chemistry of Nanostructured Materials
  http://www.people.fas.harvard.edu/~hpark/

- Nanopore Group
  http://www.mcb.harvard.edu/branton/projects-solid.htm

Massachusetts Institute of Technology (MIT)
- BioInstrumentation Laboratory
  http://biorobotics.mit.edu/
- MIT Institute for Soldier Nanotechnology (ISN)
  http://biorobotics.mit.edu/
- MIT Microsystems Technology Laboratories
  http://www-mtl.mit.edu/mtlhome/
- MIT Nanostructures Laboratory
  http://nanoweb.mit.edu/
- MIT Surfaces and Structure
  http://web.mit.edu/CHEME/research/surfaces.html
- MIT NanoMechanical Technology Laboratory
  http://web.mit.edu/nanolab/
- MIT Space Nanotechnology Laboratory
  http://snl.mit.edu/

Michigan State University (MSU)
- Carbon Nanotubes
  http://www.pa.msu.edu/cmp/csc/nasa/main.html
- David Tománek "The Nanotube Site"
  http://www.pa.msu.edu/cmp/csc/nanotube.html

New York University
- Center for Advanced Materials and Nanotechnology
  http://www.nyu.edu/projects/nanotechnology/

Northwestern University
- Institute for Nanotechnology
  http://www.nanotechnology.northwestern.edu/
- Nanoscale Science and Engineering Center (NSEC) for Integrated Nanopatterning and Detection Technologies
  http://www.nsec.northwestern.edu/index.html
- Center for Nanofabrication and Molecular Self-Assembly
  http://www.nanofabrication.northwestern.edu/index.html

- Center for Transportation Nanotechnology
  http://www.ctn.northwestern.edu/

Penn State
- Atomic-Scale Measurements and Control
  http://stm1.chem.psu.edu/
- Center for Molecular Nanofabrication and Devices
  http://www.cmnd.psu.edu/
- Nanofabrication Facility. Part of the National Nanofabrication Users Network (NNUN)
  http://www.nanofab.psu.edu/
- Materials Research Institute
  http://www.mri.psu.edu/
- Allara Research Group
  http://london.mri.psu.edu/Allara-Group.htm

Princeton University
- Nanostructure Laboratory
  http://www.ee.princeton.edu/~chouweb/
- Ceramics Materials Laboratory
  http://www.princeton.edu/~cml/html/research.html

Purdue University
- Center for Nanoscale Devices
  http://www.nanodevices.ecn.purdue.edu/
- David Jane's Group
  http://www.ece.purdue.edu/~janes/index.htm
- Laboratory for Chemical Nanotechnology (PLCN)
  http://www.chem.purdue.edu/Nanochem_lab/nano.htm
- Purdue University NanoHub
  http://nanohub.purdue.edu/

Rice University
- Center for Nanoscale Science and Technology
  http://cnst.rice.edu/
- Colvin Group
  http://nanonet.rice.edu/

- Halas Nanophotonics Group
  http://www.ece.rice.edu/~halas/
- Tour Group
  http://www.ruf.rice.edu/~kekule/
- Center for Biological and Environmental Nanotechnology
  http://www.ruf.rice.edu/~cben/

Stanford University
- Stanford Nanofabrication Facility
  http://snf.stanford.edu/

University of California at Berkeley
- Berkeley Sensor & Actuator Center - MEMS Reference Database
  http://www-bsac.eecs.berkeley.edu/memsdb/
- Microstructured Materials Group
  http://eande.lbl.gov/ECS/aerogels/
- Professor Connie Chang-Hasnain Optoelectronics Research Group
  http://photonics.eecs.berkeley.edu/web/
- Alivisatos Group
  http://www.cchem.berkeley.edu/~pagrp/index.html
- Institute for Bioengineering, Biotechnology and Quantitative Biomedical Research, QB3. (In conjunction with UC San Francisco, UC Santa Cruz)
  http://www.qb3.org/

University of Arizona
- Nanomechanics and Mesoscopic Physics
  http://www.physics.arizona.edu/~stafford/
- AFM Lab
  http://www.physics.arizona.edu/~smanne/

University of California at Los Angeles
- Nanoelectronics Research Facility
  http://www.nanolab.ucla.edu/
- California NanoSystems Institute (CNSI), with UCSB
  http://www.cnsi.ucla.edu/

University of California at Santa Barbara

- Nanofabrication Facility. Part of the National Nanofabrica-tion Users Network
  http://www.nanotech.ucsb.edu/
- Nanoscale Physics - Cleland Group
  http://www.iquest.ucsb.edu/sites/cleland/
- Awschalom Group
  http://www.iquest.ucsb.edu/sites/Awsch/
- Institute for Quantum Engineering, Science and Technology (iQUEST) (formerly known as the Quantum Institute)
  http://www.iquest.ucsb.edu/

University of California at San Diego

- Physics Department - Thin Film Lab - Nanoscience Group. Professor Ivan K. Schuller
  http://physics.ucsd.edu/~iksgrp/
- California Institute for Telecommunications and Infor-mation Technology (Cal-(IT)2)
  http://www.calit2.net/

University of Nebraska – Lincoln

- Quantum Device Laboratory
  http://www.ee.unl.edu/
- Nanomachining / Nanofabrication Laboratory
  http://excimer.unl.edu/facility/nanomachining.htm

University of North Carolina at Chapel Hill

- North Carolina Center for Nanoscale Materials (NCCNM)
  http://www.physics.unc.edu/~zhou/muri/
- Nanoscale Science Research Group (NSRG)
  http://www.cs.unc.edu/Research/nano/
- The Nano Manipulator
  http://www.cs.unc.edu/Research/nano/cismm/nm/index.html

University of Notre Dame

- Center for Nano Science and Technology
  http://www.nd.edu/~ndnano/

- Nanofabrication Facility
  http://www.ee.nd.edu/ndnf/
- Nano Science and Technology Center
  http://www.nd.edu/%7Endnano/index.htm

University of Texas
- NanoTech Institute
  http://www.utdallas.edu/dept/chemistry/nanotech/
- Center for Quantum Electronics
  http://www.utdallas.edu/research/quantum/
- MEMS Research Group
  http://www.utdallas.edu/%7Ejblee/research/

University of Wisconsin – Madison
- Center for NanoTechnology
  http://www.nanotech.wisc.edu/
- Applied Superconductivity Center
  http://www.asc.wisc.edu/
- Center for Plasma-Aided Manufacturing
  http://cpam.engr.wisc.edu/

IMPORTANT CENTERS FOR NANOTECH

Albany NanoTech
http://www.albanynanotech.org/
"Albany NanoTech is a university-based global research, development, technology deployment and education resource supporting accelerated high-technology commercialization. Co-located with the new College of NanoScale Science and Engineering at the University at Albany (SUNY), it seeks to leverage resources in partnership with business, government and academia to create jobs and economic growth for the nano-electronics-related industries. Small, medium and large industrial partners have access to state-of-the-art laboratories, super-computer center, shared-user facilities and an array of scientific centers."

Lawrence Livermore National Laboratory
http://www.llnl.gov/

"Lawrence Livermore National Laboratory (LLNL) is a premier research and development institution for science and technology applied to national security. We are responsible for ensuring that the nation's nuclear weapons remain safe, secure, and reliable. LLNL also applies its expertise to prevent the spread and use of weapons of mass destruction and strengthen homeland security."

Los Alamos National Laboratory
http://www.lanl.gov/index.shtml

"The mission of Los Alamos National Laboratory is national security. Most Los Alamos employees are working to help ensure the safety and reliability of the nuclear weapons in our country's stockpile. Many others work to prevent the spread of weapons of mass destruction and to protect our homeland from terrorist attack. Much of their work relates to Laboratory's work on national security and must be kept secret. There is, however, a great deal about national security and the nuclear weapons work being done at Los Alamos that is unclassified."

NASA Nanotechnology Team
http://www.nas.nasa.gov/Groups/SciTech/nano/

"Atomically precise manipulation of matter is becoming increasingly common in laboratories around the world. As this control moves into aerospace systems, huge improvements in , for aircraft and launch vehicles, and other systems are expected. Studies suggest that it may be possible to build:

- 1018 MIPS computers
- 1015 bytes/cm2 write once memory
- Aerospace Transportation single-stage-to-orbit launch vehicles

and which sense their environment and react intelligently. All of NASA's enterprises should benefit significantly from molecular nanotechnology. Although the time may be measured in decades and the precise path to molecular nanotechnology is unclear, all paths (diamondoid, fullerene, self-assembly, biomolecular, etc.) will require very substantial computation."

FOUR FASCINATING BOOKS FOR NON-SCIENTISTS (ALL OF THESE BOOKS ARE AVAILABLE AT WWW.NANOTECHNOLOGY.COM)

Scientists and non-scientists alike will find these four books thoroughly engrossing and mind expanding. While physics/math-oriented (but no weird math or physics equations with multiple Greek letters and strange symbols to deal with), they are real "page-turners," and will give you a sense of awe at the unseen world around and in us, and the basic working premises of the nanoscientists that are changing our world.

A Brief History of Time: From the Big Bang to Black Holes, Stephen Hawking, 1988, Bantam Books. This short book says a lot. The famed British physicist challenges us with the central questions of existence, and how science has answered some of them, so far.

Fermat's Enigma: The Epic Quest to Solve the World's Greatest Mathematical Problem, Simon Singh, 1997, Walker & Company. This scientific/historical work takes off way beyond its genre. Singh pulls us into the minds and souls of mathematicians through the ages, struggling with an esoteric mystery. Math majors might get a few inside jokes I missed, but you do not even need to remember Algebra II to enjoy this fascinating, true yarn.

Genius: The Life and Science of Richard Feynman, James Gleick, 1992, Pantheon Books. *The Father of Nanotechnology,* and the most famous physicist of the 20th Century not named Einstein gets a full treatment in this remarkable biography. Gleick is great here, helping us know the bongo-playing, womanizing, man of many contradictions and paradoxes as well as we can know anyone from a book.

The Ultimate Einstein, Dr. Donald Goldsmith, 1997, Pocket Books. This little book does a great job detailing and explaining Einstein's life, thoughts, theories, triumphs and failures. You will actually "get" relativity, the unified field, anti-matter, and why you get younger when you travel at the speed of light. Really.

THE BOOKS I RECOMMEND FOR PEOPLE WHO WANT TO LEARN HOW TO MAKE MONEY IN THE MARKETS (AVAILABLE AT WWW.NANOTECHNOLOGY.COM)

The Art of the Start, Guy Kawasaki, 2004, Penguin. It is amazing that you have to pay good money just for common sense. But Guy Kawasaki's wonderful book about how to start and build a successful entity is well worth it, and shows how rare common sense is. Great for investors, nanotech startups, and more mature companies as well.

Beating the Street, Peter Lynch, 1993, Simon & Schuster. Talk about common sense: the legendary Magellan manager makes investing a down to earth process, and teaches simple, winning approaches to fundamental and business analysis.

How to Make Money in Stocks: A Winning System in Good Times or Bad, William J. O'Neil, 1995, McGraw-Hill. The head of *Investor's Business Daily* easily conveys momentum investing and technical analysis in the best senses of words. This contains tons of useful information for anyone who can buy a stock without saying, "I am buying it for the long term."

The New Market Wizards: Conversations with America's Top Traders, Jack D. Schwager, 1992, Harper-Collins. Schwager has a bit of a series going based on this device. He interviews famous, extremely high performing speculators about how they win, how they deal with losses, and what makes them the way they are. Fascinating.

Tools and Tactics for the Master Trader, by Oliver Velez & Greg Capra, 2000, McGraw-Hill. So many books on technical analysis and system trading are dead wrong at worst or written by dilettantes at best. Velez and Capra present a strong, highly readable book based on real life experience.

Trader Vic – Methods of a Wall Street Master, by Victor Sperandeo, 1991, John Wiley & Sons. Full of enlightening cynicism, great stories, and great hardcore trading ideas, this is a look into the mind of one of our market wizards, warts and all.

Running Money: Hedge Fund Honchos, Monster Markets and My Hunt for the Big Score, Andy Kessler, 2004, Harper Business. This is a real insider's view into the hedge-fund/VC world of the late 1990s in Silicon Valley. Be a fly on the office wall; hear the uncensored conversations of the participants, and, most interestingly, Andy Kessler's own uncensored thoughts when the ludicrous gets surreal. I was not present at any of the meetings in the book, but I certainly was in dozens of more-than-similar ones. The whole thing rings true. Great work and great fun.

GLOSSARY OF NANOTECH INVESTOR TERMINOLOGY

Absolute Zero: The point at which all molecular motion stops; -273 degrees Celsius.

Accredited Investor: An investor who meets certain SEC requirements for net worth and income: enabling participation in some restricted stock offerings.

Adaptive System: A self-sensing system of hardware and software capable of some self-correcting.

AFM (Atomic Force Microscopy) uses an extremely small cantilever, similar to the arm and needle of a record player, in which the needle runs over the "grooves" of a specimen to "visualize" contours and structures as small as an individual atom.

Algorithm: A formalized mathematical instruction.

Angel Investor: An individual investor who provides startup capital to young companies.

Angstrom: One ten-billionth of a meter, the length scale used to describe the dimensions of a single atom. A tenth of a nanometer.

Assembler: A theoretical nanomachine that can assemble atoms into molecules or materials.

Benchtop: The first successful attempt of a technical application of a pure science concept.

Binary: The computing code based on a series of zeros and ones.

Biomimetic: The imitation of nature in human made processes, materials, devices, or systems.

Bionanotech: Biomolecular nanotechnology is the use of biomolecules as replicators, assemblers, or components for nanotechnology. It tends to be more reliable than inorganic nanotechnology.

Biosensor: A sensor used to target biological molecules.

Bit: The smallest unit of computer data, the one or zero in binary code.

Brownian Motion: The random motion of small particles suspended in a medium.

Buckyball: A nanoscale ball of carbon atoms arranged in a soccer ball like structure. The buckyball is formally known as the buckminsterfullerene.

Burn Rate: The rate at which a company which is not making a financial profit uses its available cash each month.

Byte: A group of eight bits.

CAD: Computer Aided Design.

Carbon Nanotube: Sheets of graphite rolled into the shape of a nanoscaled straw, resembling chicken wire, commonly referred to as CNTs.

Catalysis: The use of an external material to initiate, accelerate, or modify a process.

Ceramics: A hard, brittle material.

CMOS: Complimentary metal oxide semiconductor used as a device in integrated circuits.

Conductor: A material which continuously allows the flow of electrons. All metals are conductors.

Coulomb's Law: The basic law of electrical interaction used to derive the force between two charges.

Covalent Bond: A relatively strong interatomic bond which is created through the sharing of electrons between atoms.

Current: The flow rate of electric charge.

Crystal Growth: The formation of crystals from a solution. Development of salt crystals on the side of a boat is an example of crystal growth.

DARPA: Defense Advanced Research Projects Agency.

Dendrimer: A synthetic, three-dimensional macromolecule with the possibility of having applications in the field of electronics and drug-delivery.

Dielectric: Any electrically insulating material.

Diffusion: The mixing of two materials at the atomic level.

DNA: Deoxyribonucleic Acid. The molecules that encode the replication process for all living organisms.

DOD: Department of Defense.

DOE: Department of Energy.

Electron: A single unit of charge.

Electron Beam Lithography: A common fabrication method in which electron beams are used to form structures on surfaces.

Electron Microscopy: The characterization of structures and surfaces using an electron beam.

Electrophoresis: The displacement of charged particles within an electric field.

Electrostatic Force: The force of attraction or repulsion between electrons and protons, similar to the attractive force of gravity between two objects in space.

Entanglement: The process of combining two pieces of information into a single entity in quantum computing.

FET: A Field-Effect Transistor is the most common transistor used in semiconductor chips.

Fiber-optics: The process of relaying information in tiny packets of light through long transparent fibers.

Fullerene: A type of nanoparticle; a buckyball of sixty or more carbon atoms.

Genome: The map of genetic content derived from DNA sequencing.

Gigahertz: One billion repetitions per second.

Hydrogen Bond: A relatively weak chemical bond consisting of a hydrogen atom between two electronegative atoms.

Hydrophilic: A material which is soluble in water. Sugar will dissolve in water, thus it is hydrophilic.

Hydrophobic: A material which will not dissolve in water.

Insulator: A material which does not allow the flow of electricity.

Ion: A particle that is electrically charged.

Ionic Bond: The columbic interatomic bond between two oppositely charged electrons. The ionic bond is the strongest bonding force.

IP: Intellectual Property, i.e. patents, copyrights, trademarks, trade secrets, and *know-how*.

IPO: Initial Public Offering. An IPO is a company's first offering of stock to the public.

LED: A Light Emitting Diode is a device which permits direct transformation of electricity into light. LED's are commonly used in display panels as low-energy light sources.

Ligand: An ion that binds atoms or molecules together.

Lithography: The transfer of patterns onto a surface.

Luminescent Tags: Nanostructures, such as quantum dots, which emit light and can be used to identify structures to which they are bonded.

Macromolecule: A complex molecule consisting of thousands of simpler molecules.

MEMS: Microelectromechanical Systems are structures at the micron scale which combine electronics with micromechanics.

METI: Ministry of Economy, Trade, and Industry (Japan).

MFM: Magnetic force microscopy: similar to AFM which senses deflections of a magnetic probe.

Molecular Manipulator: A device used to position molecular tools or atoms with great precision.

MOSFET: Metal oxide semiconductor field-effect transistor.

MRAM: Magnetic random access memory stores data in the spin of electrons.

MRI: Magnetic resonance imaging: a form of spectroscopy that identifies particular atomic nuclei in the body or other biological systems.

Multi-Wall Nanotube: A nanotube of multiple cylinder walls commonly referred to as MWNT.

Nanocomposites: A composite material in which there exist nano-materials.

Nanocrystal: A material consisting of multiple crystals, where the grains within the crystals are of nanometer dimensions.

Nanomachine: A device in which the smallest component is of nanometer dimensions.

Nanometer: A billionth of a meter. The width of a human hair measures about 80,000 nanometers.

Nanotube: A straw-like object at the nanometer scale.

Nanowire: A long, thin wire of diameter within the nanometer range. Nanowires have been known to demonstrate light emitting properties.

NEMS: Nanoelectromechanical Systems, similar to MEMS.

NIH: National Institute of Health.

NNI: National Nanotechnology Initiative.

NSF: National Science Foundation.

Optics: Referring to the science of light and its interactions with matter.

Photoelectric: The conversion of light into electricity.

Photoresist: A thin film used to protect a substance or material when exposed to light.

Photosensor: A device for detecting the presence and frequency of light.

Photovoltaics: Devices which transform light energy into electrical current through a photoelectric process.

Piezoelectric: A material which can transform current into motion or motion into current.

Pixel: The smallest element in a digital picture. With a large number of pixels a display will have a high resolution.

Plasma: A form of matter in which electrons move freely among the nuclei of atoms.

Polymer: Usually a plastic, this material is composed of many repeating patterns.

Private company: A company which has not sold stock to the public.

Public company: A company which is listed on a stock exchange and has sold stock to the public.

Quantum: The physics of quantum mechanics.

Quantum Computer: A computing device based on the behavior of particles at the subatomic level.

Quantum Dots: Isolated semiconductor islands capable of containing single units of charge. Commonly referred to as QDs or Q-dots, quantum dots have been used in single electron transistors.

Qubit: The unit of computing power for a quantum computer.

Replicator: A device which is capable of making copies of itself. Bacteria are examples of natural replicators.

Resistance: The efficiency of electron flow through a material. A high resistance will produce low efficiency in flow.

Ribosome: Manufactures all the proteins used in all living things.

ROI: Return on investment.

SBA: Small Business Administration.

SBIR: Small Business Incentive Research Program.

SEC: Security and Exchange Commission. SEC is the federal agency regulating the trade of stocks.

Self-Assembly: The process in which structures are created through the chemical and physical interactions of surrounding materials.

SEM: Scanning Electron Microscopy uses electron beams to image an object.

Semiconductor: A material that is capable of controlling the flow of electrons conditional to the presence of other electric fields.

SIA: Semiconductor Industry Association.

Single Electron Transistor: A device capable of controlling the flow of a single electron between a source and a drain.

Spintronics: The manipulation of the spin of an electron, rather then charge.

STM: Scanning tunneling microscopy is a technique which measures electrons tunneling between a probing tip and a conducting surface. Nearly atomic resolution is possible with STM.

Subatomic: Refers to dimensions smaller then an atom.

Superconductor: A material which allows the flow of electrons with no resistance.

Swarm: A collaboration of many devices toward a common goal.

Terahertz: One trillion cycles per second.

Thin Film: A layer of material a few atoms thick.

Transistor: A device capable of regulating the current or voltage flow of electrons.

UV: Ultraviolet light is a relatively short wavelength used in semiconductor fabrication. It is not within the range of visible wavelengths.

Van der Waals Bond: A relatively weak bond between molecular dipoles.

VC: A venture capitalist is an investor in start-up or early stage companies. Because of the risk inherent in this type of investing, they seek large returns.

Wafer: A small plate of silicon used as the base for integrated circuits.

Yield Strength: The strength required to create any permanent deformation.

INDEX

ABOUT THE AUTHOR

Darrell Brookstein read Drexler's *Engines of Creation* in 1988; ideas about nanotechnology stuck in his head waiting for the right moment to emerge. After closing his highly successful Internet, resource, and high-tech private equity fund in August of 2000, and returning substantial profits to his investors, he began looking for *the next big thing*. Like someone else's book title says, he decided it was "really small," and the timing was right to lay the groundwork for *Nanotech Fortunes* to come. In 2001, he enlisted National Academy of Sciences member, and noted bio-nanoscientist, Erkki Ruoslahti, M.D., Ph.D to help him co-found and develop a leading nanotech financial services and corporate development advisory firm.

In previous work, Darrell edited and authored the key source books and newsletters related to the analysis of speculative natural resource stocks, especially precious metals mining equities. He is responsible for significant financing of more than a dozen of the most successful mining and natural gas companies started in the last 25 years. He has been president of an investment bank, venture capital, hedge and private equity funds, several Registered Investment Advisors, and managed and invested hundreds of millions of dollars for more than four thousand individual investors and dozens of institutions. He is a graduate of Duke University. Born in DC and raised in the Washington suburbs, Darrell has lived in Santa Barbara, Vancouver, and Prague. Since 1996 he makes his home in the worldwide center of the confluence of wireless, biotech and nanotechnology, San Diego. He is the Managing Director of The Nanotech Company, LLC and nanotechnolgy.com. His beautiful family: wife, Helen, and daughters, Kimbra and Shannon, make him crazy and happy.

Throughout this book I have gathered in for you other interesting and sometimes controversial points of view from friends of mine who offer a smorgasbord of professional and fresh perspectives to help you make your *nanotech fortune*. Look for them. They are set aside with a by-line for each. There is much wisdom, and much to learn from them. I thank them so much for their great efforts and immeasurable contributions to this book.